The Cambridge Companion to the Cello

The Cambridge Companions to Music

The Cambridge Companion to the

CELLO

EDITED BY
Robin Stowell
Professor of Music, Cardiff University

CAMBRIDGE
UNIVERSITY PRESS

PUBLISHED BY THE PRESS SYNDICATE OF THE UNIVERSITY OF CAMBRIDGE
The Pitt Building, Trumpington Street, Cambridge CB2 1RP, United Kingdom

CAMBRIDGE UNIVERSITY PRESS
The Edinburgh Building, Cambridge CB2 2RU, UK http://www.cup.cam.ac.uk
40 West 20th Street, New York, NY 10011–4211, USA http://www.cup.org
10 Stamford Road, Oakleigh, Melbourne 3166, Australia

First published 1999
Reprinted 2000

Printed in the United Kingdom at the University Press, Cambridge

Typeset in Adobe Minion 10.75/14 pt, in QuarkXpress™ [SE]

A catalogue record for this book is available from the British Library

ISBN 0 521 621011 hardback
ISBN 0 521 629284 paperback

Contents

Illustrations

The contributors

Peter Allsop is a Lecturer in Music at Exeter University and specialises in Italian seventeenth-century instrumental music. He is the author of *The Italian 'Trio' Sonata* (Oxford University Press, 1992) and General Editor of New Orpheus Editions (devoted to the publication of the trio sonata repertory), and he contributed a chapter to *The Cambridge Companion to the Violin*. He is currently completing a life and works study of the Italian violinist-composer Arcangelo Corelli.

R. Caroline Bosanquet studied at the Royal Academy of Music and later continued her cello studies with Christopher Bunting and in the USA. She also gained a B. Mus. degree externally from the University of Durham. A Senior Lecturer at Anglia Polytechnic University, Cambridge, from 1966, she has taught the cello, musicianship and numerous academic courses to students of all ages from beginners to degree and diploma level, and has given courses for cello teachers with Joan Dickson. Her book devoted to harmonics, *The Secret Life of Cello Strings* (1996), has received critical acclaim and her *Elégie* for cello and piano has received many performances world-wide. She has also written many articles on cello-related subjects in *The Strad* and in the journal of the European String Teachers' Association.

Margaret Campbell is the author of *The Great Cellists*, *The Great Violinists*, *Dolmetsch: the Man and his Work*, and has been editor of the *British Journal of Music Therapy*. She began her career as a Fleet Street journalist and has been a regular contributor to *The Strad*, *Musical Opinion*, *Music in Education*, and other journals.

John Dilworth graduated from the Newark School of Violin Making in 1979. He has since worked for Charles Beare in the London workshops of J. & A. Beare Ltd. as a restorer of violins, violas and cellos, but now runs his own workshop in Twickenham. He has made several instruments, including reproductions of Classical examples. A contributor to *The Cambridge Companion to the Violin*, he also writes for *The Strad* and *Das Musikinstrument*, contributing articles based on practical experience and research into the history of the violin and its makers. He is currently working on a volume on *The Masterpieces of Giuseppe Guarneri del Gesù*.

David Wyn Jones is a Senior Lecturer in the Department of Music, Cardiff University. His publications include *Haydn, his Life and Music* (co-authored with H. C. Robbins Landon; London, 1988), a study of Beethoven's Pastoral Symphony (Cambridge, 1995), an edited volume entitled *Music in Eighteenth-Century Austria* (Cambridge, 1996) and *The Life of Beethoven* (Cambridge, 1998). He is currently completing a project on manuscript sources of eighteenth-century Austrian music in the Royal Palace, Madrid, and compiling the *Oxford Companion to Haydn*.

Bernard Richardson is a Lecturer in the Department of Physics and Astronomy at Cardiff University. His research activities in musical acoustics stem from a long-standing passion for making and playing musical instruments. He has written numerous articles and lectured world-wide on the subject.

Robin Stowell Educated at the University of Cambridge and the Royal Academy of Music, Robin Stowell is a Professor of Music at Cardiff University. He is a professional violinist and Baroque violinist as well as a music editor and author. He has written extensively about the violin and stringed instruments in general, as well as about the conventions of performing early music. The author of *Violin Technique and Performance Practice in the Late Eighteenth and Early Nineteenth Centuries* (Cambridge, 1985), he has also written articles for a wide variety of music journals, including *Early Music, Music & Letters* and *The Strad*, and contributed chapters to several collaborative volumes. He is editor of and principal contributor to *The Cambridge Companion to the Violin* (Cambridge, 1992), editor of *Performing Beethoven* (Cambridge, 1994) and has recently completed a study of Beethoven's Violin Concerto (Cambridge, 1998).

Frances-Marie Uitti, solo cellist and composer, is a concert artist active in performing throughout Europe, the United States and Asia. She is the inventor of the two-bow technique of playing the cello, wherein four- three- or two-part chordal and polyphonic playing is now possible. Luigi Nono, Giacinto Scelsi, György Kurtág, Jonathan Harvey and many others have written for her using this innovation.

Ms Uitti has worked with a vast array of composers and has premièred concertos, solo pieces, theatrical works, and other music dedicated to her by such composers as Louis Andriessen, Iannis Xenakis, John Cage, James Tenney, Jonathan Harvey, Brian Ferneyhough, Richard Barrett and Per Nørgård.

Ms Uitti is ongoing guest Professor at the Rotterdam Conservatory. She is currently working on a book for the University of California Press detailing the major technical and musical innovations from 1915 until the present.

Valerie Walden A resident of California, Valerie Walden studied the cello with William van den Burg, Gabor Rejto, Laszlo Varga and Coral Bognuda. She holds an M.A. and Ph.D from the University of Auckland, New Zealand, and is an adjunct instructor for the South San Joaquin Valley branch of Chapman University. Her performance credits include being principal cellist with the Tulare County Symphony and cellist of the Kings Classical Trio. She is also active as a cello teacher and adjudicator. Dr Walden is the author of *One Hundred Years of Violoncello: Technique and Performance Practice, 1740–1840*, published by Cambridge University Press (1998), and is a contributor to the *Revised New Grove Dictionary of Music and Musicians*.

Preface

The chapters which make up this volume were commissioned from various friends and colleagues, all experts in their fields. Their principal aim has been to demonstrate that the cello deserves similar treatment to the other instruments in this series and to provide the reader with a compact, composite survey of the history of the cello from its origins to the present day, drawing on the resources of contemporary scholarship. They offer as comprehensive a coverage as possible, focusing in particular on four main areas: the instrument's structure, development and its fundamental acoustical principles; its chief exponents; its repertory; and its technique, pedagogical literature and aspects of historical and contemporary performance practice. Inevitable limitations of space have resulted in the need for authors to be selective in their essays, illustrations, musical examples and bibliographical references, but if we have been successful in stimulating constructive, penetrating thought about the past, present and future of the art of cello playing and its numerous related aspects, our joint purpose will have been realised. As editor, I must take full responsibility for this volume's overall content and proportions and I very much regret my negligence if there are significant areas which have been inadvertently overlooked.

We have written for all who have an interest in the cello – 'amateurs' as well as students and professional musicians. Although some technical knowledge has been assumed of our readers, those unversed in 'musical mechanics' will find help to hand in the explanatory glossary of technical terms included at the end of the volume. There is also a useful appendix and a selective bibliography, and numerous illustrative plates and musical examples have been included to enhance the text and contribute to a balanced publication. Dates of birth and death of significant figures in the cello's history are sometimes included in the text to clarify historical perspective, but such details are consistently provided in the index as points of reference in respect of most personalities cited.

My good friend Timothy Mason was to have contributed to this book. It is deeply regrettable that this volume has been deprived of a chapter from such a fine cellist whose enquiring mind and whose energies and enthusiasms for so many different aspects of his profession made him an especially influential force in the fields of contemporary music (for example, with Capricorn) and period performance (with the London Pianoforte Trio, the English Baroque Soloists, the Orchestra of the Age of the Enlightenment and numerous other orchestras/ensembles). I dedicate this volume to his memory.

It is a pleasure to acknowledge the help given so willingly and by so many in the preparation of this Companion. I am indebted to my contributors one and all for their co-operative attitude, promptness of response to various problems and queries and for giving readily of their expertise in their various fields. I am also grateful for the assistance of Joanna Pieters and Naomi Sadler (*The Strad*), and

Howard Cheetham (Cardiff University). Cardiff University of Wales has also been generous in its help, granting me a period of study leave in order to bring this volume to completion, and I am indebted to my wife and family and many friends and colleagues who have assisted and encouraged me during the course of this project. Last, but not least, I must extend my sincere thanks to Penny Souster and her team at Cambridge University Press, and especially Ann Lewis, for their helpful advice and firm but unobtrusive encouragement in bringing the book to press.

Robin Stowell

Acknowledgements

Acknowledgement for kind permission to reproduce illustrations and music examples is due to the following:

Illustrations

J. & A. Beare Ltd.: Fig. 1.2d

Colourstrings International Ltd.: Fig. 12.3

Dr Carleen Hutchins: Fig. 3.4

Mr Arthur Montzka: Fig. 3.5

Mr Peter Oxley: Figs. 2.4, 2.5, 2.6

Mr William Pleeth: Fig. 12.2

Schott and Co. Ltd. London: Fig. 12.1

Courtesy of *The Strad*: Figs. 6.5, 6.6, 6.7, 6.8

Music examples

Ex. 10.3 Universal Edition Ltd., London. Reproduced by permission.

Ex. 12.2 Schott and Co. Ltd., London.

Ex. 13.1 Morton Feldman: *Intersection 4*, Edition Peters No. 6960. © 1964 by C. F. Peters Corporation, New York. Reproduced on behalf of the Publishers by kind permission of Peters Edition Ltd., London.

Ex. 13.2 Brian Ferneyhough: *Time and Motion Study II*, Edition Peters No. 7223. © 1966 by Hinrichsen Edition, Peters Edition Ltd., London. Reproduced by kind permission of the Publishers.

Ex. 13.3 John Cage: *Etudes Boreales*. Edition Peters No. 66328. © 1960 by Henmar Press Inc., New York. Reproduced on behalf of the Publishers by kind permission of Peters Edition Ltd., London.

Abbreviations, fingering and notation

amp vc amplified violoncello
bc basso continuo
br brass
ch ens chamber ensemble
ch orch chamber orchestra
cl clarinet
db double bass
elec org electric organ
fl flute
hn horn
hpd harpsichord
Hz Hertz
ob oboe
orch orchestra
orchd orchestrated
org organ
perc percussion
pf pianoforte
sax saxophone
str strings
str qt string quartet
timp timpani
va viola
vc violoncello
vle violone
vn violin
ww woodwind

Cello fingerings are indicated in the usual manner:
ǫ thumb
0 open string
1 the index finger (not the thumb as in keyboard fingering) and so on

Pitch registers are indicated by the following letter-scheme:

Under this scheme the notes to which the cello is normally tuned are represented as C–G–d–a.

1 The cello: origins and evolution

JOHN DILWORTH

Introduction

Although it is the noblest and most profound in tone of the violin family, the cello is probably the youngest member and certainly the most recently perfected in form and proportion. Although its large size makes it particularly vulnerable to damage, its design (as with its smaller relatives, the violin and viola) has given it a remarkable longevity, and instruments made three hundred years ago are still used and treasured by discerning players.

The cello is a mechanically simple but acoustically complex instrument. (See Fig. 1.1.) The four tapered tuning pegs for adjusting the strings, tuned C–G–d–a, are made usually from hard rosewood (*dalbergia latifolia*) or boxwood (*buxus sempervirens*) for durability, and project laterally from a backward-curving pegbox. Proportionally, the pegbox is much broader than that of the violin, in order to accommodate thicker strings, and has distinctive squared shoulders at the lower end. At the upper end is the scroll, a Baroque adornment which is a characteristic feature of all the instruments of the violin family. The slope of the pegbox tensions the strings across the ebony nut, which is slotted to locate and raise them just clear of the surface of the ebony fingerboard, against which the strings are stopped by the fingers of the left hand.

The fingerboard is glued to the neck, which is carved in one piece with the pegbox and scroll from maple (*acer pseudoplatanus*). It has a curved top in cross-section, usually with a flattened area beneath the C string to allow for the wider vibration of this, the heaviest string. The fingerboard increases in width from the nut to permit wider string spacing at the bridge, allowing easier movement of the bow in string-crossing. The neck joins the body of the cello at the root, which extends to the full depth of the ribs, whilst the fingerboard extends further above the body.

The framework of the body is the rib structure, assembled from six thin maple strips bent to shape by dry heat and reinforced at the joints by interior blocks – one in each of the four outward-curving corners, one at the lower end, and the top block, into which the neck-root is fitted with a tapered mortice (prior to the nineteenth century, the neck was either glued to the outside of the ribs and secured with nails through the top block, or

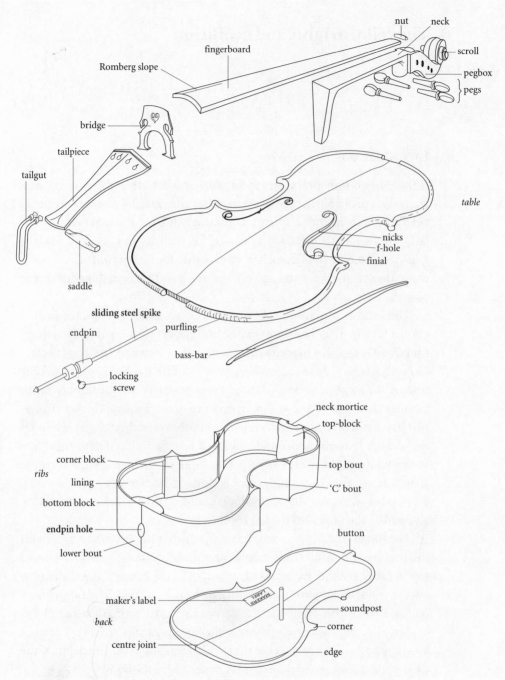

Fig. 1.1 An 'exploded' view of a cello

simply continued inside the body of the instrument forming its own top block, with the upper ribs inserted into slots cut in either side). The six ribs correspond to the six main curves of the cello outline: the upper bouts, the inward-curving middle or 'C' bouts, and the wide lower bouts, symmetrically arranged on treble and bass sides. To ensure a strong glue-joint between the extremely thin ribs and the table and back of the cello, strips of pine or willow, known as the linings, are glued along the upper and lower inside edges of the ribs.

The Classical makers of seventeenth- and eighteenth-century Italy assembled the ribs around a shallow hardwood mould, and this remains the accepted method today. Proportionally, the ribs of the cello are much deeper than those of the violin or viola (and consequently more vulnerable to damage), so many makers, including the greatest of all, Stradivari, chose to reinforce the inside of the ribs with linen strips.

The back of the cello is usually made from one or two matched pieces of maple jointed along the length. Maple trees of sufficient girth to provide flawless planks wide enough for cello backs are not easy to come by, and poplar, willow and even beech are not infrequently substituted, the softer woods often seeming well suited to the mellow tone-quality of the cello. Once jointed and planed flat, the outline of the cello is drawn and sawn out from the timber, and the arching (the outward swell of the back) is carved with gouge, planes and scrapers. The inner surface is also carved out to give a finished thickness in the centre of about 7 mm, reduced around the edges to about 4 mm. The height and shape of the arching, in combination with the precise finished thicknesses, are fundamental factors in determining the tonal quality of the instrument.

The appearance and strength of the back are also affected by the way in which the wood is cut from the tree (See Fig. 1.2a). The most common and strongest method is to join two pieces cut 'on the quarter' (Fig. 1.2b). This shows the horizontal 'figure', resulting from ripples in the grain of the wood, to good effect, matching mirror-fashion on either side of the joint. If the back is made from a single piece of quarter-sawn wood, it is usually made from the larger varieties of poplar or willow, which rarely show horizontal figure (See Fig. 1.2d). If the wood is cut 'on the slab' (See Fig. 1.2c), the figure is more diffuse in maple, although the 'contour lines' formed by the grain are more apparent. Wood so cut is not quite as stiff and is slightly more vulnerable to splits, but can yield a particularly warm and rich tone. Whichever variety is chosen, from the most desirable imported Balkan maple to the plainest local-grown willow, the back is always made from hardwood, which has a complex structure of interlocking cells and is relatively dense and strong.

The table is made in a similar way, but using spruce (*picea abies, picea*

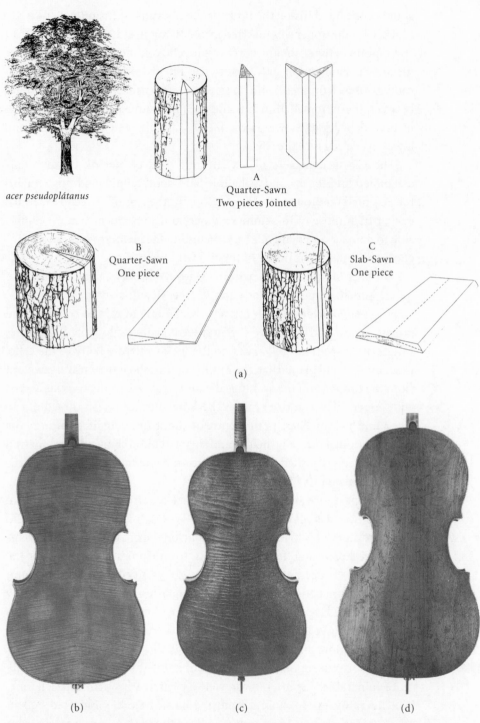

acer pseudoplátanus

A
Quarter-Sawn
Two pieces Jointed

B
Quarter-Sawn
One piece

C
Slab-Sawn
One piece

(a)

(b)   (c)   (d)

Fig. 1.2(a) Cutting the back of the cello: three different methods. **(b)** The back of a cello by G. B. Rogeri of Brescia, dated 1714, showing the characteristic transverse markings of quarter-sawn maple. **(c)** The back of a cello by Francesco Rugeri of Cremona, *c.* 1690, showing the more diffuse and irregular pattern of slab-sawn maple. **(d)** The back of a cello made by Bartolomeo Cristofori in Florence, 1716, a single piece of poplar wood of typically plain appearance

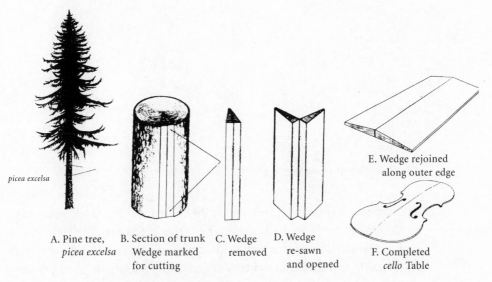

picea excelsa

A. Pine tree,   B. Section of trunk   C. Wedge   D. Wedge
picea excelsa   Wedge marked   removed   re-sawn   E. Wedge rejoined
for cutting   and opened   along outer edge

F. Completed
cello Table

Fig. 1.3 Cutting the table of the cello

excelsa or *picea alba*), always cut on the quarter and carefully selected for straight and even grain, and the finished thickness is usually about 4.5 mm throughout (see Fig. 1.3). The wood is thus a coniferous softwood whose simple, light and rigid structure is essentially a bundle of hollow tubes which transmit vibration more readily along the grain rather than across the width.

Just inside the edge of the front and back is a narrow inlay, known as the purfling. This comprises three separate strands of wood, the outer two of ebony or pearwood stained black, the inner strand generally of poplar, the whole approximately 1.4 mm thick. As well as being decorative, the purfling serves an important purpose in inhibiting the development of cracks from the edges, which are especially vulnerable since they project outside the delicate ribs by a margin of 3–4 mm. On the back, this overhanging margin incorporates the button which substantially strengthens the neck joint and assists it in resisting the considerable tension of the strings.

The table, sometimes called the belly or front, is pierced by two sound-holes, known by their shape as f-holes. They comprise three elements: a long curving arm, at each end of which is a circular finial. The bridge, whose precise location on the table is indicated by the small nicks cut in the middle of each f-hole, is held in place by the pressure of the strings alone and is cut from a wedge of hard maple. Its intricate shape is designed to reduce the mass of wood, without reducing its strength and rigidity beyond practical limits. The top curve of the bridge matches that of the fingerboard (though without the flattened section under the C string), and allows the bow to sound one string at a time, without fouling

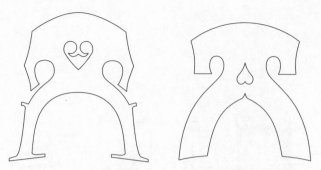

Fig. 1.4 Modern and seventeenth-century bridges contrasted

the adjacent strings (Fig. 1.4). Inside the cello, just behind the outer edge of the bridge 'foot' on the a-string side is the soundpost. This is a spruce rod, 11 mm in diameter, which is fitted precisely to the interior contours of the table and back and lightly wedged into position. Its exact position and 'tightness' are carefully regulated to adjust the instrument's tone to optimum effect for each player and for differing conditions. In a symmetrical position beneath the bass 'foot' of the bridge on the inside of the table is the bass-bar, a supporting strut of spruce which is roughly three-quarters of the length of the table.

The strings, having passed over the bridge, are secured to the tailpiece, traditionally made of rosewood, ebony or boxwood, but often now from lighter materials such as plastic or metal alloys and incorporating mechanisms for fine tuning. The tailpiece is secured to the cello by a loop of gut, or more commonly now nylon or wire, which runs over a saddle of ebony let into the bottom edge of the table, and around the endpin. This latter is a hardwood plug set into the lower block, through which runs the retractable metal spike which supports the instrument in its modern playing-position.

The adhesive used throughout the construction process has always been traditional animal glue, which is extremely tenacious but can easily be released when necessary with hot water, for repair work. That it is possible for the cello to be quite readily dismantled and repaired is a major factor in its remarkable longevity, enabling it to be modified to accommodate the various changes in sound ideal.

The cello is covered with a protective varnish, the quality of which is more than merely an indicator of the quality of the instrument. The Classical Italian makers appear to have used different formulations for the ground coat, which seals and protects the wood and can bring out the natural beauty of even the commonest plank of poplar wood, and the top coats, which were tinted with rich red, yellow and golden brown colours. Different combinations of oils and resins give different degrees of hardness and flexibility; a well-judged varnish allows the cello to speak with its full voice for centuries, whilst a poor one will stifle it. Re-creating the varnish of past masters has been one of the greatest challenges to present makers; recent research suggests that walnut or linseed oil was the major constituent of the finest old Italian varnish, which was later supplanted by inferior recipes based on shellac and alcohol.

Origins and antecedents

Tracing the origins of the cello is not easy. Instruments played with a bow appear in European iconography from around AD 900, but interpretation is difficult and terminology seems to vary and overlap. Broadly speaking, however, these instruments fall into four main categories: the rebec, the medieval and Renaissance fiddle, the lira da braccio and the viol. Of these, the first three are generally accepted as ancestors of the violin and viola, because of their playing positions and sizes. It has also been suggested that they were all originally carved out of a solid block, with a simple sound-board added, a technique only practical with the smaller sizes of instrument.

With the viol, however, more complex and sophisticated constructions and musical applications are apparent, and the idea of the consort of instruments of the same family, but played in different registers, became fixed. This idea was very quickly applied to the violin after its appearance, probably at the beginning of the sixteenth century. In the fresco decorating the cupola of Saronno Cathedral, painted by Gaudenzio Ferrari in 1535 and thought to be amongst the very earliest depictions of the violin family (see Fig. 1.5), recognisable violins and also at least one three-stringed cello are discernible. In short, the distillation of the various families of instrument, such as the three-stringed rebec and the seven-stringed lira, into the four-stringed violin with carved back and front, provided a form which could easily be extended to the larger sizes for the consort, the viola supplying the middle voice and the cello as the bass instrument. The full name of the instrument, the 'violoncello', did not become widely agreed until the late seventeenth century, the instrument being described variously as 'violoncino' or even 'violone' in Italy,[1] the 'bas de violon' or 'basse de violin' in France and 'bass violin' elsewhere until well into the eighteenth century.

The oldest surviving cello is the work of Andrea Amati, the maker also of the earliest attributable violins, and is dated 1572. It was made as part of a group of instruments for Charles IX, King of France 1560–74, and shows that the cello was established as a member of the violin family at a very early stage.

Fig. 1.5 Detail from the cupola of Sarrono Cathedral painted by Gaudenzio Ferrari (1535), showing a cellist. Although distorted by the curved surface of the painting, the cello is clearly depicted, and appears to have three strings.

Development

The development of the cello as a distinctive and formally acknowledged instrument was inhibited by the practice, which continued well into the seventeenth century, of preferring the viol to the cello as the bass instrument in string ensembles. The fretted six- or seven-stringed viol with its flat, rather than carved, back evolved from a quite different background to the violin family. In England particularly, the viol enjoyed a reputation for refinement and delicacy of performance even into the eighteenth century, as it was capable of greater articulation than the early cello, with its rather clumsy tones. The practice derived from the slow acceptance of the violin as a court instrument, it having previously been regarded as the instrument of the street musician to whom volume of sound was more important than articulation. Nevertheless, cellos made by the earliest violin makers still survive today, though in a greater variety of forms than the violin.

Seventeenth-century paintings which depict the cello are much rarer than those which show either the violin or viol. In Dutch and Flemish paintings, the cello is almost invariably shown in the hands of street musicians or in tavern scenes, whilst courtly settings are usually graced by viols.

The early cello would probably have been more suited to supplying simple bass lines than the agile counterpoint associated with the viol. Indeed, the first description of a bass violin, by Martin Agricola in 1529, mentions only three strings, tuned to F–c–g;[2] and the beautiful cellos of Andrea Amati were probably made to accommodate only three strings, the pegbox having been modified later to accept a fourth peg.

Tuning is the first problem encountered in tracing the early development of the cello. After Agricola, most descriptions cite four strings,[3] the extra one being added below the F to give a tuning of Bb^1–F–c–g, a tone below modern tuning. This 'Bb^1' tuning was suggested quite logically by moving downward in fifths respectively from the tunings of the violin (g–d^1–a^1–e^2) and viola (c–g–d^1–a^1). However, having the instrument pitched naturally in a flat key made ensemble playing awkward, and the present tuning, with the cello doubling the viola an octave below, was current in Italy in the early seventeenth century;[4] it spread only slowly, the old 'Bb^1' tuning continuing to appear in England until the following century.

The early cello was not only tuned in different ways, but it was also made in a wide range of sizes. The first instruments made in Cremona by Andrea Amati and his family were of large size, sometimes referred to as the 'bassetto', *c*. 79 cm in length of back. However, almost contemporary with these were smaller cellos made in Brescia, with the back measuring only *c*. 71 cm. These two sizes seem to have persisted as alternatives well into the eighteenth century, and they have provoked some discussion amongst modern scholars as to whether they were one and the same instrument or, rather, two variants designed for different usages and tunings. The *c*. 71 cm shorter model obviously derived from doubling the back length of the 35.5 cm violin, but other considerations must have given rise to the *c*. 79 cm larger model. Makers seem to have chosen one model or the other, but a few, such as Gofriller of Venice (working between 1690 and 1720), seem to have produced almost equal quantities of both. Two of Stradivari's surviving templates for cello necks bear the interesting inscriptions 'measure of the ordinary cello neck', and on another, some 31 mm longer and 5 mm deeper at the root (indicating the height of the ribs), 'measure of the Venetian cello neck'. In England, the first cellos appeared at the end of the seventeenth century; an example by William Baker of Oxford, attributed to 1672 when the low Bb^1 tuning was commonplace in this country, is of the smaller *c*. 71 cm size.

The unfortunate result of the preference for the larger model in Cremona is that most seventeenth-century cellos made by the greatest violin makers have been cut down for modern use and have thereby lost the original integrity of their design. Those which survive in their original

Table 1.1
Measurements for the Stradivari 'Forma B'
cello, which is now an accepted standard
(although dimensions of the body can still
vary considerably)

length of body	756 mm
widths: upper bout	342 mm
middle bout	229 mm
lower bout	437 mm
depth of ribs at neck	117 mm
depth of ribs at endpin	123 mm
length of neck, from nut to belly edge	280 mm
length of stop, from bridge to belly top edge	400 mm
length of scroll	205 mm
maximum width of scroll	68 mm

form are not popular with players accustomed to the ease of playing the modern size of instrument.

The standard measurement today is a back length of approximately 75 cm, a median measurement between the two earlier sizes which was first arrived at in Cremona towards the end of the seventeenth century. Stradivari had already made several instruments of the larger pattern when Francesco Rugeri began to work to a 75 cm model. Stradivari's revised pattern on that size, the 'B' form introduced after 1707, was one of the greatest achievements of his distinguished career, and a wonderful legacy to modern cellists (see Table 1.1).

Stradivari's work did much to gain for the cello its current status in music, his refined designs giving a greater range of expressiveness and sheer power of tone to the soloist and ensemble player. Early cellos largely follow a very bulbous form, with the back and front highly arched; this can provide a resonant bass, which was mostly all that was required of the cello in the seventeenth century. By flattening the arch, Stradivari increased the projection and focus of sound on all four strings. The balance between a dark, powerful bass, and a bright, singing treble has always been the greatest challenge to the cello maker, and Stradivari has come the closest to achieving that ideal (see Fig. 1.6).

These improvements were made possible by progress in the manufacture of strings. Early bass strings were enormously thick strands of gut and were difficult to play with clear articulation. Rope-twist and overspun (i.e.

Fig. 1.6 Cello by Antonio Stradivari in Cremona, 1712. Made to the 'B' form and known as the 'Davidoff', this cello was played by Jacqueline du Pré.

gut with a wire wrapping) strings made the bass register in particular more agile, and allowed subsequent developments in playing technique and refinements in instrument design.[5]

At first, the cello was made with a comparatively short neck and a short, wedge-shaped fingerboard, since little demand was made on the instrument's upper registers (see Fig. 1.7). Few instruments show precisely how the cello was set up in the earliest period; seventeenth-century instruments by Gaspar Bourbon and Martin Kaiser in the Brussels collection are the only important instruments to have survived in original condition. Information also accrues from contemporary accounts, such as the 'Talbot Manuscript'[6] and iconography. Many of Stradivari's original templates and patterns still exist, however; housed in the Stradivari Museum, Cremona, these enable reliable reconstruction to be undertaken.

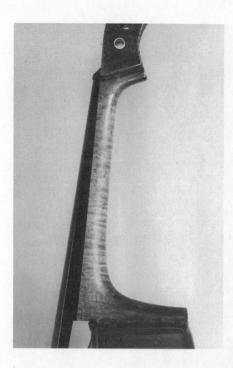

Fig. 1.7 Early cello neck with wedge-shaped fingerboard, fixed to the ribs by nails, rather than the mortising method employed today

Seventeenth-century pictures show the cello being played in three ways: with the cello resting on the floor and between the player's calves; the cello supported on a stool or chair, again with the player seated; or with the player standing or marching, the cello hung from a strap running over the musician's shoulder. Most seventeenth-century cellos have a large plugged hole at just above the mid-point of the back, generally assumed to be the position of a peg to which a carrying strap was fastened. The cellos of Andrea Guarneri (1626–98) often have this feature, whilst those of his son, Giuseppe, and other Cremonese makers of the following century, including Stradivari himself, do not. On many eighteenth-century English instruments the front face of the neck-root, where it projects above the belly to the underside of the fingerboard, is rounded off; this is clearly the place where a carrying strap was secured, the other end being tied to the endpin.

Many other aspects of the cello were the subject of wide variation and experimentation well into the eighteenth century. Most Cremonese makers made instruments that were a hybrid between the cello and bass viol. Stradivari made at least two cellos before 1700 with a flat back, while other luthiers, including Amati (one example, in the Ashmolean Museum, Oxford, is dated 1611) and Joseph 'filius Andrea' Guarneri (dated 1702), made bass viols in cello form, illustrating the overlapping role of the two instruments and indicating the quest for a design which incorporated the agility of the viol and the sonority of the cello. The English violist Christopher Simpson claimed in his *Division Violist* (London, 1659) that

Fig. 1.8(a) & (b) Five-string piccolo cello by Antonio and Hieronymous Amati in Cremona, *c.* 1615. Note the extended pegbox with provision for five pegs.

viols of the cello shape were better for sound; furthermore, viols were converted into cellos by replacing the neck and restringing. Concurrent with these models were the 'violoncello piccolo' and the five-string cello (with an additional e string), possibly one and the same instrument. An example made by the Amati brothers from around 1620 (see Fig. 1.8a and b) has a very short body of about 66 cm, and the pegbox is elongated and drilled to receive five pegs. This may have been the prototype for other such instruments made elsewhere – notably the extant English examples by William Baker (dated 1682), Barak Norman, a celebrated maker of both viols and cellos in the early eighteenth century, and Edmund Aireton (as late as 1776). All that can be said with certainty about the role of such instruments is that they seem to fit the requirements of Bach's Sixth Cello Suite (BWV1012).

While the design of the cello reached its ideal with Stradivari's 'B' form, changes in detail and fittings have continued to the present day. The short, stocky eighteenth-century neck was gradually made slimmer to facilitate playing in the upper positions; in the process, the old system of nailing the neck to the body (see Fig. 1.7), or setting the ribs into slots cut in the side of the neck, was abandoned in favour of the modern system of mortising the neck into the upper block, thus making repair and restoration of the instrument more practicable. The fingerboard has been lengthened to extend the range on each string, but it is now made of solid ebony rather than veneered wood in order to resist the wear caused by metal-covered strings. The bass-bar has increased in length and depth to provide more support for the lower-register strings. The bridge is now lighter, yielding greater volume of sound, and its delicate form has evolved into two basic designs: the French, which is more common, and the even lighter Belgian model, which is used to gain greater volume rather than tonal breadth. A further refinement to the fingerboard was introduced by Bernhard Romberg (1767–1841), who flattened it beneath the length of the C string to provide increased clearance for the wide vibration of that heavy string when played *forte*, and thus avoid its grating buzzes and rattles against the fingerboard surface.

The most important development for the player was the adjustable endpin, introduced by Adrien Servais *c.* 1845 to give the instrument greater stability during large shifts of the left hand. Various types of fixed or screw-in wooden extensions were tried for the endpin, which was originally similar to that of the violin, in order to support the instrument from the floor. The adjustable endpin is fitted directly to the cello; its metal spike can slide into the body of the instrument during transportation and out to the required length to raise the cello into a comfortable playing position. Increasing in popularity today is the bent endpin, which has been particularly associated with Rostropovich. In addition to the sliding action, this model is hinged so that it can be locked into a downward position, lifting the cello into a more horizontal plane. This has advantages for bowing, as it allows the weight of the bow to be addressed more directly downwards on to the string than when the cello is in a more upright position.

Principal centres of cello making and their chief representatives

Cremona and Brescia

Andrea Amati (pre-1505–1577) was the first recorded maker in Cremona, the greatest centre of violin and cello making, and the first of four generations of luthiers who spanned the entire period of Cremona's dominance. His work is marked by elegance and an awareness of geometrical principles in design. His modelling is of great delicacy, from the regular winds of the scroll to the tips of the f-holes. The instruments made for Charles IX of

France were also decorated in polychrome with the Royal arms and are particularly striking. The oldest surviving example, dated 1572, is the earliest cello in existence. Unfortunately, the philistine efforts of past repairers have reduced the large dimensions of these instruments to the smaller modern size, thereby destroying their harmony and integrity. Significantly, the pegboxes were originally made to contain only three strings, like the instrument depicted by Ferrari in 1535 (see Fig. 1.5). The addition of a fourth string to the cello was probably an innovation of Andrea's own lifetime, since later instruments made by him were clearly originally designed to accommodate four tuning pegs. Andrea and his family were consummate craftsmen: his two sons, Antonius (1540–?) and Hieronymus (1561–1630) continued to use their father's glorious golden brown varnish, which was perhaps the greatest possession of the Cremonese makers, but modified the patterns, most noticeably the f-holes, whose circular finials are smaller, and tips, or 'wings', are wider.

Nicolo Amati (1596–1684) was the son of Hieronymus and perhaps the greatest maker of the dynasty, although surviving cellos are rare compared to those of his father and uncle. However, his son, Hieronymus II (1649–1740), contributed some wonderful cellos of the large size.

Equally important in the history of the cello is Francesco Rugeri (1620–*c.* 1695). When plague decimated Cremona in 1630, Nicolo Amati had no immediate heirs and took on apprentices from outside the family. Of these, Rugeri proved a most prolific and innovatory cello maker. His fully arched designs borrow much from Amati, but have a distinctive style of their own (see Fig. 1.9). Often made from modest slabs of poplar wood, yet sometimes from spectacular pieces of flamed maple, they are brought to life by a luscious and richly pigmented varnish. More importantly, Rugeri pioneered the reduced *c.* 75 cm model which, after a century of variation, became the accepted standard for the next fifty years.

Another pupil of Nicolo Amati, Andrea Guarneri (1626–98), began to make cellos of similar size towards the end of his career, but with an original pattern: broad across the lower bouts and with fully rounded upper bouts. Generally high in the arching, they are magnificently modelled, with impulsive workmanship (see Fig. 1.10). Much of the work on his later instruments was probably carried out by his son, Giuseppe Guarneri (1666–1739), who continued to produce fine cellos on the smaller pattern, introducing a more slender form of f-hole but using inferior varieties of wood: beech appears as often as poplar, and sometimes a poorer quality of dark-brown varnish is used.[7]

Guarneri was overshadowed throughout his career by Antonio Stradivari (1644–1737), who was probably also a pupil of Nicolo Amati and was by far the most gifted and successful luthier of all. His earliest cello

Fig. 1.9 Cello by Francesco Rugeri in Cremona, *c.* 1690

dates from 1667 and already shows great originality. His craftsmanship was impeccable and hardly faltered throughout his seventy-year career, allowing him to concentrate all his energies on a steady refinement of design. Taking as a starting-point the work of Nicolo Amati, Stradivari gradually imbued the already graceful style with a noble aspect, a majestic quality to match the resulting profound sonority. His most important early innovations to the large-pattern cello were his flatter and more powerful archings and a new system of graduating the thickness of the plates. His f-holes are longer and less curved and his scrolls are more substantial than those of his predecessors. Stradivari also introduced a stronger red pigment to his varnish, which gives his best-preserved instruments a

Fig. 1.10 Cello by Andrea Guarneri, Cremona, *c.* 1680

seemingly bottomless depth of colour. Although many of his earlier instruments, like those of the Amatis, have subsequently been reduced in size, some magnificent specimens survive, such as the 'Medici' (1690), the 'Castelbarco' (1697) and the 'Servais' (1701).

During the first decade of the eighteenth century Stradivari experimented with the cello. These experiments resulted in his greatest achievement, the 'B' form – a designation appearing on some of the original paper patterns housed in the Stradivari Museum in Cremona. This completely original design made to the smaller *c.* 75 cm back-length spawns a succession of superb instruments such as the 'Gore-Booth' (1710), the 'Duport' (1711), the 'Davidoff' (1712; see Fig. 1.6) and the 'Batta' (1714), representing sustained work of a genius unsurpassed in cello making. These cellos have a remarkable clarity of focus and potential for tonal projection, and they have been owned and played by the greatest artists – from Servais and Piatti to Du Pré, Rostropovich and Yo-Yo Ma.

Stradivari did not rest there, however. By 1730, at the age of eighty-six, he had produced other designs, first reduced in length by 2–3 cm or so, and subsequently reduced in width, as exemplified by the 'De Munck' cello, ascribed to 1730. Judging from the workmanship of these late instruments, however, it is probable that the old man delegated much of the construction to his son Francesco (1671–1743).[8]

After Stradivari's death, no cellos appeared from the workshops of Cremona until the inferior instruments of Lorenzo Storioni (1751–*c.* 1800), but the city remains an influential centre. Its International School of Violin Making has trained many of today's leading makers, and Cremonese luthiers have never failed to find a market for their work, despite a certain inconsistency during the present century.

The first rival to Cremona as a centre for cello making was Brescia. Only a short distance from Cremona, Brescia nevertheless had a distinctive style of work in the sixteenth century. Gasparo da Salò (1540–1609) was its first known maker of cellos; his instruments, though very rare, have a rugged finish and a charm quite different from his Cremonese contemporaries, the brothers Amati (see Fig. 1.11). They were made in both the large size (over 76 cm), and in a small 71 cm length which is more suited to modern performance than the monstrous *bassetti* of the early Cremonese makers. Their flat arching, with no discernible modelling around the edge, yields a strong tone. Da Salò's purfling, though crudely laid in, is sometimes doubled or led into decorative traceries on the back. Significantly, few (if any) of his cellos have survived with their original scrolls; it may be too late to speculate what eccentricity of their design led to their replacement, but it is possible that they were made to carry only three strings.

Da Salò was succeeded in Brescia by his pupil Giovanni Paolo Maggini (1581–1632), whose early work is almost indistinguishable from that of his master. However, Maggini seems to have been aware of the high level of craftsmanship in Cremona, and aimed to emulate it, though with only limited success. The plague, which claimed the life of Maggini, seems to have closed the workshops of Brescia until the arrival *c.* 1675 of Giovanni Baptista Rogeri (active 1670–1705). A pupil of Nicolo Amati, Rogeri at last brought to Brescia the level of finesse which had escaped Maggini. One of the most elegant craftsmen to benefit from Amati's teaching, he nevertheless adopted important aspects of the Brescian tradition in his work. He made some of his cellos on the small Brescian size of 71 cm, but with a characteristic width and with very flat, stiff archings recalling those of da

Fig. 1.11 Cello by Gasparo da Salò in Brescia, *c.* 1580. In common with most other cellos from Brescia, the scroll of this cello has not survived.

Salò. Thus they anticipated the cellos of Rugeri and even Stradivari in Cremona, combining the tonal quality of Cremona with the throaty power of Brescian work. Nevertheless, Rogeri was sometimes tempted to take short cuts: although he used fine wood, he frequently omitted the purfling on the back, merely scratching two black lines around the edge.

Venice

More important than Brescia in the later development of the cello is Venice. Matteo Gofriller (1659–1742) was a cello builder of the first rank, founding a tradition which has challenged Cremona as the home of the

Fig. 1.12 Cello by Matteo Gofriller in Venice, *c.* 1690

finest instruments. Instructed by the Tyrolean maker Martin Kaiser, Gofriller established the Venetian style, distinguished largely by a deep red varnish which now characteristically shows a crackled and wrinkled finish (see Fig. 1.12). The standard of his workmanship falls between that of Brescian and Cremonese makers, but it is marked by great character, revealed especially in his diminutive and casually carved scrolls. He adopted several patterns of quite voluptuous form, ranging from the smallest 71 cm model to the largest *bassetto* size, most of which have been cut down to modern proportions. His arching is generally quite low, and the noble sound has substantial carrying power. His son, Francesco (1692–*c.* 1740), though by no means his equal in terms of his craftsman-

Fig. 1.13 Cello by Domenico Montagnana in Venice, *c.* 1740

ship, also produced successful instruments, one of which served Pablo Casals as his concert instrument.

Matteo Gofriller's pupil, Domenico Montagnana (1687–1750), was to have the greatest impact as a cello builder. Known as the 'Mighty Venetian' because of the dramatic appearance and equally dramatic tone of his cellos, his name is the only one to merit serious comparison with Stradivari. Very different in style to those of Stradivari, his cellos are broad, uncompromising and sometimes difficult to play, but in the hands of the best virtuosos they are capable of the most expressive and passionate tone (see Fig. 1.13). The curves of the outline are barely controlled, the back seeming ill-matched to the front on occasion, and the arching is low but strongly modelled with a deep hollow around the edges. The scrolls are profoundly ripped from the wood, but retain a decent regularity, and the whole is set off by an extravagant covering of curdled ruby-red varnish.

Montagnana found first an assistant, and later a serious rival, in Pietro Guarneri (1695–1762), the son of Andrea Guarneri of Cremona, who arrived in Venice around 1717. He proved as flexible as Rogeri in adapting the traditions of Cremona to his new environment: the example of Montagnana allowed him to incorporate a certain freedom of design into his more formal level of craftsmanship, with the result being clothed in the more vivid Venetian varnish. It is only the comparative rarity of his cellos that keeps his reputation below that of Montagnana.

Several other notable cello makers flourished in Venice – probably more than in any other Italian city – among them Carlo Tononi (1675–1730), Francesco Gobetti (1675–1723) and Sanctus Serafin (1699–1758). Venetian makers seem to have developed a particularly appropriate style of work for the cello, and their success was sustained until the end of the eighteenth century.

Other Italian centres of cello making

Of the other Italian centres of stringed-instrument making, Rome is distinguished by the presence of the German David Tecchler (*c.* 1666–*c.* 1747), who was a prolific maker of cellos. His style was firmly rooted in the German tradition – with highly vaulted archings deeply hollowed around the edge – but his workmanship gained a certain Italianate flair (see Fig. 1.14). His varnish is often pale in colour but deeply crackled, and the wood is of variable quality and often of local growth. He remained faithful to the large *bassetto* model, and although most of his instruments have now been cut down, they remain imposing in both proportion and tonal resource.

Florence was the home of several distinguished makers, notably Bartolomeo Cristofori (1655–1731),[9] Giovanni Gabbrielli (active 1740–70) and the Carcassi brothers, Lorenzo and Tomasso (active 1750–80). Cristofori was a pupil of Nicolo Amati; his work, though rare, is of the large size and very refined in the Cremonese manner. However, his successors Gabbrielli and the Carcassis turned to the increasingly fashionable German style, which most makers of the mid-eighteenth century adopted with varying degrees of success. Gabbrielli managed to keep within the bounds of an exaggerated style, whilst the Carcassis often did not.

Milanese makers produced cellos of mixed quality. The best were from the workshop of Giovanni Grancino (active 1685–1726), whose varnish tends towards a clear yellow or pale brown and is tender and fine textured. His modelling and design were greatly influenced by Amati and extended

Fig. 1.14 Cello by David Tecchler in Rome, 1714

to the flatter arching (although not so effectively shaped) and slender
model of Stradivari. Mostly made to the larger size, Grancino's instruments nevertheless produce a reliable sound – clear, strong and with undeniable Italian quality. Amongst his notable successors were members of
the Testore family, the eldest of whom, Carlo Giuseppe (active 1720–60),
was a fine craftsman; however, the skill and patience of succeeding generations deteriorated dramatically, despite retaining the ability to produce
some instruments of excellent tonal potential.

Almost on a par with Stradivari and Montagnana was Alessandro Gagliano of Naples (active 1700–35), who produced a tantalisingly small number of cellos of superb quality. Finely worked, of large scale yet beautifully proportioned, and with a glorious red varnish, his refined style died with him; his large and prolific family subsequently populated Naples with instruments whose quality ranges from fine to indifferent. Omobono Stradivari spent some time in the city before the death of his father Antonio in 1737, and it is probably his influence which prompted the change of style evident in the work of Alessandro's sons, Nicolo and Gennaro. Usually Stradivarian in style, their work is let down by an inferior varnish, though the sound can be satisfying and effective; like the energetic makers of Milan, the Gagliano family have provided many discerning players with excellent sounding instruments, although these are not of the very first rank.

Giovanni Battista Guadagnini (*c.* 1711–86) was probably the last of the truly inspired Italian makers. He adopted a very idiosyncratic cello model: it was of the short 71 cm size, yet broad and deep with a long string-length, and offered excellent sound and ease of playing. His varnish varied considerably, doubtless on account of his unsettled career which took him from his birthplace, Piacenza, to Milan, Cremona, Parma and, finally, Turin, where his contact with the dealer and expert Count Cozio di Salabue aided the latter's efforts to piece together for the first time the history of the craft in Italy. Guadagnini's successor in Turin was Giuseppe Rocca (1807–65), a member of the new generation of nineteenth-century makers who abandoned altogether the notion of an independent style and successfully copied Stradivari's patterns to produce a small number of excellent cellos.

Europe outside Italy.

Beyond Italy, many fine makers originated from the Tyrol but settled in cities throughout Europe. The town of Fussen in the Algau was a centre for lute making as early as the fifteenth century, and many of its craftsmen left the town after their apprenticeship to travel throughout Europe as journeymen, taking the crafts of instrument making with them to the cities of Italy. The greatest violin maker of the region was Jacob Stainer (1617–83), whose skill rivalled that of Nicolo Amati, but it is unlikely that he made any cellos. Those ascribed to him are generally converted bass viols, but his influence on other cello makers was considerable. Stainer single-handedly developed a style which gradually diverged from that of Amati, with a stiff, high arch, deeply worked around the edges, and small curling soundholes. This style quickly established itself amongst other luthiers, and Stainer was elevated to the rank of the great Cremonese. However, his style proved less adaptable to the violin as it developed a stronger voice in the eighteenth century. Nevertheless, makers throughout Italy and northern Europe, including the British Isles, persisted with the Stainer model for their cellos with considerable success, until the ultimate demands of the concert hall prompted the final triumph of the Stradivari model. Many cellos of the Stainer pattern, with the added benefit of age, are capable of out-performing newer instruments of Italian form, and examples by Peter Wamsley (active *c.* 1725–1744), Benjamin Banks (1727–95) and William Forster (1739–1808) of England and Leopold Widhalm (1722–76) of Nuremberg are greatly sought after.

The cello became particularly popular in England in the eighteenth and nineteenth centuries, and instruments were made in large numbers, many of them to very high standards. Thomas Dodd (active 1785–1830) and John Betts (1752–1823) of London were quick to see the advantages of making careful copies of the Stradivari instruments which they bought and sold in their shops. Employing a skilled workforce of craftsmen from Germany and Italy, they raised the standards of instrument making in England considerably and produced a valuable quantity of first-class cellos, whose reputation is steadily increasing amongst musicians the world over.

The master of the art of copying the great instruments of Stradivari was the French maker Jean-Baptiste Vuillaume (1798–1875). An ingenious and gifted craftsman, he was also a very successful dealer and business-man. His copies of Stradivari instruments are of clinical accuracy right down to the worn varnish, making his instruments very attractive to players, despite a slightly dry sound-quality (see Fig. 1.15).

Contemporary makers

Instrument making has undergone a minor renaissance in recent years, due in some part to the success of the various schools of violin making in Cremona in Italy, Mittenwald in Germany, Salt Lake City in the USA, and Newark in England. Many young makers are choosing to specialise in the cello, and very fine instruments are once more being produced in good numbers – the designs based on the Classical forms of the old Italians are being steadily developed to meet players' demands. The Manchester Cello Festival – a biennial event based at the Royal Northern College of Music – has become a major international fixture, and the competition for cello making has awarded prizes to today's leading makers such as the Frenchmen Frank Ravatin and Patrick Robin. In this country, David Rubio and Helen Michetslager have devoted a large proportion of their work to the cello. Roger Hargrave, an Englishman trained in Newark but currently

Fig. 1.15 Cello by Jean-Baptiste Vuillaume in Paris, 1848, after Stradivarius

working in Germany, has won a gold medal for cello making at the Cremona Triennale competition and is now well established as one of today's leading cello makers. Many young Italian makers have also been successful in national and international competitions, while Peter and Wendy Moes, Joseph Grubaugh and Sigrun Seifert are among numerous significant American makers. Of this present generation, some have specialised very successfully in making exact replicas of Classical instruments, in the manner pioneered by John Betts and Vuillaume in the previous century, whilst others work to produce individual designs.

Modern developments have included Carleen Hutchins' new family of violins – comprising eight instruments constructed on the basis of

mathematical design, acoustical theory and Classical violin-making principles (see chapter 3, pp. 45–6) – and the electric cello. The latter is a solid
mahogany skeletal cello designed to replace the combination of acoustic
cello and pickup and offer greater facility in the electronic modification of
sounds.[10] An electric transducer system is normally set into a specially
designed bridge. A five-string electric cello developed in the late 1990s by
Philip Sheppard seems destined to equip players with a new flexibility and
versatility for the third millennium. This instrument can be played
acoustically but offers an almost limitless sound-world at the flick of a
switch.

2 The bow: its history and development

JOHN DILWORTH

The bow has a far longer history than the cello, but the instrument's rapid development made new demands on the existing bows of the sixteenth century. Although it appeared in many forms before 1500, the bow is most often depicted as a simply curved stick with a skein of horsehair stretched between the ends (see Fig. 2.1). The hair was kept in permanent tension, and the deep curve of the stick gave it a high centre of gravity, making it difficult to control. The curve was made flatter during the sixteenth century with the addition of the frog, a wedge which kept the hair clear of the stick at the handle. Early bow makers remain anonymous, and it is not clear whether instrument makers made and supplied their own bows. Only from the eighteenth century did bows begin to appear with the maker's name branded on the stick or the frog.

Nowadays, the craft of the 'archetier', or bow maker, is entirely separated from that of the 'luthier', or instrument maker. The major innovations in bow making during the Baroque period are associated with musicians rather than craftsmen; violinists generally set the pace for development, while cellists were able to make good use of the designs produced for viol players. The bow-type named after the violinist and composer Arcangelo Corelli (1653–1713) has a longer and straighter stick and a down-turned tip to raise the end of the stick away from the hair, matching the frog and increasing the usable length of hair. The tip evolved into various elegant shapes, referred to as 'pike head' or 'swan bill'. The 'clip-in' frog allowed the tension of the hair to be relaxed, prolonging the life of both hair and bow (see Fig. 2.2). The hair was fixed to the stick at each end, and the frog provided the tension when wedged into place. The screw-adjustment mechanism by which the frog is made to travel along the stick in order to tension the hair was anonymously developed c. 1700 and was eventually universally adopted.

Giuseppe Tartini (1692–1770) promoted the introduction of a deeper, more modern shape of tip, although elements of the 'swan-bill' form have remained in the design of the cello bow, which is still rather more elongated in the tip than the violin bow. Another violinist, Wilhelm Cramer (1745–99), introduced the incurved or concave stick. This last development – made possible by previous changes to the frog and tip, and the use of stronger varieties of wood – is the most crucial, and provides the essen-

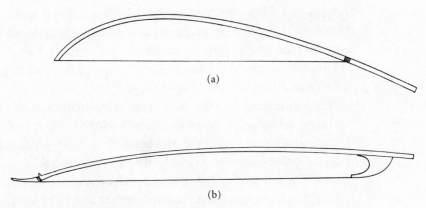

(a)

(b)

Fig. 2.1 Types of medieval and Renaissance bows

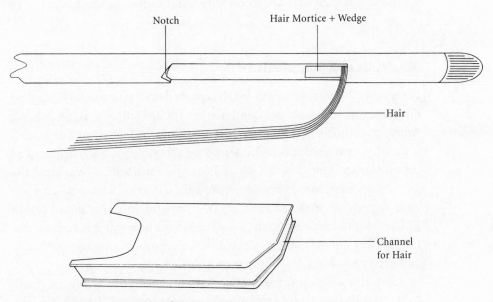

Notch   Hair Mortice + Wedge

Hair

Channel
for Hair

Fig. 2.2 'Clip-in' bow frog

tial playing qualities of the modern bow. The Cramer bow is now known as
a transitional type, with a squat 'hatchet' or taller 'battle-axe' head and an
open frog (lacking the slide which covers the hair over the bottom face),
often ornately carved from ivory. Much experimentation was undertaken
in England and France to decide the optimum size of the head and curve of
the stick, and the playing length and width of the band of hair was gradually increased.

The final form of the bow was determined by the great French craftsman François Tourte (1747–1835), known as the 'Stradivari of the bow'.
Although it cannot be proved that he invented any of the individual

features that define the modern bow, he was the first to employ them effectively. He refined the shape of the head, and equipped the ebony frog with the slide and 'D-ring', or ferrule, to maintain the hair in a uniform ribbon. He also perfected the incurved shape of the stick to produce an ideal balance, weight and spring in the pernambuco wood.

The period since 1850 has been marked by attempts at innovation; the steel bow and the self-hairing bow were developed by J.-B. Vuillaume. The first was intended to solve the problems of the relatively fragile wooden stick; however, steel was found to be equally vulnerable – to rust and fatigue. The self-hairing bow could be rehaired with prepared lengths of hair by the player, rather than requiring the skills of a bow maker, but this idea never caught on. Modern experiments have been directed towards replacing pernambuco (which is now threatened with extinction) with synthetic materials such as carbon fibre – and with some success.

Materials and manufacture

Pernambuco (*echinata caesalpina*) has proved the best material for a good bow, because of its unique combination of strength and resilience. An Amazonian timber, named after the port from which it was first exported, it is now a protected species under severe threat by the encroachment of the rainforests. The 'Corelli' bow of the seventeenth century was generally made from snakewood (*brosimum aubleti*), a heavier Amazonian variety with a speckled, snakeskin-like grain. It was the introduction of South American timbers to Europe in the sixteenth century which made possible the changes in bow making, since only these woods have the suppleness and strength needed in a long, straight bow.

In making a bow, great care and attention is paid to selecting the wood. Close and flawless grain is required in order to work the wood to the required weight without losing strength. The stick is first sawn out straight, with the rough head incorporated at one end, and bent to the correct curve with dry heat. It is then finished with very small planes and files to the correct tapering diameter. This work is highly skilled, and it is the maker's appreciation of the qualities of the wood which determines the final shaping, since the final weight, strength and balance must all fall within very fine tolerances. To make the bow easier to control, the tip must be reasonably light yet responsive to the player. To achieve this, the stick is made thinner, and the curve, or 'spring', made progressively deeper towards the head. In the finished bow, the stick will normally be closest to the hair approximately two-thirds of its length towards the head. Bows are made with either an octagonally faceted or round cross-section, those

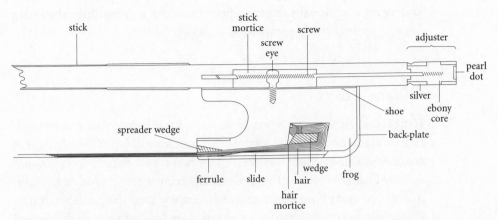

stick

stick
mortice   screw

screw
eye

adjuster

pearl
dot

silver

shoe   ebony
core

spreader wedge

back-plate

ferrule   slide   hair   frog

wedge
hair

hair
mortice

Fig. 2.3 Cross-section of the frog of a modern bow

made of heavier snakewood in the pre-Tourte period often being fluted along the length of each facet for lightness.

Once the stick has been shaped, the head can be carved and given its protective face of ivory lined with ebony, and a mortice cut to receive the hair and its retaining limewood wedge. At the other end, an elongated mortice is cut in the stick to accept the screw eye, and a hole of small diameter is drilled in from the end to meet the mortice to accommodate the adjuster (see Fig. 2.3).

The frog is carved from a block of ebony. Although tortoiseshell and ivory have been used in the past, these materials are now legally controlled and rarely employed. The top surface of the frog is carefully fitted to the stick, which is left faceted at the handle so that the frog cannot twist around the stick. The thin edges of the frog are protected by a silver lining shoe. A groove is then cut in the lower face to receive the mother-of-pearl slide which covers the hair mortice. The front is shaped to accept the silver D-ring, and a silver back-plate is fitted. The sides of the frog are carved with a concave form, and a mother-of-pearl dot is inlaid in each side, sometimes surrounded by a silver ring. The brass screw-eye is threaded into the top face, and the frog can then be fitted to the stick by means of the adjuster, which is a silver tip often decorated with ebony and mother-of pearl, set on to a threaded steel shaft.

The finished stick is oiled, waxed or french-polished, according to the taste of the maker, and the handle is given a lapping of leather, thread, silver wire or whalebone to protect it from wear by the player's hand. The maker shows his own individual style in the choice of these fine decorative materials and devices. On a particularly fine stick, gold is often substituted for silver, and may sometimes be chased and engraved. On cheaper grades of bow, nickel silver is frequently used in place of silver, and is even occasionally found on fine bows made during times of scarcity of silver or financial hardship for the maker.

Famous makers

Little is known about early bow makers. An English reference *c.* 1670 mentions a violin by a named maker with a 'stockman's bowe', implying that the bow was an accessory supplied by another tradesman. A violin bow has survived with the brand of Tononi, the eighteenth-century Venetian violin maker, and many bows with eighteenth-century English brands are extant. It was common practice, however, for makers to stamp the work supplied by others, and the fine cello bows of John Dodd, for example, are found with the brands of Forster, Betts and Banks superimposed. The collection of Stradivari tools and templates in the Civic Museum in Cremona includes patterns for bow-frogs, but of the bows attributed to his hand only two fluted snakewood bows in the collection of W. E. Hill & Sons have any real claim to authenticity.

The Cramer type and other transitional bows are the first to be attributed to specialist bow makers. In Paris, Louis Tourte *père* (*c.* 1740–1780)[1] and Jacques Lafleur (1757–1832) made bows with incurved sticks and elegant ivory frogs, adopting various head shapes. In London, Edward Dodd (1705–1810) has been credited with many transitional bow-types in England, but his son John (1752–1839) is historically more important. His bows evolved in tandem with those of François Tourte in Paris, but he takes second place to the great Frenchman because of his less consistent craftsmanship.

France

François Tourte (1747–1835) was apprenticed as a watchmaker before becoming a bow maker like his father and brother. He possessed not only the ingenuity to bring the bow to perfection,[2] but also the skill to make bows of unsurpassed quality which are still sought after by players and emulated by makers. He was succeeded by several native French bow makers who maintained their country's unassailed supremacy in the art of the 'archetier'. Tourte's bows are mainly octagonal in section, the profile in fact being slightly 'egg-shaped', especially near the tip, with the broadest part of the stick a little below the centre (see Fig. 2.4). Jean Dominique Adam (1795–1865) and his son, known as Grand-Adam (1823–69), both followed this tradition. Like many other great French bow makers, they were born in the town of Mirecourt and worked in Paris.

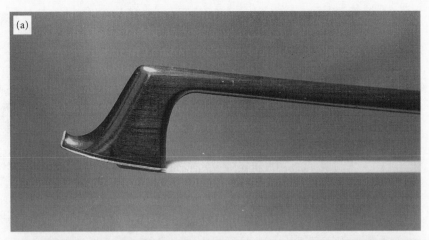

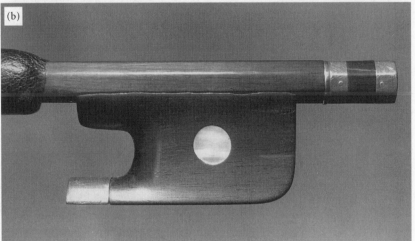

Fig. 2.4 Cello bow by François Tourte (a) tip; (b) heel

Also born in Mirecourt, Dominique Peccatte (1810–74) seems to have been Tourte's natural and most gifted successor. He worked for Vuillaume until 1837 and continued his association with him thereafter, with the result that many of Peccatte's bows bear the Vuillaume brand. Peccatte developed the Tourte bow, giving it a rounded cross-section (but with the 'egg-shape' accentuated), probably in an attempt to increase the lateral strength of the bow. Pierre Simon (1808–82) and Joseph Henry (1823–70), both pupils of Peccatte, continued to work in his style.

Mirecourt-born François Voirin (1833–85) made the last significant variation on the Tourte model. He resolved the more masculine 'hatchet'-type head into a finer, more delicately rounded form and likewise made the stick more perfectly round in section and more slender, with the camber increased in the first section near the head to regain any lost rigidity (Fig. 2.5). His cello bows are in fact often thought to be too light for modern

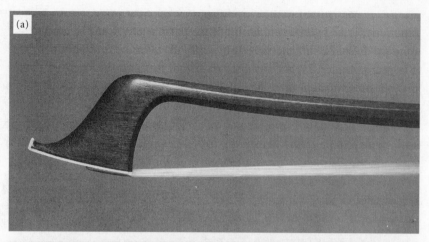

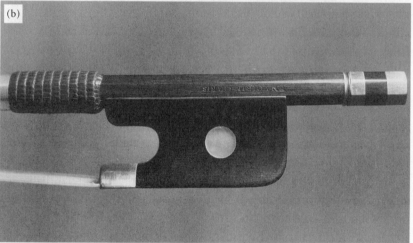

Fig. 2.5 Cello bow by François Voirin (a) tip; (b) heel

playing, rarely weighing more than 80 grams. Voirin's successors included Alfred Lamy (1850–1919) and Eugène Sartory (1871–1946).

Centres of bow making outside France

In England, the work of John Dodd (1752–1839) developed towards the modern bow but retained the 'open' frog. Through his efforts the bow attained an almost equal degree of sophistication in England as had been attained in France during the late eighteenth century. Dodd's cello bows, though variable and often a little short, are particularly successful and still in use (see Fig. 2.6). He was the most important member of a large family of instrument and bow makers; his nephew, James (*fl. c.* 1864), continued the tradition after his uncle's death.

The work of Thomas Tubbs (1790–1863) around 1840 defines the English style of the subsequent period, with large square heads, octagonal

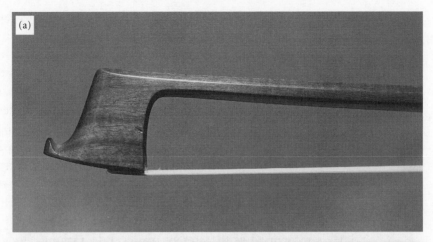

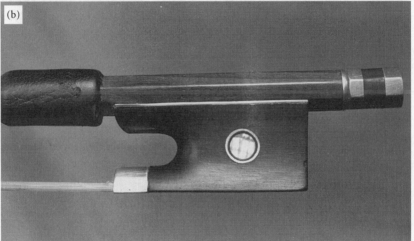

Fig. 2.6 Cello bow by John Dodd (a) tip; (b) heel

sticks, and eccentric inlays in the frog. This represented a stylistic dead-end, when attention was diverted briefly from the Classical model. However, the work of James Tubbs (1835–1921), the best-known maker of the family, returned English bows to a prominent position, equalling any example produced in France at the time; his work for W. E. Hill and Sons provided the impetus for an entire school of English bow makers trained by the Hills. Their bow workshops continued under William Retford (1875–1970) and others and have employed and trained many of the finest English bow makers.

Germany has produced some respected archetiers, such as Nikolaus Kittel (who worked in St Petersburg between 1839 and 1870), Ludwig Bausch (1805–71) and Albert Nürnberger (1854–1931). The name of Bausch, however, has been added to numerous factory-produced bows.

Today, fine bow makers are active throughout the world, including a number in the French tradition, and English makers trained by Hill and Sons. In France, Stephan Tomachot is the leading archetier of his generation. He studied in Mirecourt with Ouchard, who has played a large part in reviving post-war French bow making and has himself passed on the French tradition to a further group of bow makers who are now active world-wide. In Germany, Klaus Grunke is the current bow maker in a long family tradition, who is also passing on his art to others. In England, the tradition of W. E. Hill and Sons is still upheld. Tim Baker, who was trained at Hill and Sons, has grown in stature through his current association with London dealers J. and A. Beare Ltd; and Peter Oxley, who worked for several years in France, is now established as one of Great Britain's best makers. In America, Charles Espey, who worked with Tomachot for some time, is recognised as the present master. Bow making, alongside cello making, has experienced a considerable renaissance in the last thirty years.

3 Cello acoustics

BERNARD RICHARDSON

There is a huge diversity of bowed stringed instruments throughout the world. Their acoustical principles, however, are common. A bow is drawn across a taut string. Friction between the bow and the string excites the string into vibration. The string has particular vibrational properties which make it an 'ideal' musical signal source, but unfortunately its small size renders it practically inaudible. The string is therefore connected to some form of resonator, which is traditionally a wooden box (as in the case of the cello), a stretched animal skin or a gourd. The function of the resonator box is to vibrate in sympathy with the strings. The larger surface area of the box interacts readily with the surrounding air, creating sizeable pressure fluctuations which we hear as sounds.

This chapter aims to provide a brief introduction to cello acoustics and to add sufficient detail to the above simple model to explain various features of practical importance to players. The last thirty years have witnessed intense activity in the study of the acoustics of stringed musical instruments. In the case of bowed stringed instruments, work has concentrated almost exclusively on the violin, and readers interested in pursuing the subject further are directed to several standard works on the subject.[1] In many respects, the differences between violins and cellos are simply a matter of scale, the acoustical principles being the same in both cases. However, the increased body size and heavier strings and structure bring particular problems associated with starting transients and wolf-notes, both of which will be discussed later.

The bowed string

At first sight, it seems very strange that the slow, uni-directional movement of the bow can excite rapid, oscillatory motion of the string. This puzzling interaction was first investigated by Helmholtz.[2] Figure 3.1a illustrates the motion of the string, which at any time is broken into two straight segments. The vibrating portion of the string is that length between the bridge and nut for the open string, or between the bridge and the fingertip for the stopped string. The 'kink' between the two segments is not static, however, but traces out a cigar-shaped envelope, which, because

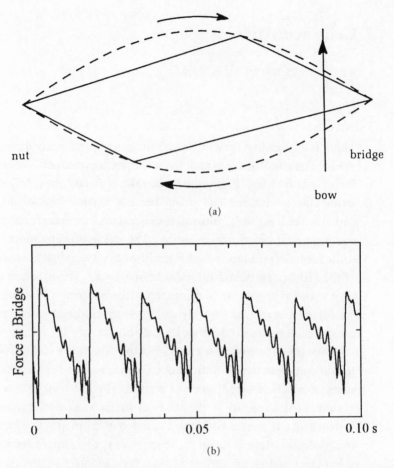

(a)

(b)

Fig. 3.1(a) Schematic diagram of the motion of a bowed string shown arrested at two different times during its vibration cycle. The kink in the string traces out the envelope of the vibration (dotted line). (b) The time-varying force signal which the open C string imparts at the bridge. This small variation is superimposed on the much larger, static down-bearing force created by the strings on the bridge. The time period is approximately 15 ms.

of the rapid movement, is all that is seen by the naked eye. Energy is supplied to the string by the frictional forces between the bow and string. The required amount of friction is generated by the rosin, which must coat both the bow and the string to work correctly. During most of the kink's cycle, the bow and string stick together and move at the speed governed by the player. Energy to sustain the oscillations is supplied during this phase. However, during the period in which the kink lies between the bow and the bridge, the bow and string are slipping, and the string moves in the opposite direction at a much higher speed. This 'slip-stick motion', as it is often called, is a consequence of static friction being greater than dynamic friction, an observation which can be most admirably made when removing the cork from a champagne bottle. Rosin, in fact, is a most interesting substance. Not only does it exhibit the usual friction characteristics described above, but it also has a melting-point very close to room temperature – one of the reasons why it feels so sticky. The frictional forces can heat the rosin such that it melts and solidifies once per cycle of the string, thereby affecting the dynamics of the process. Different rosins exhibit different frictional properties, which is why players are so choosy about using a particular brand of rosin.

Figure 3.1a shows that the strings make a variable angle with the bridge during each cycle of their motion. This alters the down-bearing force of the strings at the bridge, and even though the variations are small in comparison with the static load, it is this time-varying force which sets up vibrations of the body of the instrument to produce the sound. A graph of the force against time has a characteristic 'saw-tooth' appearance (see Fig. 3.1b). The perceived pitch of the sound is governed by the time-period of the motion, that is the time taken for the kink to travel once around the envelope; short time-periods give high pitches and long-time periods give low pitches. The inverse of the time-period gives the fundamental frequency of the motion. In the example given, the open C string has a fundamental frequency of 65 Hz (Hertz) or cycles per second.

The fundamental frequency (f) of the string is determined by its vibrating length (L) and the wave speed of the kink, the latter being given by the square-root of the ratio of the tension (T) and the mass per unit length (m) of the string. This relationship is summed up neatly in Mersenne's law:

$$f = \frac{1}{2L}\sqrt{\frac{T}{m}}$$

This law is qualitatively explored during tuning or string selection or whilst playing notes of different pitches. It is soon established that increasing the tension of the string increases the pitch. Similarly, shortening the vibrating length increases the pitch – for each semitone rise, the vibrating length of the string must be reduced by about 6 per cent. For a given length and comparable tension, as found across the four open strings, heavier strings give lower pitches. The fundamental frequencies of the open strings on the cello range from 65 to 220 Hz, with a playing range which extends to about 1000 Hz.[3]

When a musician bows an individual note on an instrument, it might reasonably be expected that this generates a sound of a single frequency. This is not the case, however. The fundamental string frequency is accompanied by a whole set of overtones, each of which is an integer multiple of the fundamental. Played individually, these overtones would form a harmonic series (see Ex. 3.1), but mixed together they invoke the sensation of

Ex. 3.1 The first eight harmonics of the harmonic series based on the open C string. The approximate frequency associated with each note is shown below the staff.

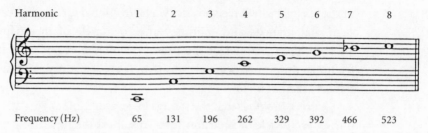

Harmonic	1	2	3	4	5	6	7	8
Frequency (Hz)	65	131	196	262	329	392	466	523

a single note with a single pitch and a particular tone-quality which depends on the relative intensities of the fundamental and overtones. The relationships between this harmonic mix and the tone-quality of the instrument will be explored further in the next section, but understanding the origin of the overtones helps to explain the musician's ability to play natural and artificial 'harmonics'.[4]

The subject of vibrating strings is most often approached by discussing the modes of vibration of a stretched string, several of which are sketched in Figure 3.2a. Modes are special vibrations which occur at resonances of the system. Near to the centre frequency of the resonance, it is easy to excite large vibrational amplitude for little effort. Individual modes of strings are rather difficult to excite without special equipment, but a good feel for modes can be obtained by playing with a 'slinky spring' (Fig. 3.2b). After establishing the fundamental mode of vibration – a simple up-and-down oscillation of the entire spring – doubling or trebling the rate at which the spring is wobbled forces it to slip into its second or third mode. In the real world, bowing, plucking or striking a string always simultaneously excites a large number of modes, and without recourse to some difficult mathematics, it rests on an act of faith to accept that the Helmholtz motion described earlier can be synthesised by adding together these string modes; hence, the force driving the body consists of a mixture of harmonically related overtones. The exact mix of overtones (i.e. their relative intensities) governs the waveform shape. More importantly, it governs the perceived tone-quality. Bowed strings can excite many overtones, which the human ear is capable of hearing up to its upper limit (about 20, 000 Hz or 20 kHz for a young adult).

The playing of 'harmonics' (in the musician's sense) then becomes clear. To take a specific example: if the string is lightly touched at the centre, the first, third and higher odd-numbered modes are inhibited. Only those modes which naturally have a node (or stationary point) under the finger are excited. This eliminates the odd harmonics from the har-

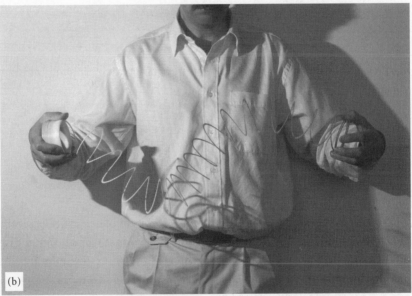

Fig. 3.2(a) Sketches of the first four transverse modes of vibration of a stretched string. The solid and dotted lines show the two extremes of the string's motion. **(b)** The second mode of vibration of a string illustrated using a 'slinky spring'.

monic series. The notes remaining form a new harmonic series based on a 'common denominator' one octave higher – thus the pitch of the note rises by one octave. The equivalent Helmholtz description would be to say that the string slips twice per cycle in this regime. Similar arguments can be used to explain that touching the string one third of the way along the length cuts out all but the third, sixth, ninth etc. modes generating a new tone one twelfth above the open string. Other simple-fraction touch-points yield higher notes from the harmonic series.

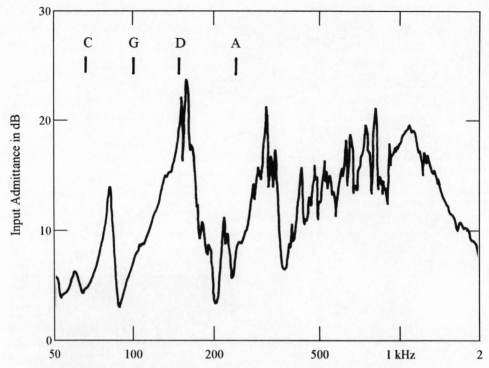

Fig. 3.3 A cello response curve showing the input admittance (velocity amplitude per unit driving force) as a function of excitation frequency. The curve was obtained by exciting the instrument at the bridge in the bowing direction. The fundamental frequencies of the open strings are also shown.

Body vibrations and sound radiation

Although the bowed string is the source of acoustical energy in the cello, the vibrating string itself is a very poor radiator of sound. The conversion of mechanical vibrations into sound relies on inducing local pressure changes in the air, so the string, with its small surface area, is a very poor source. The strings are therefore coupled to a soundbox, whose sole purpose is to increase the instrument's radiation efficiency. The tiny movements of this wooden structure, driven by the strings, make the sounds we hear.

It will come as no surprise to learn that the ease with which different cellos convert the strings' vibrations into sound is very variable. What may be surprising, however, is the huge variability across the playing range of an individual instrument. Figure 3.3 shows the input admittance (or velocity amplitude per unit driving force) measured at the bridge as a function of frequency; each change in 20 dB of the curve represents a tenfold increase or decrease in the vibrational amplitude – the higher the input admittance, the more readily vibrations are set up. The sound-pressure response varies in an equally alarming manner.[5] The effect of the unequal response of the body is very profound – it modifies the harmonic content of the radiated sound such that the driving signal (which always looks like Fig. 3.1b) bears little resemblance to the radiated sound waveform (e g. Fig. 3.6c) apart from having the same periodicity. This 'filtering' effect of the body is different for every note. Even the pitch variations encountered playing vibrato are sufficient to alter the harmonic mix during each vibrato cycle, adding interest to the sound. The filtering effect also varies from instrument to instrument. The response curve is thus a sort of 'acoustical fingerprint', and the unique details of this curve, which are in turn determined by the instrument's construction, ultimately govern the sound-quality and playing qualities of a particular instrument.

The unequal response of the cello is the result of the body exhibiting mechanical resonances. Each peak in Figure 3.3 is a resonance. When the body is driven at a frequency close to a resonance, it tends to vibrate predominantly in one of its modes of vibration. These modes are similar to those considered earlier on the string, except that the vibrations now spread out over a two-dimensional surface and, very importantly, the mode frequencies no longer have simple (harmonic) relationships. Relatively few studies have been undertaken on the body vibrations of cellos, but recent work by Bynum and Rossing[6] shows that the vibration patterns are similar to those found in violins (except that, because the cello is larger, comparable modes are found at lower frequencies). The resonance frequencies and vibrating shapes of the modes are related in some complex way to the construction and dimensions of the instrument and to the mechanical properties of the material from which it is made. The most critical factors affecting the final sound-quality of the instrument are the thickness variations and arching of the table and back, and the densities and elasticity (Young's moduli and shear moduli) of the wood both along and across the grain.[7] The elasticity of wood tends to be very variable, even in specially selected 'tone woods'. When one considers the huge number of variables involved in the construction of an instrument, it is small wonder that each one has its own individual characteristics.

The modes of vibration of the body which generate the most sound are those which couple readily to the strings and also create sizeable volume changes in the air. These are usually soundbox modes. Though they contribute little to the sound radiation, vibrations of the neck and fingerboard are also important because they absorb energy and also give tactile feedback to the player. In the low-frequency range the vibrations spread around over the entire body and the deformations are relatively simple, involving corporate motion of the table, ribs and back. The lowest mode (often referred to in the literature as the 'air resonance') involves both structural vibrations and significant air displacement in and out of the f-holes. At higher frequencies body deformations become more complex, splitting into smaller and smaller vibrating patches (rather like the string, see Fig. 3.2a). The air cavity then plays a less direct role in sound production, with most of the radiation coming directly from the exterior of the body shell. The higher modes are particularly sensitive to the construction and materials of the instrument; control over these modes largely determines the luthier's ability to make consistent instruments.

The mechanical action of the soundpost and bridge are worthy of further discussion. Mode studies of bowed stringed instruments show that, at low frequencies at least, the soundpost and 'treble' bridge foot lie near to nodal (non-moving) lines. The soundpost does not, as is often supposed, convey vibrations from the table to the back, but it instead creates a fixed point about which the bridge can rock. The rocking motion of the bridge encourages conversion of the side-to-side forces of the bowed string into up-and-down forces of the 'bass' bridge foot. These in turn drive the body in its most susceptible direction. If the soundpost is removed, the fullness of tone of the instrument is lost.[8]

Like the body, the bridge also has resonances. There are two important resonances at about 1 kHz and 2 kHz in which the upper part of the bridge rocks or sways laterally on the tall legs.[9] These bridge resonances further 'colour' the sound of the instrument. Bridge modifications (or soundpost adjustments) can be used to fine tune an instrument to impart improved tonal characteristics or better playing qualities. The addition of a mute represents a gross change. The mute adds significant mass to the bridge. The extra mass at this strategic point inhibits the transfer of energy from the strings to the body and hence reduces the loudness of the instrument. The added mass also shifts the bridge resonances, imparting a characteristically different sound.

The cello is not a scaled violin

The lack of concerted scientific study on the cello inevitably invites comparison of the acoustics of violins and cellos. Although historically the violin, viola and cello have rather different ancestry, there is an obvious similarity in form. (The same cannot be said of the double bass, of course, which proudly and stubbornly proclaims its lineage from the bass viol.) The increase in size from violin to viola and from viola to cello clearly accommodates longer and lower-pitched strings, but the body size is also increased to promote lower resonance frequencies, which enhance the low-frequency radiativity and ensure adequate bass response and a full sound in the lowest registers of each instrument.

Acoustical 'scaling' of the violin family was first discussed in a seminal paper by Schelleng,[10] in which he uses the violin as an arbitrary starting-point. Tuned a twelfth below the violin, the scaled cello would require a body size three times larger than the violin for equivalent acoustical action. Most cellos are, in fact, just over twice the size of the violin and this 'compromise' in size leads to some specific acoustical problems. Increased rib height helps to keep the 'air resonance' sufficiently low for bass enhancement, but otherwise the cello relies on comparatively thinner construction to keep resonances sufficiently low. Lighter construction makes the cello rather more reactive, substantially increasing the coupling between the shorter, heavier strings and the body. The result is the dreaded wolf-note, a cyclic stuttering of the bowed string which plagues many fine cellos in their lower ranges.

The origin of the wolf-note is relatively easy to explain. In order to produce sound, the string must induce motion of the bridge and body. When this motion is modest, the bridge acts more or less like a node and the string modes are set up and excited as previously described. However, when the string fundamental drives the body within a semitone or so of its main resonance, the motion at the bridge becomes comparatively large. The bridge movement perturbs the modes of the strings to such an extent that stable oscillations become almost impossible. In physical terms, the coupling becomes so strong that it is no longer possible to talk about 'string' modes and 'body' modes – instead the system exhibits a pair of 'string–body' modes whose resonance frequencies are separated by a few Hertz (neither of which is harmonically related to the overtones). When the string is bowed, these two closely spaced modes 'beat' with each other creating a modulation in the intensity of the note at a rate equal to the frequency separation.[11] Thus, wolf-notes always coincide with frequencies of strong body resonances. Unfortunately, since strong acoustical response inevitably accompanies strong body response, wolf-notes are an almost unavoidable feature of a good instrument. The player can control wolves to some extent by increasing the downward pressure of the bow or by choosing lower-tension strings, but they are most easily tamed using wolf-note suppressors. These work on the principle of tuning another resonator to the same frequency as the offending body resonance to help dissipate energy. They can be as simple as modelling clay stuck on the segment of string between the bridge and tailpiece. More complex devices comprise mass-spring oscillators which can be fixed permanently inside the instrument. In either case, the suppressor must be correctly tuned to be effective.

The concept of acoustical scaling was developed further by Carleen

Hutchins to create the Violin Octet,[12] a set of eight instruments in which physical dimensions and principal resonances are appropriately scaled to the violin. No attempt at homogenising families of bowed stringed instruments had been attempted since the era of the viols, though a number of instruments in the Octet resemble earlier transitory instruments which have since fallen from favour. There is no reason to suppose that the violin is any more 'ideal' than the viola or cello; however, it has a much lower susceptibility to problems such as wolf-notes, so it is reasonable to conclude that its body size is more appropriately matched to its strings. Interestingly, none of the orchestral stringed instruments has a body size which is large enough to radiate effectively at the fundamentals of its lowest notes.

The Violin Octet constitutes an interesting scientific experiment which turns out to be of particular relevance to the cello. Its major achievement, however, is that as well as opening up new musical possibilities, it challenges (or strengthens) our preconceptions of the current violin 'family' and the role of its members within an ensemble. Figure 3.4 shows the tuning and size comparison of the instruments. The Baritone Violin employs the same tuning as the cello, but it has a body size about two-and-a-half times that of the violin, not unlike the large cellos built in the fifteenth and sixteenth centuries (many of which have since been cut down to modern dimensions). The greater power and deeper sonorities of the Baritone are appealing to some players. There is also a smaller instrument, the Tenor Violin, tuned one octave below the violin, which bridges the otherwise large gap between cello and viola. This has an attractive, light voice, which some cellists might find suitable for solo work in the higher registers.

What is interesting in this context is that the properly scaled Baritone Violin, with larger table dimensions and narrower ribs, failed to satisfy the musical expectations of many cellists (see Fig. 3.5). Two types of Baritone were made, one with deep 'cello' ribs, and the other with narrow 'violin' ribs. The deeper ribs substantially modify the placement of the principal resonances, which in the violin are tuned about a fifth apart, whereas in the conventional cello they have a near-octave tuning. Acoustical scaling of the violin to cello dimensions gives the instrument a new voice, which, whilst blending admirably with the remaining instruments of the Octet, evidently fails to fulfil the instrument's full potential in its more traditional role. This is not a surprising conclusion, particularly in the case of the cello, which must act as bass and tenor both in heavy orchestral texture and in lighter contexts such as string quartets. The current violin family has evolved over many generations, and its physical evolution has been interwoven with its musical developments. Vast quantities of music have been written with specific tonal qualities in mind, and it is thus difficult to

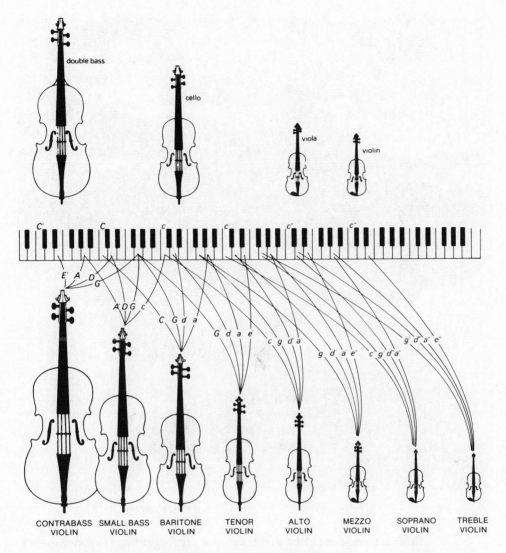

Fig. 3.4 The Violin Octet and its relationship with the violin, viola, cello and bass.

introduce all but the smallest of changes to the current family without losing something of this heritage.

Performance

Whilst the vibrating string and body may physically create the sound of a cello, it is the player who makes the music. To the beginner, the instrument might present a host of seemingly impossible mechanical obstacles, but to the expert performer the instrument almost becomes part of his physical being. The more subtle aspects of musical performance and the criteria by

Fig. 3.5 The Violin Octet. The Baritone Violin, tuned like the cello, is third from the back.

which players select instruments are only just beginning to receive the scientific attention they deserve.[13]

The player and instrument form a closed loop with auditory feedback. The player can thus actively modify the sound being produced. Players learn by trial and error that acceptable sounds are made only when the downward pressure of the bow falls within relatively tight constraints. These depend on the bow speed and the bowing distance from the bridge. Bowing nearer the bridge produces a louder, more brilliant sound, but greater bow pressure is then required for stable oscillations. More importantly, the tolerance in bow pressure is much reduced, and it is small wonder that beginners naturally gravitate to playing towards the fingerboard. On the other hand, the accomplished player, with highly developed bow control, has a much wider range of tonalities and dynamics at his or her disposal. Even then, there are muscular instabilities which prevent the amplitudes of long notes being maintained at an absolutely constant level, as can be seen from the fluctuations in the 'envelope' of the waveform shown in Figure 3.6a.

Whilst feedback-control is useful for long notes, starting the notes predictably is far more difficult, and this is where a player needs to know his or her instrument well in order to play effectively. Periodic vibrations of the instrument are not established immediately. Figures 3.6b and c compare the transient and 'steady-state' parts of the sound waveform of a cello. The transient is always a period of uncertainty, and recent research has focused on how transients affect the 'playability' of bowed stringed instruments. It seems that many instruments are chosen for their 'ease of response' rather than 'beautiful tone'. Transient phenomena are complicated, but they are related to the mechanical response of the body, the choice of strings, the mechanics of the bow and the muscular actions of the player.

In instruments with heavy strings, transients can last for substantial portions of notes in rapid passages, requiring special bow techniques and exact muscular control. Various researchers are now starting to look carefully at bow dynamics (i.e. the modes of vibration and resonances of bows) and the subtleties of bow pressure and bow speed used by players in a variety of conditions both on violins and the larger orchestral instruments.[14] Transients tend to be at their longest when the string must be brought into action from rest. One 'trick' to shorten the transient (and to help with intonation) is to slap the string with the left-hand finger to initiate string vibrations prior to contact with the bow. With suitable bow control, the string can then be 'picked up' at an appropriate point in its cycle to shorten the onset of periodic vibrations.

Needless to say, choice of strings has a large impact on the playability and sound-quality of a cello. High-tension strings are capable of generating higher bridge forces (and hence greater sound intensity), but, as shown by Mersenne's law, the vibrating masses must then also be increased, making the strings harder to control and increasing the likelihood of wolf-notes. Players have the choice of gut, synthetic or steel-cored strings. The latter offer higher reliability as well as greater power. String construction and materials vary considerably, but most are made of a central core overspun with various types of metal wire or tape, with some sort of floss or braided material between the core and windings. Overspun strings allow manufacturers to increase the vibrating mass of the string whilst maintaining a low bending stiffness, without which the string resonances become inharmonic. The precise construction and any mechanical processing of the internal and external surfaces critically affect the damping and harmonicity of the string, both of which have an important

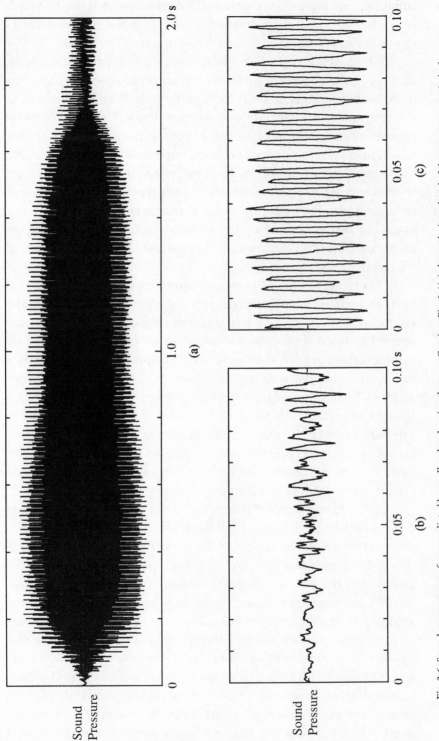

Fig. 3.6 Sound-pressure waveforms radiated by a cello when bowing the open C string. Fig. 3.6(a) shows the 'envelope' of the note over a period of two seconds. The initial build-up of the transient and the decay at the end of the note can be seen. The time-scale is too small for the individual cycles to be seen. Fig. 3.6(b) shows details of the transient, and Fig. 3.6(c) shows details of the 'steady-state' portion of the waveform. The time-scales of the latter two are expanded by a factor of about ten so that the individual cycles can be seen.

influence on the final harmonic content and the playing quality of the bowed string.

Technological improvements in string materials and manufacture have been of great benefit and offer the current player considerable choice from a wide range of reliable and consistent products. New materials and methods are actively researched by the major manufacturers, and it is reasonable to assume that players will be able to look forward to 'improved' string quality. Although bound by tradition, music and performance are forever changing. Cellists now face the difficulties of playing in diverse acoustical environments, ranging from vast modern concert halls to the confines of small recording studios. These make new demands on technique and with time will undoubtedly influence the players' choice of both strings and instruments. The better-quality instruments are still made by hand using traditional techniques and traditional materials. There have been concerns that appropriate timber is becoming scarce; this is the result of over-exploitation, poor forestry, environmental factors and devastation due to war. There have been some serious attempts to find synthetic alternatives to wood, but at present these are expensive, somewhat unreliable and difficult to use outside automated factories. More significantly, they do not have the inherent beauty of straight-grained spruce or curly maple. It may be that yet again the cello may have to change its face a little, but this is just part of the long acoustical development of the instrument.

4 Masters of the Baroque and Classical eras

MARGARET CAMPBELL

Until the beginning of the nineteenth century, musicians were largely dependent for their livelihoods upon either the goodwill of royal or noble patronage or regular employment by a municipality or the Church. A gradual emancipation subsequently took place, due to the growth of public concerts and operatic performances, and substantial developments in music printing and publishing.

The first public opera house was opened only in 1637 and the first public concerts did not take place until the late seventeenth century. The earliest and most consistent patron of music was the Church, although at first it was concerned more with composition – and with vocal rather than instrumental music. Most of the royal and aristocratic families kept a musical establishment as part of their state and were therefore of vital importance to musicians. The enormous development of instrumental forms and styles during the late sixteenth, seventeenth and eighteenth centuries was almost entirely associated with court and aristocratic support. There were, for example, over three hundred states and courts in Germany; these provided musicians with more opportunities for employment than in France, where there were few, or in England, where there was only one.

As with the violin, Italy was undoubtedly the birthplace of the cello; and it was employed increasingly as a solo instrument during the seventeenth century. The first known executant and composer for the instrument was Domenico Gabrielli from Bologna. His contemporary Petronio Franceschini, employed at San Petronio, Bologna, encouraged composers to write specifically for the cello, and he was also one of the founders of the Accademia Filarmonica. Giovanni Bononcini, born in Modena into a famous family of musicians, enjoyed many appointments in the Church and with the nobility in Rome, Vienna and England, where from 1720 he was composer and conductor of the King's Theatre. Sarah, Duchess of Marlborough, was a strong supporter and employed him to play at the twice-weekly concerts at her house in St James's. Antonio Tonelli (De'Pietri), from Carpi, played a number of instruments but favoured the cello, as it was then making its way into the orchestra and the concert room. However, the first virtuoso cellist to make an impact on the public was the Neapolitan, Francesco Alborea, known as 'Francischello'. When

Quantz heard him in Naples, he described him as 'incomparable'.[1] Alborea was also the first to make the cello known in eastern Europe.

Giacobbe Cervetto, born in Italy of Jewish parents, came to London in 1728 and set up shop as a dealer in musical instruments. He also played the cello well enough to become a member of the theatre orchestra at Drury Lane. He was one of the first to promote interest in the cello in England, and, according to Burney, 'brought the violoncello into favour and made us nice judges of that instrument.'[2] Cervetto eventually went into theatre management and became very rich, but he continued playing and teaching the cello; one of his most talented pupils was his son, James.

Among other Italians who helped to popularise the cello in England were Pasqualini, Salvatore Lanzetti and Andrea Caporale. Salvatore Lanzetti was born in Naples, studied at the Conservatoro di S Maria di Loreto and entered the service of Vittorio Amedeo II in Turin. He came to London in the 1730s, where he lived for about twenty years, achieving numerous successes as a cellist. As a composer he was very advanced in his thinking; the technical demands of his cello writing, particularly with regard to bowing, are almost on a level with the Venetian violin concertos. Little is known about Andrea Caporale except that he spent ten years in London (*c.* 1735–45), becoming a celebrity as a soloist and playing in theatre and pleasure-garden orchestras, including Handel's opera orchestra. Burney writes that he possessed 'a full, sweet, and vocal tone', and as such attracted large audiences to the concerts established by the Royal Society of Musicians to raise money for the 'Support of Decay'd Musicians and their Families.'[3]

Giovanni Battista Cirri, who was born in Forlì in Italy, originally took Holy Orders in 1739 but preferred a career in music. He was attached to the chapel of San Petronio, Bologna, and became a member of the Accademia Filarmonica in 1759. He gave concerts in Paris and London, where he settled in 1764. In addition to his concert activities, he became chamber musician to the Duke of York and director of music to the Duke of Gloucester. In 1764 he played in a concert at the Spring Gardens, St James's, at which the eight-year-old Mozart made his first public appearance in London. He returned to Italy in 1780 and became *maestro di cappella* at Forlì Cathedral in 1787. His cello compositions show an unusual harmonic and formal control with virtuoso parts high in the upper register; they also possess a melodic freshness which accounts for their popularity.

By the middle of the eighteenth century the cello had become so popular in Italy that it had ousted the viola da gamba. The key figure in its progress was Luigi Boccherini. He was born in Lucca and studied first with his father Leopoldo, a double-bass player, before continuing with

Francesco Vanucci, *maestro di cappella* of the cathedral at San Martino. Boccherini and his father were regular members of the Imperial Court Theatre Orchestra in Vienna, but they received so little encouragement on returning to Lucca that Luigi decided to settle abroad. After the death of his father in 1766, he teamed up with the violinist Filippo Manfredi; as a duo they toured throughout northern Italy and sojourned in Paris, where they met the Spanish ambassador, who invited them to give some concerts in Madrid. This led to Boccherini's appointment in 1770 as 'violoncellist of Don Luis's Chamber and composer of music, authorised by Charles II'. He received a generous salary and was also permitted to have his music published. After Don Luis's death in 1785, the king continued to guarantee Boccherini a pension. Although still domiciled in Spain, in 1786 Boccherini was conferred with the title 'composer of Our Chamber' by the Crown Prince Friedrich Wilhelm of Prussia and was paid handsomely for a number of quartets and quintets, a situation which continued after the prince succeeded to the throne.

After 1787 Boccherini's name disappears from the records, reappearing in 1796 through his letters to Ignace Pleyel, a Viennese composer who settled in Paris and established himself as a music publisher and later a manufacturer of keyboard instruments. Pleyel was an avaricious opportunist who recognised Boccherini's genius as a composer and entered into an agreement to publish all his music. Boccherini was delighted and sent all his manuscripts to Paris, but unfortunately his letters relate a sad account of broken promises, unanswered letters, unreturned manuscripts and money withheld. He had been suffering from tuberculosis since 1765 and his final years were spent in anonymity and poverty.

The gamba was still a favourite instrument in northern Europe, whilst in France the cello was regarded as a crude impostor. However, Martin Berteau from Valenciennes did not ascribe to this view, and he is regarded as the undisputed founder of the French school of cello playing. Berteau began his career as a gambist, studying with the Czech teacher Kozecz; on hearing the legendary Franciscello he was immediately attracted to the cello, although he continued to hold the bow gamba-fashion with the hand underneath, as was also customary in Germany and England. In 1739 he played a concerto of his own composition at the Concert Spirituel in Paris, after which he achieved much success in the salons of that city. His playing was praised for its beauty of tone and depth of expression; he also made considerable use of harmonics and developed an advanced system of fingering.

A notable contemporary of Berteau was Jean Barrière, who through his virtuoso performances and compositions also contributed greatly to the development of cello playing in France. Little is known about him except that he came from a humble Bordelaise family and was living in Paris in 1730 as a *Musicien ordinaire de notre Académie Royale de Musique.* He went to Rome in 1736 for three years, after which he returned to Paris to continue composing for his instrument. His writing overall was idiomatic and technically advanced, especially in those works composed after his stay in Italy.

François Cupis was a pupil of Berteau at the age of eleven, became solo cellist at the Grand Opéra in Paris and toured successfully throughout Europe. He wrote much cello music and was the teacher of numerous famous cellists such as Jean Henri Levasseur and Jean Baptiste Bréval. Bréval is remembered mainly for his large number of cello compositions.

Another pupil of Berteau, Jean-Baptiste-Aimé Janson from Valenciennes, made his debut at the Concert Spirituel at the age of twenty-four; he achieved such success that he was engaged to accompany the Prince of Brunswick to Italy, where he stayed until 1771. Thereafter, he toured extensively throughout Germany, Denmark, Sweden and Poland to great acclaim. The richness and beauty of his tone was said to be outstanding. In 1789 he returned to Paris, where he was invited to be the first professor of cello at the Conservatoire on its establishment in 1795. Sadly he was drawn into the notorious quarrel between Jean-François Lesueur and Bernard Sarrette which resulted in the entire reorganisation of that institution in 1802. Janson was dismissed, could not come to terms with the disgrace and suffered a nervous breakdown, dying within a year.

One of Berteau's most famous pupils was Jean-Pierre Duport, known as Duport *l'aîné* to distinguish him from his even more celebrated brother, Jean-Louis. Sons of a Parisian dancing master, both had shown early musical talent. Jean-Pierre made his debut at the Concert Spirituel in Paris and was immediately appointed a member of Prince de Conti's private band. After his solos in the *Concerts de la Quinzaine de Paques* in 1762, the *Mercure de France* reported: 'In his hands the instrument is no longer recognisable: it speaks, expresses and renders everything with a charm greater than that thought to be exclusive to the violin'.

In 1769 Jean-Pierre gave up his position with the prince in order to travel, visiting Spain and England. When he was in London he played at the 'Professional Concerts' (managed by Lord Abingdon at the Hanover Rooms), with the violinists Pierre Lahoussaye and Maddalena Lombardini Sirmen, both of whom were pupils of Tartini. In 1773 Duport took up an appointment in Berlin with Frederick the Great as chamber musician to the Royal Chapel and solo cellist for the Royal Opera. He also tutored the crown prince, who later became Friedrich Wilhelm II. When the prince ascended the throne in 1786, Duport became Director of the Royal Chamber Music and played only at court. During his stay in Germany he met both Mozart and Beethoven; Mozart's 'Prussian' Quartets (K.575, 589 and 590), demand an advanced cello technique indicative of Duport's influence.

Jean-Louis Duport began his musical studies as a violinist but, swayed by his elder brother's success, turned to the cello and took lessons with him. He made his debut at the Concert Spirituel in 1768 and the *Mercure de France* described his execution as 'brilliant and astounding', predicting a great future for 'his fine talent'. He visited London in 1783 at the invitation of his friend and co-student, John Crosdill, also his brother's pupil. They appeared together in a number of concerts and Duport also played in the 'Professional Concerts', just as his brother had done some fifteen years before. At the onset of the French Revolution in 1789, Jean-Louis joined his brother in Berlin; he, too, was appointed to the Royal Chapel, where he remained for seventeen years until the death of his royal patron. At this time Europe was perpetually at the mercy of invading armies, so he was obliged to change his domicile many times, returning to Paris in 1807. After five years in Marseilles, playing in the band of ex-King Charles IV of Spain, he finally returned to Paris, where he experienced the most successful period of his career. He was appointed professor at the Conservatoire, solo cellist to Napoleon and member of the empress Marie-Louise's chamber music group, which performed regularly in private concerts at the Tuileries.

Joseph Bonaventure Tillière, yet another pupil of Berteau, was active in France as a performer and composer. In 1760 he played in the orchestra of Prince Conti, and in 1770 he was a member of the Académie Royale de Musique and performed in the Paris Opéra orchestra. His *Méthode pour le violoncelle* (Paris, 1764) follows Michel Corrette's *Méthode, théorique et pratique* (Paris, 1741, and probably the first tutor for the instrument), and treats the cello as a solo instrument, it includes exercises for string-crossing, double-stopping and use of the thumb-position. He also wrote a number of sonatas and duos, as well as a concerto.

In England, the viol reigned supreme until the middle of the eighteenth century, principally because it was favoured by the upper classes; in other words, it was 'a gentleman's instrument'. The violin was regarded as vulgar and fit only for use in taverns and fairgrounds; thus, any member of the violin family was looked on as being of the same ilk. King Charles II had modelled his 'Twenty-four Violins' on Louis XIV's 'grande bande'; one of its members, William Saunders, played the 'bass' violin, but his influence was not felt beyond the court.

It was not until about 1733 that the cello superseded the bass viol in English orchestras, and even then the players were mostly Italian. A remarkable exception was Bartholomew Johnson, who appeared as a soloist in London around 1770 and for seventy years was one of the 'town waites'. Benjamin Hallett, probably the first child prodigy on the cello, appeared at the age of six, dressed in female clothes. A surviving picture shows that he held the instrument like a double bass, supporting it with the left hand; but he also held the bow at a point at least one-third of its length from the heel.

Another important cellist of this time was James Cervetto, son of the *émigré* Italian Giacobbe Cervetto, who received his early instruction from his father and appeared at the Little Haymarket Theatre when he was only thirteen. He was said to be an expressive player with a 'nobility of style' and became popular not only in England but also in the principal cities of Europe. His numerous compositions display a distinct advance in technical demand over those of his Italian predecessors. John Crosdill, a contemporary of Cervetto, began his musical education as a choirboy at Westminster Abbey and had his first cello lessons as a nine-year-old from his father, a pupil of Jean-Pierre Duport. He was elected a member of the Royal Society of Musicians when he was only seventeen and was appointed first cellist in the Three Choirs Festival at Gloucester a year later. In 1775 he furthered his studies with the elder Duport, becoming a fellow student and friend of Jean-Louis Duport. As we know, it was Crosdill who persuaded Jean-Louis to play in London. Crosdill's career went from strength to strength; he was appointed first cellist of the Concert of Antient Music when it was established in 1776 and was also a member of the Chapel Royal, the King's Band of Music and chamber musician to Queen Charlotte. He gave cello lessons to the Prince of Wales (afterwards George IV) and, as a result, became a favourite in court circles as the most fashionable cello teacher of the day. His pupils included many aristocrats but also several who later became professional musicians, the most distinguished being Robert Lindley. John Gunn, from Edinburgh, taught the cello in Cambridge and moved to London in 1789, where he published many learned treatises on instrumental playing.

It is important to remember that there were few instruction books at this time, so techniques and performing conventions were generally passed down by word of mouth from teacher to pupil. One of the first tutors, Robert Crome's *The Compleat Tutor for the Violoncello* (London, *c.* 1765), contains some advice on what is obviously a forerunner of the spike:

> This instrument may be Consider'd as a large Fiddle only held the contrary way, and the fourth string is next to the Bow Hand, as the Body is turn'd downward, the lower part to rest on the Calves of the Legs supported with the knees, but for the greater ease of a Learner we would advize him to have a hole made in the Tail-pin and a Wooden Peg to screw into it to rest upon the Floor which may be taken out when he pleases.[4]

Crome therefore implies that once the learner has control of his instrument he can dispense with the peg. This was written over a hundred years before the introduction of the endpin.

It is not known exactly when the cello superseded the viol in Germany. As there appear to have been numerous cellists in that country before 1700, it may be reasonably assumed that the transition coincided with that in Italy. One of the first names on record is Gregor Christoph Eylenstein, from Gelmroda near Weimar, who was chamber musician to the Duke of Weimar. Johann Sebald Triemer, also from Weimar and a pupil of Eylenstein, was one of the first virtuoso cellists. His musical education was sponsored by the duke and he became a member of the court orchestra; he later travelled extensively in Germany, France and Holland. Another excellent cellist was Riedel from Silesia, who in 1727 went to St Petersburg, where Czar Peter II appointed him to the court orchestra and as a teacher of cello and fencing. Johann Baptist Baumgartner, from Augsburg, was chamber musician to the prince bishop at Eichstadt. He toured successfully throughout Europe, England and Scandinavia, and also composed for his instrument. Johann Christoph Schetky was born in Darmstadt into a musical family with whom he toured throughout Europe, astounding audiences with his virtuosity. He appeared in London in 1770, where he found a patron in Johann Christian Bach. He also composed extensively for the cello.

The Bavarian Joseph Weigl was appointed, on Haydn's recommendation, to the private band of Prince Esterházy and went on to play in the opera orchestra in Vienna, eventually becoming a member of the emperor's private band. One of the most outstanding virtuosi of his day was Johann Konrad Schlick, from Munster in Westphalia. He held many court and church appointments, and with his wife, the violinist Regina Strinasacchi, he toured most of Europe's principal towns. In the winter season of 1799–1800 he was engaged as a soloist for the Gewandhaus concerts, a sign that opportunities for the cello soloist were increasing.

Although the foregoing executants all contributed to the popularity of the cello as a solo instrument, they did not stem from any main roots. It is Bernhard Heinrich Romberg who is regarded as the undisputed 'father' of the German school. He was not only considerably gifted as a player, but also a fine composer. Born in Dinklage into a family of musicians, he received his first lessons from Johann Schlick and appeared in public at the age of seven with his violinist cousin, Andreas. They later successfully toured Europe, meeting Viotti at the Concert Spirituel in Paris in 1784. Both Romberg's playing and composition were said to have benefited from this French influence.

Romberg met Beethoven in Bonn and the two became friends. During this time, the violinist Franz Ries and Andreas and Bernhard Romberg formed a string quartet with Beethoven on the viola. The Rombergs also played in a piano trio with Beethoven. Beethoven admired Romberg's playing, but Romberg found it hard to understand his friend's compositions. He thought the Op. 18 quartets 'absurd' and the Razumovsky quartets 'unplayable'.[5] Romberg's career took him to Vienna, the main cities in England, Spain and Portugal, and Paris, where he spent two years as a professor at the Conservatoire. He held a number of court appointments in Berlin, St Petersburg and Moscow and also travelled widely in Russia, promoting considerable interest in the cello.

Romberg's compositions are now regarded as being only of academic interest, but are of considerable value if considered in the light of their time. He employed a number of new ideas which later led other composers to extend the capabilities of the instrument. He made greater use of the thumb-position than any other composer since Boccherini, and paid tribute to Jean-Louis Duport for the establishment of a system of fingering, which in turn he used to develop left-hand technique to an advanced level. Despite his perpetual travels as a performer, he wrote operas, concertos, sonatas, duets, divertimenti and countless other works, including a cello method. Romberg also used his inventiveness to suggest modifications to the instrument itself (see pp. 14 and 242n29), and he was a fine teacher, counting among his many pupils Pierre Norblin, Mathieu Wielhorsky, Adolf Press, Friedrich Kummer and August Prell. He undoubtedly had a significant influence on cello playing in his time, especially on Friedrich Dotzauer, founder of the Dresden school.

Many virtuoso cellists of the eighteenth century were of Bohemian origin, notably Johann Cermak, who was heard in Warsaw by Joseph Fiala and deemed an excellent player. The Neruda family were all accomplished musicians. Johann Georg Neruda played both violin and cello and, for thirty years, was master of the Chapel Royal at Dresden. Little is known about the cellist Kozcek except that he was apparently a fine teacher, counting E. Václav Petrik among his pupils. Petrik, from Libachovice in Bohemia, was considered one of the best cellists of his time and an excellent teacher; he was also famous for playing violin compositions on the cello. One of his pupils, Ignaz (Hynck) Mara, went to Berlin where he was appointed to the king's private music, a position he held for thirty years. Ignaz's son, Johann Baptist Mara, was a highly talented cellist who was engaged by Prince Henry of Prussia as one of his chamber musicians. Unfortunately, he was a drunkard and a gambler and died in poverty in Holland. Joseph Reicha from Prague, uncle of the composer Antoine Reicha, was a member of both the court and theatre orchestras in Bonn, in which the fifteen-year-old Beethoven played the viola.

The Kraft family also plays a prominent part in the history of the cello. Anton Kraft, born in Rokitzau in Bohemia, originally studied law, but his progress on the cello was such that he was engaged for the Chapel Royal in Vienna. Haydn secured for him a place in Prince Esterházy's court orchestra, and Kraft was later employed in a similar capacity by Prince Grassalkowitz in Vienna. In 1793, with Ignaz Schuppanzigh as leader, Prince Lichnowski as second violin and Franz Weiss on viola, Kraft formed the famous Schuppanzigh Quartet, which performed the works of Haydn, Mozart and, later, Beethoven, directed by the composer. He was an important influence in that he brought the Czech traditions to Vienna and combined them with those of the Viennese Classical school. His playing was known for a beautiful singing tone and an impeccable technique. Anton's son, Nicolaus Kraft, studied initially with his father and later with Jean-Louis Duport in Berlin. He also had a distinguished career as a member of the Lobkowitz chapel orchestra and as a soloist. An injury to his right hand forced him to give up performing in 1834, but his compositions represent a significant contribution to the cello literature.

Bernhard Václav Stiastny, from Prague, was not a virtuoso cellist but a meticulous ensemble player, and for many years was principal cellist in the Prague Opera Orchestra. He was also an excellent teacher and was first professor at the Conservatoire until 1822. His published writings include a tutor for his instrument. His brother, Jan, held a number of court appointments and surpassed him both in playing and composition, contributing much to the cello repertory; his *Six Duos for Two Cellos*, for example, contain passage-work showing an ingenuity that, at the time, must have been a revelation.

By the close of the eighteenth century musical composition was pointing more and more towards the Romanticism that would flower so profusely in the nineteenth century. As far as the cello is concerned, it was Romberg who formed the main link between the Classical and Romantic periods, and in so doing looked forward to the developments of the nineteenth century.

5 Nineteenth-century virtuosi

MARGARET CAMPBELL

By the turn of the eighteenth century, French cellists had achieved standards of performance equal to those of the Germans, who had taken over the lead from Italy. Individual characteristics were in evidence in each country; German players were renowned for a highly developed left-hand technique and a vigorous tone, while the French favoured elegance, as exemplified by the courts of Louis XV and XVI. Tone production was influenced strongly by Viotti, the Italian founder of the French school of violin playing.

The Paris Conservatoire was the main teaching centre in France. Two of its most respected professors, who contributed greatly to the improved standards, were Jean-Baptiste Bréval (see p. 55) and Jean Henri Levasseur, both of whom had studied with François Cupis. Levasseur, who had also studied with Jean-Louis Duport, was appointed first cellist of the Opéra orchestra in 1789, and later became a member of Napoleon's Private Music, continuing in that position after the defeat of the emperor. He was also one of the contributors, with Baillot, Catel and Baudiot, to the *Méthode de Violoncelle et de Basse d'Accompagnement* (Paris, 1805), regarded as one of the most significant instruction books for the instrument at that time.

Jacques Michel Hurel Lamare, one of the most prominent of Levasseur's pupils, was born in Paris into a very poor family; but he had such outstanding musical talent that he entered the Institute of the Pages of the Royal Music as a seven-year-old, and at fifteen became a pupil of Jean-Louis Duport. At the outbreak of the Revolution in 1789, he left his royal employers and in 1794 was appointed principal cellist at the Théâtre Feydeau, appearing frequently as soloist; he was also a professor at the Paris Conservatoire. He relinquished both appointments in 1801 in favour of a solo career and received acclaim in Moscow and St Petersburg and in many countries throughout Europe. Lamarre admired the violinist Pierre Rode and was once described as 'the Rode of the bass'.[1] Fétis writes of him: 'He had a most wonderful execution, but his main strength lay in the rendering of chamber music. He entered more deeply into the spirit of works of that class than any other violoncellist I have ever heard, and he succeeded better than any of them to bring out all the beauties of such compositions'.[2]

Charles Nicolas Baudiot, one of Jean-Baptiste-Aimé Joseph Janson's most distinguished pupils and his successor at the Conservatoire, was born in Nancy; he managed to combine a post in the Ministry of Finance with a career as a soloist and appointments as first cellist in the Chapel Royal and professor at the Conservatoire. As a soloist, he had a well-developed technique and perfect intonation, but his playing lacked expression, a criticism levelled at many French cellists of the time. Baudiot exhibited his true talents as a teacher, as exemplified by two of his most distinguished pupils, Norblin and Vaslin. He wrote much for his instrument including a *Méthode*, 2 vols. (Paris, 1826–8) in which he was assisted by Norblin. It contains helpful advice and strong views on the teaching of children: 'It is generally recognised', he claims, 'that in science, literature and art, as well as in our social life, the first education requires the greatest care; its neglect leaves traces which sometimes prove indelible'. He also recommended a bow-hold similar to that of the violinist, whereby the fingers were placed on the stick in front of the nut.

Another pupil of Jean-Louis Duport, Nicolas-Joseph Platel, was born in Versailles, the son of a musician in the French Chapel Royal. He received his first musical training as a singer in the Institute of Pages of the Royal Music. By the age of ten he had shown talent for the cello and studied for two years with Duport; from this age his playing was marked with the beauty of tone for which he and his pupils were celebrated. When Duport went to Berlin in 1789, Platel continued his studies with Lamare. He held a number of appointments in theatre and opera orchestras and appeared with success in the Concerts de la rue de Cléry. In 1813 he was engaged as principal cellist of the Opera Orchestra in Antwerp, and from 1819 held a similar position in the Royal Opera in Brussels. Here he met the Prince de Chimay, who appointed him teacher of the cello for the newly established Royal School of Music in Brussels. When it was reorganised as the Conservatoire de Musique in 1831, Platel was appointed professor of cello. He was regarded as the founder of the Belgian school of cello playing, which was perpetuated by his pupils, Servais, Batta and De Munck. At Platel's death in 1835, he was succeeded at the Conservatoire by De Munck.

One of the most prominent French cellists of the time, Louis Pierre Norblin, was born in Warsaw; his father, a painter, had married a Polish woman. Norblin studied at the Paris Conservatoire with Baudiot and Levasseur, and in 1811 became solo cellist at the Paris Opéra. In 1846 he succeeded Levasseur as professor at the Conservatoire, where his most celebrated pupil was Franchomme. Besides being an eminent soloist Norblin was also a fine quartet player and was for many years a member of the Baillot String Quartet. In 1828 he founded the Concerts du Conservatoire with the violinist and conductor François-Antoine Habeneck.

The name of Vaslin appears frequently in association with Norblin's many pupils, who also include the operetta composer Jacques Offenbach. Little is known about Olive-Charlier Vaslin except that he was born in 1794 and entered the Paris Conservatoire at the age of fourteen as a pupil of Baudiot; a year later he was a member of the orchestra of the Théâtre Variétés. He claimed that he formed his style of playing by watching the great violinist Baillot, and he was nicknamed 'Le Baillotin'. He wrote much for his instrument, most notably his *L'Art du Violoncelle* (Paris, 1884), which gives precise directions for the bow-hold and condemns the habit of allowing the wrist to sink below the level of the arm.

August Franchomme was one of the great French masters of the cello. Born in Lille, he began his studies at the Lille Conservatoire; after winning first prize, he studied with Pierre Baumann. He entered the Paris Conservatoire in 1825, studying with Norblin and Levasseur; whilst still a student, he played in the orchestra of the Théâtre Ambigue-Comique and was later appointed solo cellist at the Théâtre Italien. Franchomme stayed only a short time with the orchestra as he preferred solo and chamber music playing. He formed a quartet with the violinist Delphin Alard and held chamber music soirées with the pianist Charles Hallé. Also a fine teacher, he was second professor of cello at the Paris Conservatoire until he succeeded Norblin as first professor in 1846. His playing was said to have a full and expressive tone with a brilliant facility of the left hand, and he was also praised for his musicianly interpretations. Franchomme wrote a number of works for the cello, including transcriptions of violin sonatas by Mozart and Beethoven.

The cello was introduced into Belgium and Holland at about the same time as in France, but made less progress, possibly because there were few exponents of the instrument. One of the early names we encounter is Peter Wilhelm Winkis from Liège, who served in the Cassel Court and later became chamber musician and cellist to the Queen of Prussia. Joseph Müntzberger was born in Brussels, the son of a German musician in the service of Prince Charles of Lorraine, Governor of the Netherlands. Fétis tells us that six-year-old Müntzberger played a concerto on a tenor viol, handling it like a cello.[3] When still in his teens, he went to Paris and held a series of appointments with theatres, including the Feydeau, where he was first cellist. He was also a member of Napoleon's, and later the king's band.

Towards mid-century, cello playing in Belgium gained momentum, thanks largely to Nicolas-Joseph Platel. One of Platel's most celebrated pupils, and by far the most important of the Belgian school, was Adrien François Servais from Hal, near Brussels. He began his studies on the violin but turned to the cello on hearing Platel, entering the Conservatoire as his pupil. He was awarded first prize after only one year and became

Platel's assistant in 1829. Servais was a member of the Opera Orchestra in Brussels and made solo appearances, but received little recognition in his own country. He was later acclaimed with enthusiasm in Paris and in London. After a further two years of advanced study in Brussels, he returned to Paris and toured throughout Europe, attracting glowing praise from critics and public alike. The main feature of his playing was his singing tone, claimed to be as beautiful in the highest positions as in the bass; his left-hand technique was often compared to that of Paganini, and he became known as 'Paganini of the Cello'. He was also a prolific composer for his instrument and his works, though rarely performed today, remain invaluable for teaching purposes. Servais made many tours of eastern Europe and Russia where he was greeted with enthusiasm.

When Platel died in 1848, Servais succeeded him as full professor at the Brussels Conservatoire. Among his numerous pupils, the best known are his son, Joseph, Jules De Swert, Ernest De Munck and Joseph Hollman. Through his performing style and his writings he created a unity that personified the age of Romantic virtuosity, in which he was a leading figure. He will also go down in history for his invention of the endpin, or spike. Besides the crude device mentioned by Crome, or the use of a small footstool, there was no other way of securing the instrument except by the legs. In his later years Servais grew very fat and experienced difficulty in holding this position, hence his brilliant invention which was to revolutionise cello technique. It also meant that women could play in a dignified manner; their only option prior to this was to play 'side-saddle', since no lady would dare to straddle her legs around an instrument in the same way as men.

Pierre Alexandre François Chevillard, from Antwerp, studied in Paris with Norblin when he was nine and won the first prize as a sixteen-year-old. After some orchestral work and solo tours, he returned to Brussels to make a successful debut and was praised for his brilliant technique and refined, stylish playing. Chevillard was also interested in chamber music and tried in vain to interest Parisian musical circles in the late string quartets of Beethoven. Eventually, assisted by Maurin, Sabbatier and Mas – who shared his aims – he founded the 'Société des derniers Quatuors de Beethoven' and gave some private concerts. Their innately musical performances attracted an ever-increasing following and, after a successful recital at the Salle Pleyel, they toured the main cities of Germany with a similar response. In 1859 Chevillard succeeded Vaslin at the Paris Conservatoire.

François De Munck, born in Brussels, was one of the most promising cellists of his generation. He studied with Platel at the Conservatoire and was praised initially for his perfect intonation and intensity of feeling. But he never realised his potential, as he led a 'somewhat disorderly course of life',[4] which affected his health and led to an early death. De Munck's younger son, Pierre Joseph Ernest, appeared in public at the age of eight and made his debut in London aged ten. He studied with Servais at the Conservatoire and later travelled as a soloist with Jullien's orchestra in Britain. He was the cellist of the Maurin Quartet in Paris for some time; in 1871 he went to Weimar as solo cellist of the Grand Ducal Chapel, where he became friendly with Liszt. After some time in the USA, he finally settled in London, where he became professor of cello at the Royal Academy of Music until his death in 1915.

Jules De Swert, from Louvain, appeared in public as a child prodigy. Servais was so impressed that he accepted him as his pupil at the Conservatoire; at fourteen, he was made 'Laureate'. He then followed a highly successful solo career, touring throughout Europe and Scandinavia. In 1868 he was appointed solo cellist of the Ducal Chapel at Weimar and the following year went to Berlin as Royal concertmaster, solo cellist of the Royal Chapel and teacher at the Hochschule. In 1876, at Wagner's request, he formed the orchestra at Bayreuth, where he was solo cellist. In 1888 he went to Ostend as director of the local conservatoire of Gand and Bruges. Although technical difficulties were unknown to him, he was a fine musician who never resorted to mere virtuosic display. He also wrote several compositions for the cello.

The cello made slow but steady progress in Holland, which could boast several first-class cellists by the middle of the nineteenth century. One such was Johan Arnold Dammen, who was born in The Hague in 1760. In 1769 he was living in London, and in 1794 was employed at Drury Lane, presumably as first cellist. Jacques Franco-Mendes who was born in Amsterdam into a Portuguese Jewish family, studied the cello with Präger and with Merk in Vienna. In 1831 he toured with his brother, a talented violinist, achieving success in both Paris and London; on his return he was appointed chamber violoncellist to the King of Holland. After the death of his brother in 1841, Franco-Mendes renounced touring for some time and played only in Amsterdam's subscription concerts. In 1845 he participated in the unveiling of the Beethoven Memorial in Bonn. He also composed for his instrument.

Alexander Batta from Maastrict had his first instruction on the violin from his father, a teacher at the Brussels Conservatoire. It was there that he heard Platel, decided to take up the cello and became Platel's pupil at the Conservatoire; he shared the first prize with De Munck in 1834. He wrote a considerable amount for the cello, of which only the studies are used today. Charles Ernest Appy, born in The Hague of French parents, at first studied the piano but turned to the cello as a fifteen-year-old pupil of Charles Montigny and, later, Merlen, first cellist of the Amsterdam Orchestra. Appy was a member of the Coenen String Quartet and for many years performed with some of the greatest artists of the time, including Clara Schumann. For around twenty years he was professor at the Maatschappij tot Bevordering van Toonkunst in Amsterdam.

Foreign musicians largely gained favour over nationals in Britain. Among the most prominent British cellists were the brothers Joseph and Hugh Reinagle, John Smith, Charles Jane Ashley, Richard Cudmore and Frederick William Crouch. However, by far the best known was Yorkshireman Robert Lindley, who started out as a violinist but soon changed to the cello. He made rapid progress and at the age of nine took the place of an indisposed soloist, achieving instant success. At sixteen years, he continued his studies with James Cervetto and in 1794 became principal cellist of the Opera at the King's Theatre in London, a post he held for fifty-seven years. At the same time, he followed a highly successful solo career, appearing in the Antient Concerts and the Philharmonic Society concerts. He also became a close friend of Domenico Dragonetti, the Italian virtuoso double-bass player, and they formed a duo partnership that lasted for over fifty years. 'Nothing could compare with the intimacy of their mutual musical sympathy'.[5] Their performances of the Corelli sonatas were famous. When the Royal Academy of Music was founded in London in 1822, Lindley was one of its first professors of cello.

The Dresden Court had always attracted gifted musicians from abroad, especially from Italy; as a result, standards were high and by the turn of the eighteenth century it had become one of the most important centres for the study of the cello in Europe. The acknowledged founder of the Dresden school was Justus Johann Friedrich Dotzauer from Haselrieth, who began his studies on the piano and later extended them to various instruments, ranging from the double-bass to the trumpet. He finally decided on the cello and studied with Kriegk, a pupil of Jean-Louis Duport. For a time, he was a member of the Leipzig Orchestra and he subsequently joined the Court Orchestra at Dresden, where he was later appointed solo cellist. In 1806 Dotzauer had a period of further study with Romberg. His interest in chamber music led to the foundation of the celebrated Leipzig Professors' Quartet. Although Dotzauer followed a successful solo career, appearing in most of Europe's principal cities, it is as a teacher that he will best be remembered. Among his many pupils were Kummer, Schuberth, Voigt and Dreschler. Dotzauer also wrote a considerable amount of music for his instrument, and although most is of purely academic interest today, his exercises still provide good material for the student.

Friedrich August Kummer was born in Meiningen and was a pupil first of his father, a court musician, and later Dotzauer. In 1817 he joined the cello section of the Chapel Royal, succeeding Dotzauer as soloist on his retirement in 1850. He was also a professor at the Dresden Conservatoire from its foundation in 1856 until his death in 1879. His many pupils included his two sons, Ernst and Max, Bernhard Cossman, Julius Goltermann, Richard Bellman and Ferdinand Bochmann. Kummer was renowned for his attention to detail and his constant striving to improve both the technical and the artistic elements in his playing. Although he was a fine cellist, his critics observed that he 'remained a stranger to the lighter and more brilliant technique of the bow, cultivated by the French and Belgian school'.[6] Nevertheless, Kummer was admired throughout Europe and Scandinavia as both a soloist and chamber musician.

Another Dotzauer pupil, Karl Dreschler from Saxony, began as a military bandsman but was noticed by the Kapellmeister to the Duke of Anhalt-Dessau, who provided the means for him to study with Dotzauer. As a soloist he toured Europe and the UK and in 1820 was appointed principal of the Dessau Orchestra. His playing was admired for its purity and refinement of feeling and good taste. He was a gifted leader and as such was sought after as principal cellist for music festivals all over Germany. He was also a first-class teacher who brought all the advantages of the Dresden school to Dessau; through his pupils, notably Cossmann and Grützmacher, he established principles which were passed on to several generations of cellists.

Carl Schuberth from Magdeburg had his first lessons at the age of five, appeared as a soloist as an eleven-year-old and at thirteen began studying with Dotzauer. He enjoyed a successful career travelling throughout Europe and Scandinavia and finally settled in St Petersburg, where he served as Director of the Imperial Band, Inspector of the Music School affiliated to the Court Theatre and Director of Music at the University. His most famous pupil was Davidoff. Bernhard Cossmann from Dessau is best known for his *Etudes de Concert* Op. 10 and his cello studies, which are still used today. He studied with Dreschler and Theodore Müller – cellist of the Müller String Quartet – and finally with Kummer at Dresden. From 1840 he was principal cellist at Paris's Théâtre Italien and in 1847 Mendelssohn appointed him solo cellist for the Gewandhaus Orchestra in Leipzig; the following year, he undertook an extensive tour to England and Ireland. He was appointed professor at the Hochschule at Frankfurt-am-Main in 1878, a post he held until his death. Hanover-born Edward Goltermann is almost forgotten today, but in the earlier part of the nineteenth century he was a celebrated touring virtuoso. In 1851 he gave up performing in order to devote himself to composition, but none of his works is of lasting value.

Friedrich Wilhelm Grützmacher, from Dessau, was one of the leading lights in the second half of the nineteenth century. He showed early talent for the cello and studied with Dreschler, thus being in a direct line from Dotzauer. He went to Leipzig in 1848 and two years later inherited all three of Cossmann's appointments – solo cellist in the theatre orchestra and the Gewandhaus Concerts and professor at the Conservatoire. He played for many years in the David String Quartet, but went to Dresden in 1860 to become principal cellist of the Court Orchestra, Head of the Dresden Musical Society and professor at the Conservatoire. He also managed to pursue a busy solo career, touring throughout Europe and Russia. His playing was noted for its technical mastery and musicality. He was forward-looking in his choice of repertory, which included works by Beethoven, Chopin and Grieg. He was the soloist in the première of Richard Strauss's *Don Quixote* in Cologne in 1898. Grützmacher was also a gifted teacher; among his most distinguished pupils in Dresden were Emil Hegar, Johannes Klingenberg, Wilhelm Fitzenhagen and Hugo Becker. Grützmacher's compositions are almost unknown today, but at the time his transcriptions and arrangements of the classics offered an invaluable exten-sion to the repertory. His 'arrangement' of Boccherini's Concerto in B flat, achieved by filching from four different works, is still used by cellists today, many of whom have no idea of its inaccuracies. Perhaps Grützmacher's most unforgivable contribution is his 'concert version' of Bach's Solo Suites (BWV1007–12), which he completely reorganised with additional chords and embellishments, so presenting a travesty of the composer's work.

Johannes Klingenberg, a Grützmacher pupil from Gorlitz, made one important contribution to the development of cello playing in the nine-teenth century. His Dotzauer–Klingenberg tutor (Hamburg and Leipzig, *c.* 1870) amalgamates three volumes of Dotzauer with exercises by Duport, and as such consolidates the Dresden influence; even today it is regarded as one of the most systematic and thorough works ever compiled for the instrument.

Robert Hausmann was born in Rottleberode in the Harz Mountains and received lessons as a nine-year-old from Theodore Müller, becoming one of the first cello students at the Berlin Hochschule after its foundation in 1869. When Müller died in 1871, Hausmann succeeded him as first pro-fessor. Violinist and fellow professor Joseph Joachim took him to London where he met Piatti, with whom he had a further period of study. Hausmann later made successful solo appearances in London with the Philharmonic Society. However, his real love was chamber music and, after a period with the Dresden String Quartet, he joined the Joachim Quartet in 1878 and remained with them until Joachim's death in 1907. In 1887 Hausmann and Joachim premièred Brahms's Double Concerto at Cologne with the composer conducting. Max Bruch dedicated his *Kol Nidrei* to Hausmann.

Carl Davidoff, born in Goldingen in Latvia, was one of the first great Russian masters of the cello. He had his first lessons with Heinrich Schmidt, principal cellist at the Moscow Theatre, and later studied with Carl Schuberth, Director of the Imperial Band and of music at the university. Davidoff's parents insisted that he complete his formal education before undertaking musical studies, so he took a degree in mathematics at St Petersburg University, before studying composition with Moritz Hauptmann at the Leipzig Conservatoire. Hauptmann's advanced ideas on musical theory had a profound influence on Davidoff, not only regarding composition but in his later work on the development of cello technique. His mathematical knowledge was helpful in understanding Hauptmann's ideas on acoustics and harmony and 'several phenomena which result from cello tuning in fifths'.[7] Davidoff was one of the first to link technique with the anatomical and physiological aspects of teaching, also investigated by Becker and later developed by Casals and Feuermann. He was acclaimed throughout Europe as the greatest cellist of his day. On his return to Russia, he was appointed principal cellist of the Imperial Italian Opera and a member of the Russian Musical Society's Quartet. In 1863 he succeeded his former teacher, Carl Schuberth, as professor at the St Petersburg Conservatoire, becoming Director in 1876; here he gained a reputation for assisting impecunious students to receive free lodging and for increasing the number of scholarships awarded.

One of Davidoff's most distinguished pupils was Hanus Wihan, from Poliza, Bohemia. He entered Hegenbarth's class at the Prague Conservatoire as a thirteen-year-old and completed his studies with Davidoff. At eighteen, he was appointed professor at the Mozarteum at Salzburg and played in numerous orchestras, including the Bilse – later the Berlin Philharmonic – and the Court Orchestra in Munich. In 1891 Wihan founded the Czech String Quartet, whose members (violinists Karl Hoffmann and Josef Suk and violist Oskar Nedbal) stayed together for over forty years. Wihan's close contacts with both Smetana and Dvořák inevitably influenced the artistic development of all three. Dvořák wrote his *Rondo* Op. 94 and his Cello Concerto Op. 104 for Wihan, as well as the attractive cello part in his 'Dumky' Piano Trio Op. 90.

One of the major influences on nineteenth-century cello playing was another Czech, David Popper (see Fig. 5.1), who was born in the old ghetto of Josephstadt in Prague, and was the son of a cantor in the synagogue. He showed musical talent from the age of three and could play both piano and violin; at twelve he was given a place at the Prague Conservatoire providing that he took up the cello. He joined the class of Julius Goltermann, an ex-student of Kummer in Dresden, and was therefore in a direct line from

Fig. 5.1 David Popper (1843–1913)

Romberg and Duport. Popper was employed in the Chapel Royal of Prince Hohenzollern at Löwenberg when he was only eighteen years old and he later became 'Kammervirtuoso'. He subsequently travelled extensively as a soloist, captivating audiences everywhere. As a twenty-five-year-old, he became the youngest principal cellist ever appointed to the Imperial Opera Orchestra. He also participated in the Sunday Philharmonic

Concerts and a series of concerts with the Hellmesberger Quartet (with Hellmesberger, Brodsky and Bachrich).

Popper left the Vienna Opera Orchestra in 1873 in order to undertake concert tours in Europe and Russia. When a string department was opened in the Royal Hungarian Academy of Music in Budapest in 1886, he was appointed its first Professor of Cello, with the violinist Jenö Hubay as Head of Department. The institution had been founded in 1875 with Liszt as president and, not surprisingly, the only instrument taught there until this time had been the piano. During the first season Hubay and Popper founded the string quartet that was commonly known as the 'Budapest'. Its members were often joined by Brahms in concerts and they performed many of Brahms's works. Popper managed to continue his solo tours, play chamber music, teach and compose, returning to Prague in 1892. His cello compositions made him world famous and his salon pieces were popular not only with cellists – many were transposed for the violin. His greatest contribution to the development of cello technique was his *Hochschule des Violoncellspiels*, published in four volumes of ten studies each between 1901 and 1905. Of Popper's pupils, the best known are Arnold Földesy, Jenö Kerpély, Mici Lukács, Ludwig Lebell and Adolf Schiffer – the teacher of Janos Starker.

After Boccherini, Italy produced few cellists of renown. However, Giuseppe Rovelli, from Bergamo, was employed by the Duke of Parma; among his pupils was Vincenzio Merighi, considered to be the founder of the Lombardian school. Merighi was professor at Milan Conservatoire where Alfredo Piatti, Alexander Pezze and Gugliemo Quarenghi were his students. The Turin school was founded by Pietrio Casella, the first in a long line of cellists.

Alfredo Piatti, from Bergamo, studied both violin and cello, played in a string quartet as a six-year-old and, two years later, joined the local orchestra. He was accepted as Merighi's pupil at the Milan Conservatoire when he was ten. In 1838 he gave a concert at La Scala which was so successful that he undertook a European tour. In 1844 he made his first appearance in London, where critics and audiences alike could not find enough superlatives to describe his playing. This adulation was reciprocal; Patti became a confirmed anglophile and often appeared in London – where he made his home – and the main provincial cities. He played frequently as principal cellist with the Italian Opera Orchestra and in a quartet comprising Ernst (first violin), Joachim (second violin) and Henryk Wieniawski (viola). He also participated in the concerts given by the London Beethoven Quartet Society and appeared regularly at the 'Pops', then held at St James's Hall in Regent Street and devoted entirely to chamber music. Piatti was the cellist in the original 'London' Joachim String Quartet which was permanently engaged for the Pops. He continued to perform in the main European cities and, despite a busy concert schedule, enjoyed a long and distinguished career as a teacher. He was continually offered teaching posts in his native Italy but declined, preferring to stay in England. He held the post of cello professor at London's Royal Academy of Music, but his attendance was sporadic; most of his teaching was private and among his best-known pupils were Robert Hausmann, Hugo Becker, Leo Stern and William Whitehouse. Piatti's compositions for the cello are not remarkable, except for his *Tarantella* Op. 23, which is a first-class virtuoso piece. His *Twelve Caprices* remain valuable items in the present teaching literature and, in contrast to Grützmacher's vandalism, his faithful arrangements of eighteenth-century works (including sonatas by Locatelli, Porpora, Veracini, Ariosti, Marcello and Boccherini) were of great significance in extending the available cello repertory. Piatti was the last of the old Romantic cello school, combining brilliant technique and good taste. Wasielewski wrote of him: 'He is not only the most important cellist in England, but belongs altogether to the highest ranks of artists at the present time'.[8]

6 Masters of the twentieth century

MARGARET CAMPBELL

Around the turn of the century, the German school was still at the forefront, its two leading figures being Julius Klengel and Hugo Becker, both representatives of the Dresden school in a direct line from Grützmacher. Despite their shared inheritance of the need for serious interpretation and rejection of the over-Romantic virtuoso style, they were totally different in their concepts of teaching; Klengel's approach was empirical, whereas Becker concentrated more on scientific aspects.

Klengel was born in Leipzig into a family of professional musicians; his first lessons were with Emil Hegar, principal cellist of the Gewandhaus Orchestra. From early childhood he played chamber music with his siblings, and at fifteen joined the Gewandhaus orchestra, succeeding his teacher as principal cellist at the age of twenty-two; the same year he was appointed 'Royal Professor' at the Leipzig Conservatoire. Klengel also appeared as a soloist in Germany and in Russia, where he gave the first performance in that country of Haydn's D major Concerto (1887); but he will go down in history for his remarkable teaching gifts. Paul Grümmer, Emanuel Feuermann, Guilhermina Suggia, Edmund Kurtz and William Pleeth are among his most famous pupils. Klengel never encouraged his students to copy, but always helped them to find their own way of playing; thus they were all individual in their approach. Klengel was also a composer who wrote imaginatively for the cello: his works include several concertos and a *Hymn for Twelve Cellos*, dedicated to the memory of the conductor Arthur Nikisch.

Becker was born in Strasbourg, the son of the famous violinist Jean Becker, and at the age of six began to learn the violin. He took to the cello as a nine-year-old with Kanut Kundinger in Mannheim, and at fifteen became second cellist in the Mannheim Court Orchestra. He later studied briefly with Grützmacher. Like Klengel, Becker developed his performance skills in chamber music, touring with the 'Jean Becker Family Quartet' in 1880. From this time he enjoyed a busy career both as solo cellist of the Opera orchestra in Frankfurt and as a quartet player. Like Klengel, Becker is best remembered as a teacher; but although he was admired and respected by many of his students, some found him too pedantic. In 1895 he became director of chamber music classes at the Hochschule in Frankfurt. From 1902 he taught at the Royal Music Academy at Stockholm

and succeeded Hausmann at the Hochschule in Berlin in 1909. He was one
of the few teachers of this era to explore the physiological aspects of cello
performance, aiming to cultivate a natural manner of playing. Among his
most famous pupils were Enrico Mainardi, Paul Grümmer, Arnold
Földesy, Boris Hambourg, Beatrice Harrison and Herbert Walenn. Becker
also composed a number of works for his instrument, but only his studies
and exercises are used today.

Paul Grümmer was the son of a court musician from Gera in Germany.
At fifteen he entered the Leipzig Conservatoire under Klengel and com-
pleted his studies with Becker. As a soloist he toured extensively, finally set-
tling in Vienna where he became soloist in the Concert Society and the
Opera House orchestras and, latterly, cellist in the Adolf Busch String
Quartet. Also an excellent teacher, Grümmer taught at the Viennese
Musical Academy, and later at the Hochschulen in Cologne and Berlin.
Many composers dedicated works to him, including Reger, Wolf-Ferrari
and Tcherepnin.

Another distinguished Becker pupil was Boris Hambourg, born at
Vorionez in South Russia into a family of famous musicians. Hambourg
studied for some time with Herbert Walenn, also a pupil of Becker, before
spending five years with Becker himself. He followed a highly successful
solo career and toured internationally with his brother Mark, the world-
famous pianist. Believing that much could be learnt about the art of
bowing from violinists, Hambourg took lessons from Ysaÿe. His studies
led to a reversal of many accepted theories, especially regarding the use of
the point and the upper part of the bow, and attacking accented notes in
the more incisive up-bow. His bowing became more elegant and achieved
greater freedom, and he developed considerable left-hand agility. He was
one of the few cellists of his time to take an interest in early music, presenting a series of well-researched recitals at London's Aeolian Hall.

A Klengel pupil who has enjoyed a successful international career is
Edmund Kurtz, born in St Petersburg and now an Australian citizen. In
Paris he was influenced by Casals, who advised him to study with
Alexanian. Kurtz followed a busy solo career and later became principal
cellist for several famous orchestras, including the Prague German Opera
and the Chicago Symphony Orchestra. In 1945 he made his solo orchestral
debut in the USA playing Dvořák's Concerto with the NBC orchestra
under Toscanini. From this time Kurtz followed a successful solo career
world-wide and he premièred several works written specially for him.
Perhaps Kurtz's most important contribution to the development of the
art of the cello is his facsimile edition of Bach's solo Suites, published in
1983.

A British pupil of Klengel who has gained an international reputation as a teacher is William Pleeth, born in London into a Polish *émigré* family of musicians. His first lessons on the cello were at the age of seven and he entered the London Cello School as a ten-year-old to study with Herbert Walenn. At thirteen he won a scholarship to study with Klengel at Leipzig, the youngest student ever admitted; in two years he learnt Bach's Suites, Piatti's *Caprices* and some thirty-two concertos. Pleeth was only fifteen when he made his debut at the Gewandhaus playing Haydn's D major Concerto to an enthusiastic reception. On his return to London during the depression he had to struggle to make a living. He served in the army during the 1939–45 war, meeting Edmund Rubbra, who became a lifelong friend. Rubbra dedicated his Sonata (vc, pf) to Pleeth and his wife, the pianist Margaret Good. In the early 1950s Pleeth became a member of the Allegri String Quartet and devoted himself both to chamber music and to teaching.

Today, teaching is his major concern and he passed on to his students much from his old professor at Leipzig. He says:

> I like to leave a lot of leeway for them to develop along the lines of their own personality. I don't want them to be a reproduction of me. They are harnessed to me in a way, but they are *attached* not *bound*. There are so many ways of being expressive. We discuss the drama and the lyrical quality together, but somehow the individual personality must come through. It is also my job to help that particular personality to bloom. One has to be a psychologist to understand one's students.[1]

Pleeth has been a visiting teacher at The Menuhin School since 1977, but for some time now has taught only at his London home. His son, Anthony, who specialises in Baroque cello, Robert Cohen and Jacqueline du Pré are outstanding examples of the countless cellists who have benefited from his expertise.

In the early twentieth century there were many fine British chamber musicians but no outstanding British soloists. One of the foremost contributors to the development of cello playing in England, especially in chamber music, was Carl Fuchs from Offenbach. He began lessons at nine with Robert Riedel and at the age of sixteen studied with Cossman at the Frankfurt Conservatory, completing his studies with Davidoff in St Petersburg. In 1887, Clara Schumann, who admired his playing, gave him an introduction to Karl Hallé (afterwards Sir Charles) in Manchester, the city which was to become his second home. On his first visit he appeared as a soloist with the Hallé Orchestra and subsequently became principal cellist, continuing long after Hans Richter had succeeded Hallé. When the Royal Manchester College of Music was founded in 1893, Hallé appointed Fuchs its first professor of cello. When Adolf Brodsky came to Manchester to assume the Orchestra's leadership in 1895, he formed a Brodsky String Quartet with Fuchs as cellist.

Another important British teacher, London-born William Whitehouse, studied the cello with Walter Petit, principal cellist of the Queen's Band, and with Piatti at the Royal Academy of Music. When he was only twenty-three he became assistant professor of cello at the Academy and was appointed a full professor one year later. He also taught at the Royal College of Music and at King's College, Cambridge, guiding some of the most prominent cellists of the early twentieth century, notably Herbert Withers, Warwick Evans, Ivor James, Felix Salmond and Beatrice Harrison.

William Henry Squire, from Herefordshire, was highly regarded as both performer and teacher. He first appeared as a seven-year-old prodigy; in 1883 he won a founder-scholarship to the Royal College of Music to study with Edward Howell and also had lessons with Piatti. Squire followed a busy solo career and was principal cellist of the Royal Opera House Orchestra, Covent Garden, the Queen's Hall orchestra and London Symphony Orchestra. He held professorships at both the Royal College of Music and the Guildhall School of Music. Squire was one of the first solo cellists to make recordings; his recording of Elgar's Concerto under Hamilton Harty (1936) was highly regarded.

Herbert Walenn (see Fig. 6.1), another Becker pupil, was born in London into a family of artists and musicians. He studied with Edward Howell at the Royal Academy of Music before going to Frankfurt. He soon achieved a reputation as a soloist and chamber musician and was a member of the Kruse String Quartet. Also a dedicated teacher, Walenn was a professor at the Royal Academy of Music for many years, counting among his students Zara Nelsova, Boris Hambourg, Douglas Cameron, William Pleeth and Giovanni Barbirolli, who later, as John Barbirolli, achieved an international reputation as a conductor. In 1919 Walenn founded and directed the London Violoncello School, where he organised a series of concerts which included not only soloists but also performances with up to a hundred cellists taking part (see Fig. 12.2). Walenn's unorthodox teaching methods involved minimal technical instruction and concentration more on musical matters; he was a good psychologist and was particularly encouraging to amateur players, raising standards considerably in what had been a neglected area.

Ivor James, a pupil of William Whitehouse at the Royal College of Music, possessed remarkable gifts as a teacher. He taught for thirty-four years at the Royal College, including chamber music classes, and was also a member of the English String Quartet. James was the pioneer of the summer school for vacation study, now an integral part of all musical education. He directed the first of these schools, at Westminster College,

Fig. 6.1 Herbert Walenn (1870–1953)

Cambridge, in 1929, sponsored by the British Federation of Music Festivals. Among his many pupils were Thelma Reiss, Amaryllis Fleming, Harvey Phillips, James Whitehead, Martin Lovett and Helen Just, who later became his wife.

Another greatly loved teacher, also a pupil of Walenn at the Royal Academy, was Dundee-born Douglas Cameron. He started his career as a chamber musician and was a member of the Kutcher String Quartet, the

Blech Quartet and, later, his own New London String Quartet. He was a professor at the Royal Academy of Music and also coached the cello section of the National Youth Orchestra of Great Britain from its foundation in 1947 until his death in 1974. Foremost among his numerous pupils have been Florence Hooton, Douglas Cummings, Keith Harvey, Derek Simpson, Christopher van Kampen and Julian Lloyd Webber.

Perhaps the most outstanding early twentieth-century British cellist was Felix Salmond, a Whitehouse pupil at the Royal College of Music who completed his studies with Edouard Jacobs at the Brussels Conservatoire. Salmond made his debut at London's Bechstein Hall in 1909. Ten years later, he participated in the première of Elgar's String Quartet in an ensemble led by Albert Sammons. In the same year Elgar entrusted Salmond with the première of his Cello Concerto at the Queen's Hall with the London Symphony Orchestra under Elgar himself, the composer accepting many of Salmond's suggested amendments to the solo part. Unfortunately, lack of rehearsal time resulted in the performance being panned by the critics. Salmond never recovered from the humiliation and emigrated to the USA. Britain's loss was America's gain, for his influence on the development of cello playing there cannot be overestimated. For some thirty years he was professor at the Juilliard School of Music in New York and the Curtis Institute in Philadelphia. His legacy through his pupils such as Orlando Cole, Leonard Rose and Channing Robbins is now reaching third-generation students, two of the best known being Lynn Harrell and Yo-Yo Ma. An indication of how deep were the wounds of that Elgar première is the fact that he never taught the concerto to his students.

Two British female cellists, May Mukle and Beatrice Harrison, achieved international status during the first quarter of the century. Mukle, born in London, was already performing as a nine-year-old. She was only thirteen when she entered the Royal Academy of Music to study with Alexander Pezze, and she won every cello prize offered there. At seventeen she was awarded the ARAM, a rare honour for one so young. She followed a successful solo career, appearing throughout Europe, Australia, Asia and the USA, and *The Times* once described her as being 'in the very front rank of living violoncellists'.[2] Besides her solo playing she also enjoyed chamber music and on many occasions joined Thibaud, Tertis, Rubinstein, Albert Sammons and others in private performances or simply for the pleasure of playing together. She was a member of many well-known string quartets and ensembles and was also closely associated with the American violinist Maud Powell. Many composers dedicated works to Mukle – she premièred, for example, Holst's *Invocation* (1911) and Vaughan Williams's *Six Studies in English Folk Song* (1926) – and she founded the MM (Mainly Musicians) club in a converted basement close to Oxford Circus tube

Fig. 6.2 Beatrice Harrison (1892–1965)

station; this club provided a meeting place and air-raid shelter for musicians during the early days of the Second World War.

Beatrice Harrison (see Fig. 6.2) was born in Roorkee in the North-West Province of India, the most musically gifted of four daughters of an army colonel. As a sixteen-year-old she went to study with Becker at the Hochschule in Berlin and became the youngest competitor and the first ever cellist to win the Mendelssohn Prize. Thereafter she enjoyed a busy solo career, becoming the first female cellist to appear at Carnegie Hall (1913) and the first to play with the Boston and Chicago symphony orchestras. Harrison had a lifelong friendship with the composer Frederick Delius, who wrote his Double Concerto (vn, vc, orch) for her and her sister, May. She also became closely associated with Elgar shortly after the disastrous première of his Cello Concerto. At his request she recorded an abridged version of the work, later recording the concerto complete in 1928, with Elgar conducting. When the BBC recorded her playing Rimsky-Korsakov's *Chanson Hindou* in duet with a nightingale in the woods at her home, Harrison became a household name the world over. Today she is remembered largely for the cello and nightingale recording, but she was considered to be one of the greatest women cellists of her day. She was also a staunch supporter of contemporary music, giving premières of works by Delius, Bax and Ireland, as well as the first British performance of Kodály's solo Sonata.

Few would disagree that Pablo Casals (see Fig. 6.3), from Tarragona in Spain, made the greatest impact on cello playing in the twentieth century. The son of an organist, Casals played both violin and organ before turning to the cello at the age of twelve. His first studies were with José Garcia at the Municipal School of Music in Barcelona and such was his progress that he was soon earning pocket-money by playing in a trio at a local café. It was at this early age that Casals first began to question the unnatural stiff-armed bowing technique then prevalent, in which pupils were required to hold books under their right arms whilst playing. It was also then that he made his legendary discovery of Bach's Suites for solo cello. At eighteen he entered the Madrid Conservatory of Music, studying composition and chamber music with Tomas Breton and Jésus de Monasterio, and three years later he was sent to complete his cello studies at the Brussels Conservatoire with Edouard Jacobs; however, an altercation with Jacobs at the first class he attended flared into a full-scale argument, and Casals left for Paris the following morning. Casals's impetuosity lost him his royal patronage; life was hard at first on his return to Spain, but he later became principal cellist in the Opera Orchestra and succeeded Garcia, his former teacher at the Municipal Music School, teaching also at the Liceu School of Music. During this time Casals taught his students the methods of fingering and bowing resulting from his own research, emphasising the benefits of creating a balance between tension and relaxation.

The turning-point in Casals's career came when he met Charles Lamoureux, founder and director of the orchestra that bore his name. When Lamoureux heard Casals play, he immediately engaged him for the first concert of the orchestra's season. Casals settled in Paris and his solo career began in earnest when he appeared in the UK and all over Europe,

Fig. 6.3 Pablo Casals (1876–1973)

America and Russia. With the outbreak of the Spanish Civil War in 1936, Casals's political affiliations placed his life in jeopardy, but he continued working to raise money for the Republicans. When the fall of Barcelona was imminent – and a fascist general had threatened to cut off both arms – he crossed the Pyrenees to Prades, where he was exiled for more than twenty years. Prades virtually became a shrine for cellists the world over; festivals were held there and throughout the year cellists came to pay homage to 'Le Maître', as he was known. The list of cellists who benefited from his teaching reads like a musical *Who's Who*: Feuermann, Cassadó,

Fig. 6.4 Maurice Eisenberg (1902–72)

Maurice Eisenberg, Raya Garbusova, Pierre Fournier, Paul Tortelier, Christopher Bunting, Maurice Gendron and Rostropovich are but a few.

Closely linked with Casals was his pupil and friend Maurice Eisenberg (see Fig. 6.4), born in Königsberg in Germany. Following his studies in Europe and the USA, he worked for some time with Casals in Spain, and became professor of the Casals class at the Ecole Normale in Paris (1929–39).[3]

Another cellist associated with Casals was the controversial Armenian, Diran Alexanian. He was a pupil of Grützmacher in Leipzig, where as a student he played chamber music with Brahms and Joachim. He first met Casals in Paris and they discovered that their revolutionary technical concepts were similar; they eventually collaborated in writing a *Traité théorique et pratique du violoncelle* (Paris, 1922). In 1937 Alexanian went to the USA where he achieved considerable success as a teacher. He encountered much opposition from the establishment but, after Casals, remains one of the most important influences in the development of cello playing in the twentieth century. Bernard Greenhouse, Raya Garbousova, Edmund Kurtz and many others derived benefit from his teaching.

The only Spanish cellist of importance after Casals, Barcelona-born

Gaspar Cassadó, started playing the cello as a seven-year-old and studied with Casals in Paris from the age of thirteen. In the period immediately following the First World War Cassadó toured internationally and became established as one of the leading cellists of the day, playing under most of the great conductors. He gave recitals with Bauer, Rubinstein and Iturbi, and joined Menuhin and Louis Kentner in piano trios. He played Brahms's Double Concerto with Huberman and Szigeti, and with Jelly d'Arányi for the Royal Philharmonic Society's Brahms Centenary Concert. In the mid-1920s he settled in Florence. He was one of the founders of the Accademia Chigiana Music Courses in Siena in 1932. He received critical acclaim for his mellow tone and subtle phrasing, but he was never accorded the acknowledgement that he deserved, perhaps because his achievements were overshadowed by Casals. Two of his pupils, Rohan de Saram and Elias Arizcuren, have nothing but admiration for his methods of teaching.

A female pupil of Casals who achieved an international reputation as a soloist was Guilhermina Suggia. She was born in Oporto, the daughter of an eminent physician whose family considered social graces to be far more important than the study of music. But Suggia had a mind of her own and made her first appearance playing the cello when she was seven. At twelve she was principal cellist of the Oporto City Orchestra and the following year became the cellist in a string quartet. The Portuguese royal family sponsored her studies with Klengel in Leipzig, where she performed as a soloist with the Gewandhaus Orchestra under Nikisch. After making her first European tour, she settled in Paris and studied for some time with Casals. In 1914 she moved to London, where she worked for many years as performer and teacher, frequently being praised for the nobility of her phrasing and 'tone of a masculine power seldom heard from a lady violon-cellist'.[4] Suggia was one of the first exponents of Casals's teaching methods and always remained a staunch supporter of his principles. However, the opinions of her own teaching ability vary from those who say she had lim-itless patience to others who claim she was often negative in her approach.

One of the greatest cellists of the twentieth century was Emanuel Feuermann from Galicia in Poland. At nine he had some lessons with Friedrich Buxbaum, principal cellist of the Vienna Philharmonic Orchestra and member of the famous Rosé String Quartet, and he later studied with Anton Walter at the Music Academy in Vienna. He was only twelve when he made his acclaimed debut playing Haydn's D major Concerto with the Vienna Philharmonic Orchestra. In 1917 Feuermann was sent to Leipzig, where he studied for two years with Klengel. Klengel wrote of him: 'Of all those who have been entrusted to my guardianship, there has never been such a talent . . . our divinely favoured artist and lovable young man'.[5]

Feuermann was sixteen when Klengel recommended him for the professorship at the Gurzenich Conservatoire at Cologne, following the sudden death in 1919 of Friedrich Grützmacher, nephew of the more famous Friedrich (Wilhelm Ludwig). The authorities accepted Feuermann in every respect but withheld the title of professor. During the next decade Feuermann gave over a thousand concerts and made numerous recordings. In 1929 he was appointed cello professor at the Hochschule in Berlin and became one of the world's most sought-after teachers. During this period he played Brahms's Double Concerto with Carl Flesch, and formed a string trio with the violinist Joseph Wolfsthal and Hindemith on viola. When Hitler came into power and Jewish musicians were given indefinite leave of absence from their posts, Feuermann made his home temporarily in Zurich, but when the *Anschluss* was signed in 1938, Feuermann was trapped with his family in Vienna; through his friend, Bronislaw Huberman, they managed to escape via Israel to the USA, where Feuermann finally took American citizenship.

Another great contemporary of Feuermann was Gregor Piatigorsky (see Fig. 6.5). Born in Ekaterinoslav into a poor but musical family, he had his first lessons at seven and two years later won a scholarship to the Moscow Conservatory, where he studied with Alfred von Glehn, a pupil of Davidoff; he later had some lessons with Brandukov. From his childhood he earned his living by playing in night clubs and at fifteen, two years after the Revolution, he became principal cellist of the Bolshoi Theatre in Moscow and cellist of the country's leading string quartet, the 'Lenin'. He escaped from the USSR via Warsaw in 1921 and went to Berlin, where he had some unsatisfactory lessons from Becker, and then to Leipzig, where he fared only marginally better with Klengel. He left Germany in 1928 in order to devote himself to a solo career; he also formed a duo partnership with Artur Schnabel and a trio with Schnabel and Carl Flesch. A triumphant debut in 1929 with the New York Philharmonic Orchestra marked the beginning of his international reputation as a soloist; he also played trios with Horowitz and Milstein and in 1949 formed another famous trio with Heifetz and Rubinstein. He settled in California in 1961 where he and Heifetz founded the chamber music series known as the 'Heifetz-Piatigorsky Concerts'.

For Piatigorsky, sound production was of the greatest importance. He combined an innate flair for virtuosity with exquisite taste in style and phrasing, and his interpretation of the Romantic repertoire was unsurpassed. He premièred several new works – among them Prokofiev's Cello Concerto Op. 58 and Walton's Cello Concerto – and many composers dedicated works to him. Piatigorsky was also a dedicated teacher. In the 1940s he was head of the Cello Department at the Curtis Institute in

Fig. 6.5 Gregor Piatigorsky (1903–76)

Philadelphia and taught chamber music for many years at the Berkshire Music Centre in Tanglewood, Massachusetts. When he settled in Los Angeles he was appointed Head of Cello at the University of Southern California Music School, where a Piatigorsky Chair was established in 1975.

It is to another remarkable Russian, Mstislav Rostropovich (see Fig. 6.6), that we look for the greatest progress in the development of cello

Fig. 6.6 Mstislav Rostropovich (b.1927)

playing in the second half of the twentieth century. Born in Baku in
Azerbaijan, the son of a professional musician, he had his first cello lessons
with his father from the age of six; he entered the Children's Music School
in Oranienburg at twelve and completed his studies with Semyon
Kozolupov at the Moscow Conservatory, where he also studied composition with Shostakovich. He then embarked upon a solo career, performing
all over the USSR and eastern Europe, and was appointed professor at the
Moscow Conservatory in 1956; that same year, completely unknown in the
West, he gave a recital in an almost empty Carnegie Hall in New York; he
fared better in the UK, where he received critical acclaim. In 1970, when
Rostropovich wrote an open letter to the press (which remained unpublished) in defence of the proscribed writer Alexander Solzhenitsyn, his
travels abroad were curtailed. He later left the USSR, returning only after
the *glasnost* period.

Rostropovich is now an international figure and has premièred almost
one hundred works for his instrument, including pieces by Prokofiev,
Lutosławski, Dutilleux and Penderecki. It was in 1960, when Rostropovich

gave the premiere of Shostakovich's Cello Concerto No. 1 Op. 107 (of which he was the dedicatee), that he first met Benjamin Britten. This resulted in an enduring friendship and professional association until the composer's death in 1976. Britten wrote a number of works for Rostropovich: the Sonata Op. 65, the Symphony for Cello and Orchestra Op. 68, and the three Suites Opp. 72, 80 and 97.

In France, the high standards of performance established in the nineteenth century have not diminished in the twentieth. Maurice Maréchal, from Dijon in Burgundy, was not only a gifted cellist but had many contacts with contemporary composers such as Debussy, Ravel and Caplet, thereby promoting a world-wide interest in French music. Maréchal had his first lessons as a small child and was performing in public at the age of ten. He studied at the Paris Conservatoire with Jules Leopold-Loeb, graduating at nineteen with the *Premier Prix*. He was first employed by the Lamoureux Orchestra as deputy-principal cellist and later as a soloist; by the 1930s he was ranked among the world's greatest cellists. During the German occupation of his country in the Second World War he refused to play in Germany or even on French radio. When Gérard Hekking died in 1942, Maréchal replaced him as professor of cello at the Paris Conservatoire. Unfortunately, Maréchal later suffered from a muscular disease that made playing almost impossible. He gave his last concert in 1950, but continued his teaching activities until his death in 1964.

Another great French cellist with an international reputation was André Navarra from Biarritz, who was so talented that he entered the Toulouse Conservatoire at nine and graduated with the *Premier Prix* at thirteen; he studied further with Jules Leopold-Loeb at the Paris Conservatoire where, as a fifteen-year-old, he was awarded the *Premier Prix*. Navarra was cellist of the Kretly String Quartet when he was only eighteen, and two years later, after his solo debut with the Colonne Orchestra in Paris, he became principal cellist of the Grand Opera Orchestra. The Second World War interrupted his activities but he later toured extensively throughout Europe, the USA and the USSR, playing under such eminent conductors as Karl Böhm, Charles Münch, André Cluytens and Sir John Barbirolli; his recording of Elgar's Concerto with Barbirolli and the Hallé Orchestra has become a classic. In his latter years Navarra concentrated on teaching; he held his professorship at the Paris Conservatoire until his death and for many years taught at the Accademia Chigiana at Siena. He also travelled widely giving master classes.

Pierre Fournier was known as 'the aristocrat of cellists',[6] not only for his elegant and stylish playing but for his refined taste in everything artistic. He was born in Paris into a military family and was first taught the piano by his mother. As a nine-year-old he suffered a slight attack of polio and was advised to change to an instrument which would not require use of the feet. Fournier's progress with the cello was such that he studied at the Paris Conservatoire with Paul Bazelaire and Anton Hekking, and graduated at seventeen. Two years later he made a successful solo debut and within the next ten years followed a solo career throughout Europe. After the Second World War he established an international career and gained a reputation also as a fine chamber musician, appearing at the 1947 Edinburgh Festival with Schnabel, Szigeti and Primrose. In his teaching, Fournier aimed for a velvety and fluid tone and insisted upon a high elbow for the bow arm, advocating Ševčík's violin exercises for perfecting bowing technique. His own playing certainly personified this approach, and he retained his powers until he was almost eighty. He gave a recital in London when he was seventy-eight, and a critic wrote: 'Fournier's perceptive sense of phrasing and his still easy command of the fingerboard transformed his recital into an object lesson in fluency of playing'.[7]

Paul Tortelier (see Fig. 6.7) was another Frenchman who became a household name in the UK, largely through his televised master classes. He came from a poor Parisian family and at the age of six was given a cello by his dominating mother, who decided his future there and then. He studied at the Paris Conservatoire with Louis Feuillard (a pupil of Delsart) and Gérard Hekking. Tortelier graduated with the *Premier Prix* at sixteen, but he had played from the age of twelve in the silent cinemas and cafés all over Paris in order to contribute to the family finances. At eighteen he took on his first orchestral job as sub-principal cellist with the Orchestra of the Paris Radio and made his solo debut playing Lalo's Concerto with the Lamoureux Orchestra.

From 1935–7 Tortelier was a member of the Monte Carlo Symphony Orchestra, and for the next two years until the outbreak of war he toured internationally as a soloist. In July 1945 Tortelier played for Casals and was later invited to lead the cello section of the orchestra at the first Prades Festival in 1950. This association with Casals blossomed into a firm friendship and had a lasting influence on Tortelier's artistic development. Tortelier held professorships at the Paris Conservatoire (1956–69) and at the Folkwang Hochschule in Essen (1969–75). He was also appointed Honorary Professor of Music at the Central Conservatoire of Peking, the first Westerner to receive this honour.

One of the last of France's great cellists was Maurice Gendron from

Fig. 6.7 Paul Tortelier (1914–90)

Nice. He studied with Jean Mangot at the Nice Conservatoire and graduated with the *Premier Prix* at fourteen. At seventeen he completed his studies with Gérard Hekking at the Paris Conservatoire. Here he met many artists and musicians, including Poulenc and Françaix; he was to give recitals with Françaix for over twenty-five years. He also learnt much from performing with the Romanian pianist Dinu Lipatti. Gendron made his London debut in 1945 with Benjamin Britten as his partner on the piano, and he later gave the European première of Prokofiev's First Cello Concerto with the London Philharmonic Orchestra under Walter

Susskind. His New York debut was at a memorial concert for his idol, Feuermann, playing the Dvořák and Haydn D major concertos. He also formed a trio with Yehudi and Hepzibah Menuhin, an association which lasted for twenty-five years. Gendron was an elegant player who always paid great attention to phrasing, and his interpretations of French music had a lucidity and transparency that placed them in a class of their own. Gendron taught at the Mozarteum in Salzburg, the Académie Maurice Ravel in St Jean de Luz and at the Menuhin School in Surrey, and was a professor at the Paris Conservatoire from 1970 until his death in 1990.

One of the notable female cellists of her generation was the Russian-born Raya Garbousova, who studied with Konstantin Miniar, a pupil of Davidoff, and later briefly with Becker, whom she found 'dogmatic . . . and obsessed with anatomy'.[8] She had also tried to study with Klengel, but he claimed he could teach her nothing. Her recital debut in Berlin had the critics raving about her 'colossal talent' and this success was repeated wherever she played. Garbousova later had lessons from Casals and he invited her to play both Haydn's D major Concerto and Tchaikovsky's *Rococo Variations* with the orchestra he conducted in Barcelona. At Casals's suggestion she also studied with Alexanian and she always regarded what she learnt from this controversial teacher as her 'musical capital'.[9] Garbousova enjoyed an international performing career as a soloist and premièred several works by contemporary composers. Barber's Cello Concerto was written for her and she gave its first performance with Koussevitsky and the Boston Symphony Orchestra; she also recorded the work. Garbousova settled in the USA, where she took out citizenship. She was sprightly well into her eighties and, although she retired from the concert platform, she concentrated on teaching at the University of Northern Illinois and gave master classes world-wide.

There are many other fine performers who have contributed greatly to the development of cello playing in the twentieth century: Bernard Greenhouse, for his superb playing in the Beaux Arts Trio; Leonard Rose, a pupil of Felix Salmond, for fine solo performances and remarkable skills as a teacher; Zara Nelsova for her charismatic platform personality and fine playing; Christopher Bunting, an accomplished soloist, teacher and composer; Radu Adulescu, a sensitive chamber music player – cellist of the Italian Trio d'Archi di Roma and teacher; and Amadeo Baldovino, a distinguished chamber musician and teacher. Of the younger generation the following should be mentioned: Erling Blöndal-Bengtsson from Denmark; Ralph Kirshbaum, Lynn Harrell, Yo-Yo Ma and Tsuyoshi Tsutsumi from the USA; Steven Isserlis and Julian Lloyd Webber from the UK; and the unforgettable Jacqueline du Pré (see Fig. 6.8) who, in her short

Fig. 6.8 Jacqueline du Pré (1945–87)

life, brought her exuberant and brilliant playing to audiences world-wide. Finally, Antonia Butler (a Klengel pupil), Florence Hooton (a Cameron pupil), Joan Dickson (a Mainardi pupil) and Amaryllis Fleming (a Fournier pupil) are just a few of the century's numerous excellent cello teachers who have contributed substantially to the ever-rising standards of playing the world over.

7 The concerto

ROBIN STOWELL AND DAVID WYN JONES

The Baroque and Classical eras

Andrea and Giovanni Gabrieli's *Concerti per voci e stromenti musicali . . .* (Venice, 1587), comprising sacred music and madrigals for voices and instruments, is the earliest known publication incorporating the term 'concerto' in its title. 'Concerto' then denoted simply an aggregation of performers and was applied to various musical genres, vocal and instrumental. The instrumental concerto emerged as an independent form towards the end of the seventeenth century and soon evolved into a genre in which virtuosity and textural contrast were significant elements.

Among the earliest Italian composers to exploit the cello as a concertante instrument were Jacchini, Della Bella[1] and Dall'Abaco. Jacchini's *Concerti per camera . . . con Violoncello Obligato* Op. 4 (Bologna, 1701) comprises ten works, six of which include brief passages for a solo cello. These passages, which appear mostly in the fast outer movements (all but No. 6 are three-movement structures), are based on scales or sequential patterns and are not technically demanding. Dall'Abaco's twelve *Concerti a quattro da chiesa* Op. 2 (Amsterdam, 1712) reconcile their adoption of forms from the sonata with solo passages principally for a violin. But the eleventh concerto, in G major, specifies 'con il Violoncello obligato', which is required to play a more extensive solo role than in Jacchini's works.

The earliest true solo concertos for cello and orchestra were composed by Vivaldi, who wrote most of his twenty-seven examples (RV398–424) for the young female cellists of the Pio Ospedale della Pietà in Venice, where he was employed irregularly from 1703 to 1740.[2] Vivaldi was the first to develop fully the formal and stylistic possibilities of the Torellian concerto model, as demonstrated in some of Torelli's posthumously published *Concerti grossi* Op. 8 (Bologna, 1709). Although few of Vivaldi's cello concertos make exceptional technical demands, they fully realise the instrument's warm, expressive sonorities, most adopting minor keys. Their extended focus on the prowess of the soloist and their consistent use of both the fast–slow–fast pattern of movements and ritornello form[3] (sometimes elaborately treated) in the outer movements carve for them an important niche in history.

Cello concerto composers of the immediate post-Vivaldian generation include Porpora, Giovanni Perroni,[4] Canavas, Vandini and Molter, each of whom contributed one work.[5] Five concertos by Lanzetti are still extant, while Platti composed some twenty-eight cello concertos, mostly in a Baroque idiom.[6] Most significant, however, were Leo's six concertos (1737–8; one, in C minor, is entitled *Sinfonia Concertante*) composed for his patron, the keen amateur cellist Domenico Marzio Caraffa, the Duke of Maddaloni. Five comprise four movements, but the D major concerto includes a fifth movement, a fugue, prior to the final Allegro. All exploit the instrument's expressive and cantabile potential rather than its technical capability.

During the course of the eighteenth century many other Italian composers wrote concertos for the cello, including Boccherini, Borghi, Cirri, Graziani and Tartini. Of these Boccherini was the most celebrated. Eight cello concertos are safely attributed to him (G.474-7, G.479-81, G.483). Most date from the 1760s when Boccherini is known to have played in public concerts in Vienna. A further concerto in B flat (G.482) has achieved notoriety. The earliest known source for the work is a nineteenth-century score which was then freely adapted, elaborated and generally mutilated by Friedrich Grützmacher (Breitkopf and Hartel, 1895).[7]

Vienna's leading instrumental composer during the 1750s and 1760s was Wagenseil, whose output included two concertos, in A major (1752) and in C (1763). The latter is contemporary with Haydn's C major Concerto and clearly shows the stylistic context of that popular work without in any way being overshadowed by it. Haydn's work is one of several instrumental concertos he wrote for members of the Esterházy orchestra in the first years of his service at the court. It was never published in his lifetime and was presumed lost until, quite fortuitously, a set of manuscript parts was discovered in the National Museum in Prague in 1961. Although Haydn's Second Concerto, in D major, dates from 1783 when his reputation was securely established, it is a curiously unconvincing work for the period, notwithstanding its technical demands. For a long time it was thought to have been composed by another cellist at the Esterházy court, Anton Kraft (himself a composer of a cello concerto), but the rediscovery of the signed autograph shortly after the Second World War would seem to disprove that.

Of Haydn's contemporaries and successors in Austria four composers contributed notably to the concerto repertory, Fiala (at least one concerto), Hofmann (eight concertos), Vanhal (four concertos) and Pleyel (six concertos). The careers of the first three remained firmly centred in Austria and the performing locale of these works was the aristocratic salon. Pleyel, however, worked for significant periods of his life in Strasbourg and London, the latter in particular having an active public concert life. Four of Pleyel's concertos (Benton 104, 105, 106 and 108) seem to be designed for the public concert hall and would certainly reward modern revival.

It is a major disappointment that no cello concerto by Mozart survives, cellists having to content themselves with the occasional solo passage in his Concertone in C major (K.190). The disappointment is aggravated by hints that there might have been two major orchestral works featuring the instrument. In 1779, when Mozart was writing the Symphonie Concertante in E flat for violin and viola (K.364), he also began a similar work in A major with a solo complement of violin, viola and cello; the opening tutti is fully scored and the solo lines as far as the beginning of the development section are given. More mysterious is a Cello Concerto in F major which the nineteenth-century French composer and musicologist Charles Malherbe apparently discovered but never made public. Only the following details are known: a six-bar incipit, date of composition (March 1775) and a scoring of two oboes, two horns and strings.[8] As the history of Haydn's Cello Concerto in C exemplifies, it is not entirely impossible that this work lies unrecognised in an archive or library.

The contribution of the many composers based or educated at the Mannheim court to the development of the symphony has tended to overshadow the fact that many were prolific composers of concertos too. A leading cellist at the court from 1754 was Anton Filtz who is credited with four cello concertos. Later cellist-composers who wrote concertos for their instrument include Franz Danzi, Peter Ritter and Carl Stamitz. Like most musicians of the day, those employed at Mannheim regarded Paris as the leading musical city in Europe, notable for its concert life and numerous publications of music. Programmes of the leading concert-giving organisations occasionally featured cello concertos, especially by Jean-Baptiste Bréval (seven concertos from the 1780s and early 90s), Daniel-François Auber (four concertos, 1806–8), Jean-Baptiste-Aimé Janson (at least twelve concertos, Opp. 6 and 15), Jean-Pierre Duport (Concerto in A) and François Cupis, but the many symphonies concertantes performed and published in the city hardly ever featured the cello.

Concert life in London replicated that of Paris in many ways and cello concertos were occasionally found in this repertory, too. Although Abel's concerto in B flat probably predates his arrival in England in 1759, local musicians such as John Garth, James George, Robert Lindley and Joseph Reinagle all wrote concertos, while Haydn's Symphonie Concertante (Hob.I: 105, 1792) includes a taxing part for solo cello.

Composers resident in north Germany produced numerous concertos for violin, flute and keyboard, but concertos for the cello are comparatively rare. Notable exceptions are works by Jean Tricklir and Carl Philipp Emanuel Bach (H.432, H.436 and H.439); alternative versions for flute and keyboard exist for C. P. E. Bach's three concertos, which date from the early 1750s. The A major Concerto (H.439) is especially attractive with a wide range of sometimes quite quirky expression. In south Germany, Stuttgart-based Johann Zumsteeg contributed ten works in the genre (1777–92). At the end of the century Jean-Louis Duport, author of a celebrated treatise on cello playing, composed six concertos for the instrument.

In Beethoven's Vienna two composer-cellists made significant contributions to the repertory. Nicolaus Kraft (son of Anton) composed four concertos and was the first cello soloist to perform Beethoven's Triple Concerto in C (Op. 56, 1804–5). Bernhard Romberg had been a colleague of Beethoven at the electoral court in Bonn but his subsequent career as a player took him all over Europe; he was especially well regarded in Vienna c. 1820, his ten concertos countering the prevalent view that the only string instrument capable of virtuosity was the violin.

The nineteenth century

Nineteenth-century composers focused chiefly on the cello's lyrical qualities and constantly sought to reconcile traditional procedures with contemporary developments in form, scale and other musical elements. Few used the genre as a vehicle for the expression of nationalistic sentiments and few exploited virtuosity for its own sake.

Schumann played the cello in his youth and had close personal contact with many eminent cellists, notably Kummer, Grützmacher, Wielhorsky, Grabau, Romberg and Bockmühl. He sketched and orchestrated his Cello Concerto in A minor Op. 129 within a fortnight (10–24 October 1850), but revised it extensively after advice from Bockmühl, completing it in February 1854, shortly before his attempted suicide.[9] It is an expressive, lyrical work whose three continuous movements merge into a kind of musical ballad unified by motivic cross-references. The transition to the ternary slow movement is made via a recitative-like solo passage, while the link to the finale recalls the opening movement's first theme (ww) and the first theme of the second movement (vc). The finale's resolute march-like idea betrays its pianistic origins, which are confirmed by the subsequent contrasting material and ensuing symphonic argument. Following a change to the major mode, Schumann's written-out, accompanied cadenza, featuring reminiscences from the first movement, is a somewhat subdued affair. Some cellists (e.g. Cossmann, Popper, Jacquard, Piatigorsky and Navarra), disappointed with the limited opportunities for technical display, have expanded it to compensate.

In 1853, Brahms visited Robert and Clara Schumann in Düsseldorf. The Schumanns were impressed with Brahms's compositions and expressive piano performance, Robert writing enthusiastically about this 'young eagle'.[10] Following Robert's death, Clara became an important personal and musical influence upon Brahms, not least in the evolution of his last orchestral work, the Double Concerto in A minor Op. 102 (vn, vc, orch). In 1880, after nearly thirty years of close friendship, Joachim had severed all relations with Brahms because of his alleged 'disloyalty' in causing (unknowingly, as it happened) the acquittal of Joachim's wife of a charge of adultery with their mutual friend, and Brahms's publisher, Simrock. After many unsuccessful attempts at a reconciliation, Brahms commenced work in 1887 on the Double Concerto for Joachim and Robert Hausmann, the cellist in Joachim's quartet, completing it at Lake Thun in the late summer. The three musicians rehearsed it with piano on 21 and 22 September at Clara Schumann's house in Baden-Baden and with the Kursaal Orchestra there the following day. But ready as he was to accept Joachim's criticism, strongly upheld by Clara herself, that the solo parts needed greater brilliance, Brahms rejected many of his friends' suggested amendments. The work was premièred by Joachim and Hausmann on 18 October 1887 in Cologne, with Brahms conducting.

After a brief orchestral call-to-attention (containing the germ of the first theme), the soloists introduce themselves at first individually, then together, in a metrical quasi-recitative passage. Announced in full by the orchestra, the first theme is linked to the more relaxed second[11] by a virile syncopated transitional theme which will later be of considerable significance, notably in its transformation immediately prior to the reprise. The ternary central Andante (D major) features an expressive, melancholy violin/cello melody, announced in octaves and characterised by its initial rising fourths, which also serve independently as an introduction to the movement (ww, hns). Its central section (F major) explores two further melodies, one characterised by parallel thirds (ww), the other by triplets (soloists), after which the two are contrapuntally combined. The main theme's rising-fourth motif is recalled by both soloists after the subtly varied reprise, preluded by a cadenza and concluded by a poetic coda, which alludes to all the movement's principal material. The cello soloist takes the lead in the sonata-rondo finale, introducing both the sprightly first theme and the expansive second idea (C major). An extended central episode substitutes for development, the soloists announcing a gypsy-like idea which is expanded by the orchestra after a contrasting section with syncopations reminiscent of the first movement. During the reprise, the second theme returns in the tonic major, heralding a triumphant major-mode conclusion.

Prominent members of the 'Dresden School', established by Dotzauer, also made significant contributions to the genre. Dotzauer himself composed nine concertos (Opp. 27, 66, 72, 81, 82, 84, 93, 100, 101) and three concertinos (Opp. 67, 89, 150) for his instrument, while his pupil, Kummer, wrote a Concerto Op. 10 and at least three concertinos, one of which – the *Concertino en forme d'une scène chantante* Op. 73 – was inspired by Spohr's Eighth Violin Concerto Op. 47. Grützmacher, who replaced Kummer as solo cellist at the Dresden Hofkapelle in 1864, composed three cello concertos but is better known for his misguided editions of Classical works. Grützmacher's pupil Fitzenhagen, the dedicatee of Tchaikovsky's *Variations on a Rococo Theme* Op. 33, left at least four cello concertos.

Other nineteenth-century German traditionalists include Molique (whose popular Concerto Op. 45 (Leipzig, 1853) was influenced by Mendelssohn's Violin Concerto Op. 64), Goltermann (eight concertos), Reinecke (Op. 82, Mainz, 1866), Julius Klengel (Opp. 10, 20, 31, 37; Concertinos Opp. 7, 41, 46; Double Cello Concerto Op. 45), Becker (Op. 10) and several composers with Lisztian connections. Raff, Liszt's assistant at Weimar between 1850 and 1856, a talented orchestrator but a composer of uneven quality, wrote two concertos (1874, 1876); Tchaikovsky described the first (D minor, Op. 193) as 'intelligent, graceful, impeccable in texture, and noble and beautiful from beginning to end'.[12] Volkmann, who served with Liszt at the Hungarian National Music Academy, composed an expressive Concerto Op. 33 (1858) after Classical models; and both Klughardt (Op. 56, 1894) and d'Albert (Op. 20, 1899) drew inspiration for their concertos from the continuous one-movement design of Liszt's Second Piano Concerto.

'Had I known that such a violoncello concerto as that could be written, I would have tried to compose it myself',[13] exclaimed Brahms on first hearing Dvořák's Concerto in B minor Op. 104 (1895) at a Vienna Philharmonic concert in March 1897. Dvořák had sketched a Concerto in A major (1865) but never orchestrated it.[14] But it was Victor Herbert's Second Cello Concerto Op. 30 (1894), performed during Dvořák's tenure as director of the National Conservatory of Music in New York, that inspired Dvořák's masterpiece. Building on the experiences of his First Concerto (Op. 8, 1884), Herbert's lyrical Op. 30, in one continuous movement and exploiting especially the solo instrument's upper register, captured Dvořák's imagination, along with his natural longing for his homeland and his affection for his sister-in-law, Josefina Kaunitzová, who, as the source of his unrequited love, had inspired many of his songs. His introduction of the melody, transformed, of one of her favourites, 'Leave me Alone',[15] in the central section of the concerto's slow movement was given added significance when, on hearing of her death soon after his return to Czechoslovakia, he refashioned the work's ending[16] to reintroduce this song as a kind of requiem.

Following the substantial opening orchestral ritornello, the soloist breathes new character into both the noble, principal theme and the expressive second idea. The short development focuses on the first theme, while the reprise, signalled by a frenetic solo chromatic passage, is marked by a full orchestral statement of the second theme (B major), the principal idea being reserved for the movement's grandiose coda. Somewhat less compact is the ternary slow movement (G major), its contrasting central episode (G minor) incorporating an expressive transformation of part of Dvořák's 'Leave me Alone'. Later developed by the woodwind over varied solo cello figuration, it is recalled in the coda. The rondo finale (B minor) opens in march-like vein, announcing several melodic fragments which together form the resolute principal theme (solo cello). The cheerful first episode is brief and its material never recurs, but the second episode, pregnant with melodic material, is expanded into a self-contained, ternary-shaped interlude. The third episode (Moderato, G major) is similarly laden, the soloist introducing a reposeful melody that eventually forms the basis of a beautiful duet with a solo violin. The andante coda, newly composed after Josefina's death, includes melodic reminiscences from all three movements before a loud, augmented version of the rondo's principal theme heralds the final allegro vivo flourish.

The distinguished French cellist Auguste Franchomme augmented the repertory with his Concerto Op. 33, while Offenbach, himself a cellist but better known as a composer for the stage, composed a one-movement *Concerto Militaire* (1848), complete with trumpet fanfares and side-drum, and a Concertino (1851). Lalo's proficiency as a cellist is also evident in his Concerto (1877), notably in its broad, rhetorical lento introduction, its powerful opening Allegro maestoso and its central Intermezzo (a combination of slow movement and scherzo), while its rondo finale combines Spanish colouring with characteristic French grace.

Widor's Concerto (Op. 41, 1882) has failed to withstand the test of time, but Saint-Saëns's association with several cellists (notably Tolbecque, Lasserre, Hollmann, Delsart, Fischer and the Russians Davidoff and Brandukov) bore fruit in two concertos (Op. 33, 1873; Op. 119, 1902). His Op. 33 mirrors the design of his First Violin Concerto, telescoping three movements into one continuous, integrated whole. It comprises a sonata-form exposition with brief development, a waltz-like intermezzo in a contrasting key (B flat major), a solo cadenza, and a delayed modified recapitulation, which also incorporates new material and concludes in the major mode. His Second Concerto Op. 119 is a four-sectional work divided into two movements. Its expansive opening Allegro moderato gives way to a poetic slow movement (E flat major), derived initially from its predecessor's principal theme, while the scherzo-like Allegro non troppo culminates in a pertinent cadenza, leading to an energetic *moto perpetuo*, which recalls the two principal themes from the opening section.

Vieuxtemps has been compared to Liszt as a reformer of the concerto. While this may be the case in his Fourth and Fifth Violin Concertos, many of his works, including his two cello concertos (Op. 46, 1877; Op. 50, 1884), are more brilliant than profound. Another Belgian, Servais, made a more lasting impression with his Op. 5 and especially his *Concerto Militaire* Op. 18, a virtuoso work whose opening Allegro moderato and final rondo fully justify its title. Austrian Joseph Merk, who served for some years in the Viennese Imperial Chapel, wrote a concerto and a concertino for the cello, while David Popper's Second Concerto Op. 24 (Leipzig, 1880) was particularly enthusiastically received. However, Popper's youthful First (Op. 8, 1865) and lively Third (Op. 59; Hamburg, 1880), both in a continuous single-movement structure, and the quasi-cyclical, four-movement Fourth (Op. 72; Leipzig, 1900) were also prominent in the repertory.

Two conservative cello concertos by Anton Rubinstein (Opp. 65, 96) and four by Davidoff (Op. 5, 1859; Op. 14, 1863; Op. 18, 1868; Op. 31, 1878) constitute the principal nineteenth-century Russian works in the genre, while Svendsen's somewhat colourless Op. 7 (1870), in one movement with a ternary-shaped slow section inserted between the development and recapitulation, is the foremost exhibit from Scandinavia. Loeffler's *Fantastic Concerto* (1894) supplements Herbert's American contribution. Surprisingly, Donizetti composed a Double Concerto (vn, vc, orch); but the most significant Italian cello concerto composer of the period was Alfredo Piatti, a composition pupil of Molique. His two concertos Op. 24 (Berlin, 1874) and Op. 26 (Leipzig, 1877) and Concertino Op. 18 (Offenbach, 1863) reflect his own technical virtuosity and expressive cantabile style. Dutchman Cornelis Dopper, the Dane Eduard von Hartmann, the Norwegian Oluf Svendsen and the English composer Sir Arthur Sullivan also contributed one concerto each.[17]

The twentieth century

The early twentieth century witnessed a consolidation of late nineteenth-century concerto traditions, many of the more radical composers deliberately eschewing a medium with such conventional associations. However, the number, range and content of concertante works for the instrument expanded towards the middle of the century. Although this expansion has not been fully sustained in recent years, performers such as Mstislav Rostropovich, Siegfried Palm, Thomas Demenga and Steven Isserlis have ensured the genre's continued prosperity.

Germany and Austria

Hans Pfitzner provides a clear link with Schumann and Brahms, his youthful, two-movement A minor Concerto (Op. posth., 1888) and his single-movement First Concerto (Op. 42, 1935) combine Classical and late Romantic elements. His Second Concerto (Op. 52, 1944), in four contrasting movements, incorporates a theme from his earliest cello concerto, apparently representing his old age greeting his youth.

Hindemith's First Cello Concerto Op. 3 (1915–16), published posthumously, was also a student effort; it comprises a heroic Straussian first movement and a Romanze and a Tarantella finale in a more individual, chromatic style. However, his *Kammermusik* No. 3 (Op. 36 No. 2, 1925) was almost defiantly anti-Romantic. In four movements, it is a neo-Classical, polyphonic work composed for cello obbligato and ten instruments, each of which plays an independent melodic line. Hindemith's three-movement Concerto (1940) employs a full symphony orchestra and is his most exhilarating cello work. The first movement, based on a memorable phrase which contains a rising and a falling fifth, is well argued and introduces a fugato near its end. The following movement's eventual combination of its andante and allegro assai elements and the finale's progressively more high-spirited elaboration of its March and Trio themes demonstrate Hindemith's imagination and sense of humour.

Helmut Degen's Concerto (1941–2) and *Kleines Konzert* No. 4 (1943) sometimes adopt a style reminiscent of Hindemith; but, apart from the concertos of Schroeder (Op. 24, 1937), Höller (Op. 26, 1940–1; Op. 50, 1949) and Trexler (1952), those of the following generations mirrored more progressive twentieth-century musical developments, notably the works of Schoenberg pupil Winfried Zillig (vc, wind orch, 1934 rev. 1952), Engelmann (Op. 2, 1948), Genzmer (vc, wind orch, db, 1950), Goldschmidt (1953) and Fortner (1951). Goldschmidt's accessible melodious idiom juxtaposes Romantic elements with more austere material – the *Caprice mélancolique* is often equated with Weill, while the opening demonstrates Spanish influences – but Fortner's complex harmonic language, governed partially by serialism, and polyphonic style result in an immediately approachable three-movement work, which culminates in a set of variations, incorporating an extended solo cadenza and climactic coda.

One of Fortner's pupils, Zimmermann, contributed a single-movement concerto (1953, rev. 1957 as *Canto di speranza*) and a *Concerto en forme de 'pas de trois'* (1965–6), a developed symphonic fresco in a quasi-Stravinskian idiom combining elements of concerto, ballet music and jazz. Its five movements, each with a title, are characterised by colourful instrumentation.[18] Stravinsky was an early influence on Günter Bialas (1962) and also inspired Blacher's method of 'variable metres', exemplified in the vivace finale of his four-movement Concerto (1964), with its demanding cadenza and final Adagio following an impetuous double-metre episode. Unusually, its third movement (Adagio) repeats in inversion the exposition of the opening Adagio. More recent additions to the repertory include Matthus's dramatic single-movement Concerto (1975) and Klebe's *Concerto in einem Satz* (1990).

Of the Austrian school, Schoenberg contributed a free arrangement for cello (1932) of a three-movement harpsichord concerto in D major by Monn (1746), expanding upon Monn's thematic material and adding more chromatic harmonies,[19] while Cesar Bresgen composed a *Venezianisches Konzert* (1938) and a Concertino (vn, vc, orch, 1972). Other notable contributions were made by Schollum (Op. 52, 1954), Angerer (*Conference*, 2vc, ch orch, 1956), Siegl (1957), Reiter (1960), Vogel (1969), Ligeti (1966) and Gruber (two concertos; No. 1, 1980). Ligeti's Concerto was probably inspired by his interest in electronic music, as instrumental sonority – relating especially to extreme, copiously annotated sound gradations and textural contrasts – is its prime concern. It explores the complementary relationship between the very low, soft music (*con sordino*) of the first movement and the more virtuosic demands of the second movement (subtitled *Aventures ohne Worte*), which is a free variation of its predecessor and whose effective concluding cadenza dies away to nothing.

Great Britain

Elgar's Concerto in E minor (1918–19), comprising four movements linked in pairs, reflects the emotions of an aging composer racked by the grief of war. Its sombre mood, established during the five-bar introductory solo recitative passage (recalled as a link to the second movement and towards the end of the fourth) and in the poignant, lilting rhythm of the ternary first movement proper, is only occasionally alleviated, notably in the central *dolcissimo* section (E major). The brief, scherzo-like second movement (G major) is more animated, but is still cloaked in melancholy. The brief, soulful Adagio (B flat major) brings some repose, ending on the dominant to link with an introduction (B flat minor) to the rondo finale (E minor), foreshadowing its robust main theme and incorporating a

short cadenza-like passage. A contrasting second theme (G major) provides some relief; at the return of the main rondo idea, the soloist plays in
unison with the orchestral cellos (and, at times, violas, double basses, bas-
soons), creating a very unusual effect. An expressive Lento follows, incorporating two new ideas as well as recalling part of the Adagio. The
restatement of the opening cello recitative leads to a final fleeting reference
to the main rondo theme.

A performance of Brahms's 'Double' by May and Beatrice Harrison
(December 1914) inspired Delius to compose his Double Concerto (vn,
vc, 1915–16). Premièred by the Harrisons in 1920, it is a three-move-
ments-in-one design in which thematic repetition is preferred to development. Delius's Cello Concerto (1921), similarly through-composed,
follows an A–B–A' scheme, the varied reprise incorporating a new *allegra-
mente* section as well as other strikingly fresh material.

While the march-like second theme in the opening section of Delius's
Double Concerto may be a deliberate reference to the First World War,
Bridge's colourful, single-movement *Oration, Concerto elegiaco* (1930),
including a grotesque march which culminates with a distorted version of
'The Last Post', reflects both his pacifist sentiments and his personal grief
and veneration for those who died in the conflict. Of similar rhapsodic
nature is Bax's Concerto (1932), composed for Cassadó (hence its
Spanish-style central Nocturne). Notable chiefly for the passionate intensity of its opening movement and its finale's thematic anticipation of the
Seventh Symphony, it also demands some remarkable instrumental
combinations, notably in the Nocturne where the soloist is accompanied
by three solo double basses. Murrill's two concertos (1935; *El cant dels
ocells*, 1950), Tovey's prolix, four-movement Concerto Op. 40 (1935) and
Scott's Concerto (1937) are of less importance, but Moeran's Concerto
(1945) is remarkable for its unity. This is achieved through subtle
manipulation of motivic cells (the opening Moderato is almost mono-
thematic), the derivation of the second theme of the central slow movement from the Moderato, and the structural function of the cadenza,
which links the last two movements and transforms the slow movement's
second theme into the principal idea of the final rondo.

Concertos by Leighton (Op. 31, 1955–6), Jacob (1955), Finzi (Op. 40,
1951–5) and Bernard Stevens (Op. 18, 1952) date from the 1950s. Stevens's
work incorporates, unusually, a closely knit first movement that includes a
fugue and a central chaconne. But the decade's most important British
cello concerto was that of Walton (1955–6). Its structure is similar to the
concertos for viola and violin, with opening material being recalled at the
end, and its melancholy character and rhythmic vigour also have clear
affinities with its two predecessors. Furthermore, like them, it is an expres-

sion of love for a woman – in this case his wife, Susanna, whom he married in 1948. The moderato first movement is lyrical and reflective, its amorous themes, enhanced by unstable harmony and exotic orchestration, providing the germ of the work. The ensuing scherzo is more virtuosic and shows resemblances to the music for Pandarus in the composer's own *Troilus and Cressida*, while the finale comprises an unusual, expressive theme with four variations, two for cello alone serving also as elaborate cadenzas. An epilogue brings further unity by recalling the first movement's principal theme and combining it with the subject of the finale's variations.

Britten's sombre, dramatic *Cello Symphony* Op. 68 (1963) is a cross between symphony and concerto. Its first movement, a compact sonata structure, explores the potential of the three themes presented in the exposition by the soloist and the detail of their orchestral accompaniments. The complex, contrapuntal development especially concerns itself with smaller motifs, including the opening ostinato pattern (in inversion), and role reversal in the recapitulation results in the orchestra playing a melodic role while the soloist accompanies. The short, restless scherzo, muted throughout and developed from the cello's initial three-note scalic motif, finds contrast in the central 'trio', while the elegiac ternary Adagio forms the emotional heart of the work, its solemn main cello theme punctuated by woodwind interludes and a ubiquitous timpani roll, heard from the outset. After a varied reprise, in which the brass become the melodists and the cellist provides the interludes, a lengthy cadenza summarises the work's thematic content and provides a link to the passacaglia finale.[20] The soloist initiates the ground bass, which eventually accompanies the main theme (trumpet), derived from the previous Adagio. The orchestral writing becomes progressively more brilliant in the ensuing six variations and culminates in a coda based on the Adagio's main theme and motivic reminiscences from the first movement.

Equally fastidious in its craftsmanship is Rawsthorne's Cello Concerto (1966). Its opening movement comprises seven free variations on a theme recalled in the boisterous finale, whose scherzando middle section is developed fugally. Hugh Wood's lyrical, through-composed Concerto Op. 12 (1969) is remarkable for its references to Elgar's Concerto, one in the slow final section framed by quotation marks in the score and another, perhaps subconscious, in the cadenza, which serves as the work's fulcrum. Among other notable works of the 1960s and 1970s are Wilfred Joseph's single-movement *Concerto Cantus Natalis* Op. 34 (1962), which commemorates the birth of his daughter and is prefaced by Louis Macniece's 'Prayer before Birth'; Bliss's light-hearted Concerto (1970); Osborne's compact Concerto (1977), inspired largely by Gaston Bachelard's *La*

Psychoanalyse de Feu and the single-pitch conceptions of Ligeti; Tippett's continuous trisectional Triple Concerto (vn, va, vc, 1978–9) with its individual cadenzas, textural variety, colourful orchestral interludes incorporating jazz and gamelan styles and its subtle use of thematic self-borrowing and recall; and concertos by Cooke (1974), Rainier (1964), Brian (1964), Whettam (1961) and Parrott (1961–2).

Several British composers have risen to the challenges of concerto composition in recent years. Most prominent among them have been Colin Matthews, Arnold, Maxwell Davies, Casken, Bryars, Macmillan and Beamish, although Schurmann (*The Gardens of Exile*, 1991), Mathias (1984), Powers (1990), Harvey (1990), Saxton (1991–2), Blake (1993), Stevenson (1995) and Nyman (Double Concerto, vc, sax, orch, 1996–7) have each made a significant contribution. Arnold's neo-Classical tendencies are especially evident in the outer movements of his Concerto (1989), for which an elegiac slow movement provides the centrepiece. Like its predecessor for oboe, Maxwell Davies's 'Strathclyde Concerto' No. 2 (1988) is predominantly lyrical and has been likened to 'a symphony with cello added'. Cast in three movements, it is based, like many of his works, on short, plainsong-like fragments. Between the tautly conceived Moderato opening movement, with its climactic cadenza, and the intense finale comes the Lento, the work's emotional core. After a dense five-part chorale-like introduction, elaborated by the soloist, this movement is remarkable for the soloist's 'bluesy' trio with two flutes, its eloquent cadenza and the final solo dialogue with bass clarinet.

Matthews's First Cello Concerto Op. 27 (1983–4), in two movements, was inspired by the sea. Unified through thematic recall, it features some powerful declamatory writing and rich orchestral colours. His Second Concerto (1996) is more complex; comprising five interlinked movements which form a musical arch, its material derives almost exclusively from the opening chord. The course of Casken's Concerto (1990–1), cast in two substantial movements spread across five sections, is determined by a poem which Casken himself 'composed alongside' the work. This overtly simple poem's complex internal relations – of metre, meaning, image and sound – have a direct bearing on the way the work evolves, such as the manner in which the two sections of the later movement (fast–slow) telescope and conflate the three sections of the opening one.

The works of Bryars, Macmillan and Beamish were also extra-musically inspired. The meditative or reflective often forms a central part of philosophy-graduate Bryars's musical vocabulary, as in his serene, seven-movement *Farewell to Philosophy* (1995). Macmillan's Concerto (1996) is the second of three works relating to the Christian events and liturgies of Maundy Thursday, Good Friday and the Easter vigil. The cellist effectively takes the role of Christ and the ensemble the baying crowd on Golgotha, and the work incorporates diverse material, ranging from Presbyterian hymns to Catholic plainchant and comic song; Macmillan even uses percussion to evoke the Crucifixion. Beamish's Concerto (1997) draws on Ted Hughes's collection of poems, 'River', and reflects that river's special qualities with interesting textures.

France

Gaubert's *Concerto Lamento* (1912) and Ibert's short Concerto (1925) have achieved limited popularity. Following Stravinsky's Concerto (pf, wind instrs, 1923–4), Ibert's is scored for cello and wind orchestra. Particularly striking is its light, pastoral character, notably in its charming polytonal opening Pastorale and its lively, gigue-like finale. The latter's virtuosic cadenza portrays a different character, as does the poetic, central Romance, which provides two more expressive cadenza opportunities for the soloist.

Beginning with a solo cadenza, Milhaud's First Cello Concerto (1934) embraces a wide variety of moods and styles, its first movement (*nonchalant*) eventually settling into a foxtrot, whose melody is freely developed and later reviewed by the soloist after a second cadenza. The central Grave uses bitonality and is a none-too-convincing elegy in ternary form, but the playful finale betrays Latin American influences and incorporates a wealth of melody and rhythmic verve. Milhaud's Second Concerto (Op. 255, 1945) is more attractive and better developed, but the texture is relatively thin in the first two movements, the second movement's opening cello cantilena being accompanied by four solo violins. Only in the extrovert finale, a dance of folk origins underpinned by a drone, does the texture fill out, the soloist being involved mostly in busy passage-work, except for the climactic cadenza.

Roussel's Concertino Op. 57 (1936) was his last orchestral composition. Its last two movements, a brief Adagio in which the cellist is accompanied by a muted string quartet and a gay rondo, are played without a break, while the opening movement is more conventionally structured, contrasting two principal ideas. Roughly contemporary with Roussel's work was Bousquet's Iberian Concerto (1937), inspired by Iberian folk song and dance, and Büsser's Concertino Op. 80.

Following a barren period in French cello concerto composition, the 1960s witnessed a resurgence of interest with works by Jolivet (1962, 1966), Bozza (Op. 57), Hubeau (Concerto in A minor), Lavagne (*Concerto Romantique*), Kubizek (*Concerto brève*, Op. 23), Pascal (1960), Leibowitz (Op. 58, 1962), Tansman (1963), Dubois (1963), Martinon (Op. 52, 1963–4) and Tisné (1965). Jolivet's two concertos are less tonal than many of his previous works and demonstrate his remarkable quest for instrumental virtuosity and orchestral sonority. Four timpani and a battery of twenty-two percussion instruments create an oppressive atmosphere in the central movement (*Hiératique*) of his First Concerto. The expressive opening movement (*Méditatif*) is also sombre, but the energetic finale offers complete contrast, apart for its somewhat restrained central episode. The virtuosic Second Concerto, a continuous trisectional structure with a long solo cadenza as its fulcrum, resembles a concerto grosso, the cellist being pitted against both a string quintet and a string orchestra.

Paul Tortelier composed two solo concertos for his own use, as well as a Double Concerto for performance with his wife Maude, while the cosmopolitan Maurice Ohana contributed two concertos (*Anneau du Tamarit*, 1976–7; *In Dark and Blue*, 1991–2), the first a moving homage to the poet Federico Lorca and the second displaying jazz influence. But the foremost French cello concerto in recent times is Dutilleux's *Tout un monde lointain* (1968–70).[21] Each of its five continuous sections carries a title and epigraph, related to the verse and prose of Baudelaire, which suggest its content. Serial in technique, rhapsodic in character, and of considerable technical demand, its thematic material develops continuously, undergoing constant minute modifications and lending continuity to the overall structure. Its orchestration is highly individual; notable are the soft cymbal strokes and string chord-clusters in the first movement's ('Enigma') introductory cadenza, the subtle use of the marimba in 'Miroirs', the unusual accompaniment to the solo recitative in 'Houles', the exploitation of the cello's highest registers in 'Regard', with its reminiscence of the introduction to 'Enigma', and the atmospheric conclusion of the final 'Hymne'.

The Netherlands

French influences were predominant in the works of Leo Smit (Concertino, 1937), while Léon Orthel (1929) studied for a time in Berlin. However, Pijper synthesised Austro-German and French influences. His Concerto (1936) bears the Latin motto 'Vulnerant omnes ultima necat' and comprises six closely linked movements, including an introduction, two scherzos and a final epilogue. Among Pijper's pupils were Badings (1930, 1939 orch. 1954) and Landré, whose Concerto (1940) incorporates a memorial to Willem Landré's wife as its central focus and a finale closely associated with strict ballet music. Hendrik Andriessen's *Concertino* (1970) is a significant addition to the repertory, while Badings' pupil Hans Kox (1969, Sinfonia Concertante, vn, vc, orch, 1976) is notable for his cycle of works entitled *Cyclophony*, the first of which (1964) is for cello and chamber orchestra.

Switzerland

French influences were also predominant in much twentieth-century Swiss music. Honegger, who studied in Zurich and Paris, composed his modest Concerto in 1929. In one continuous movement, it comprises a judicious mixture of expressive solo cantilena, a lighter, jazz-influenced episode, a harsh central Largo, a cadenza (written by the work's dedicatee, Maurice Maréchal) and a vigorous concluding Allegro marcato (again with jazz overtones), which eventually recalls the melodic material of the opening Andante and its lighter corollary prior to a presto coda. Frank Martin's Concerto (1965–6) is in sharp contrast. Its expressive, central Adagietto leans towards serialism with its twelve-note theme, and its ternary-form first movement incorporates opening and closing Lento sections for unaccompanied cello. The rigid rhythms of the final Vivace seem to have affinity with Prokofiev's march-like ostinatos.

Prokofiev's influence is particularly evident in the finales of both Sutermeister's cello concertos (1954–5, 1971) and in the opening march of No. 2. Russian links are further enhanced in the finale of the Second Concerto by its use of episodes from Davidoff's 'At the Fountain' as a kind of collage. Schooled in Russian-German musical traditions, Vogel (1954) turned towards serial methods in the late 1930s, while Burkhard's Concertino Op. 60 (1940) demonstrates his neo-Classical propensities in a largely contrapuntal style reminiscent of Hindemith. German Romanticism is strongest in the work of Schoeck, whose four-movement Concerto Op. 61 (1947) is expressive and highly accessible, as are Sturzenegger's four cello concertos (1933, 1937, 1946–7, 1972).

The Americas

The cello concerto took time to blossom in the USA. Apart from the works of Sowerby (1917, 1929–34), Diamond (1938) and the eclectic Schuller (1945), the earliest notable concerto was Barber's demanding Op. 22 (1945 rev. 1947), whose three movements reflect the anguish of war in a lyrical and neo-Romantic language tinged with elements of American folk music and jazz. The first movement's opening bars introduce its thematic substance and prepare for the soloist's entry with a bravura cadenza-like soliloquy, the first of two such passages. The central Andante, a sad and tender siciliano, is worked out imitatively between the cellist and the orchestra, while the finale, a kind of rondo fantasy, begins stridently with an orchestral 'fanfare'. Its restless mood is contrasted by interjections of a sombre dirge-like theme over an ostinato bass. A toccata cello episode, framed by cadenzas, and a tarantella section completed by a recitative-like coda bring the final chords.

Virgil Thomson's characteristic quotation of Baptist hymn tunes is

exemplified in his Concerto (1950), which many have dismissed as a sterile
hotch-potch of styles and ideas. However, it has much to offer cellists, not
least its central 'Variations on a Southern Hymn Tune', incorporating a
cadenza played in harmonics (with celesta), and the brilliant coda of its
rondo finale ('Children's Games'). Among other conservative contributors to the genre are those of Mennin (1956), Halsey Stevens (1964), Rózsa
(Sinfonia Concertante Op. 29, vn, vc, 1968; Op. 32, 1971), Albert (1990)
and Zwilich (Double Concerto, vn, vc).

Several composers were attracted to experiment. Of Canadian Jean
Papineau-Couture's five *Pièces concertantes* (1951–63), No. 2 (vc, ch orch,
1959) bears the title 'Eventails', relating to its fan-like changes in density.
Perle's Concerto (1966) dates from the period in which he developed his
'twelve-tone modal system', while Lazarof's two concertos (1968–9, 1991)
are individual, atonal works which also lean towards dodecaphony.
Sessions's continuous three-movement Double Concerto (vn, vc, 1970–1)
involves much contrapuntal interaction and dialogue between the two
soloists and concludes with an unaccompanied statement of the original
form of the note-series by the solo violinist, followed immediately by the
retrograde inversion from the cellist. Lukas Foss uses tape with amplification in his four-movement *Concert* (1966), his experiments including distorted reproduction, mechanical replay and superimposition of tape. With
organ substituting for woodwind in the orchestral background, the soloist
'competes' with a cello cadenza on pre-recorded tape and, in the finale,
shares and gradually distorts the Sarabande from Bach's Fifth Cello Suite
with his recorded partner. Kupferman's Concerto (vc, tape, orch) is essentially an electro-acoustic concerto grosso, with two additional cello lines
pre-recorded by the soloist. Styles mix freely, opening in neo-Classical lyricism and continuing through Romantic and twelve-note writing into an
extended jazz passage. Among those who have experimented with
amplification is Wuorinen, whose 'Five' is a five-movement concerto (amp
vc, orch, 1987–8) based on material originally used in a ballet.

Of those who took American citizenship during the century, Toch
contributed a highly chromatic concerto in four movements (Op. 35,
1925). Other notable concertos by adopted Americans include those of
Korngold (Op. 37, 1946), Dukelsky[22] (1946), Rieti (1934, 1969), Vainberg
(Op. 43, 1948 rev. 1956) and Krenek (1953, 1982). The musical renaissance
in Latin America featured several composers who displayed nationalistic
sentiments in their work. One of the foremost Brazilian proponents of
musical nationalism was Villa-Lobos, who was himself a cellist. However,
his two concertos show few glimpses of his nationalistic spirit. The 'Grand
Concerto' Op. 50 (1915), a continuous three-movement work, has neo-
Classical inclinations – its central movement is a Gavotte – while his

Second Concerto (1953) post-dates his intense cultivation of Brazilian popular music and is characterised by its virtuosity. Its four movements comprise a vigorous Allegro, which includes orchestral motifs that recur in later movements, a ternary slow movement, a vivacious scherzo with cadenza, and a finale of primitive dance character. More nationalistic are Siqueira's two concertos (1952, 1974), which use folk material and are written in his own 'Brazilian trimodal' and 'Brazilian pentatonic' systems, adopting the modes of north-eastern folk music and their associated harmonies and rhythms. Siqueira's Second Concerto, *Paniel sonoro*, is scored, unusually, for woodwind orchestra. He also composed a Concertino (1971). Mexican Carrillo considered himself a nationalist, his experiments with microtonal composition bearing fruit in numerous works involving the cello, notably a Concertino (1927) and a solo Concerto (1958). Argentinian Ginastera had essentially outgrown his 'nationalistic period' by the time he wrote his two concertos (Op. 36, 1968 rev. 1977, Op. 50, 1980–1), which date from his period of neo-expressionism, although his serial technique was never rigorous.

Russia

Glazunov 'succeeded in reconciling Russianism and Europeanism'[23] and his *Concerto-Ballata* Op. 108 (1931), though old-fashioned, is notable for its melting melodic phrases and vein of rich rhapsodical emotion. Of similar language is Myaskovsky's Concerto Op. 66 (1944–5); a war-time work cast in two movements, it offers fascinating parallels with Elgar's Cello Concerto, particularly since both composers tap a similar vein of intense lyricism and nostalgic melancholy. Myaskovsky's pupil, Mosolov, began with avant-garde ambitions but soon fell prey to Stalinist repression and turned to composing traditional, folk-inspired material, as exemplified by his Concerto (1945), which nevertheless shows glimpses of his more adventurous past.

After his return to Russia from Paris in the mid-1930s, Prokofiev revised some of the works conceived in the West. Thus, the structure of his Concerto Op. 58 (1933–8), poorly received in Moscow (1838), was tightened, its orchestration was substantially modified and the revised work was renamed *Sinfonia concertante* Op. 125.[24] Prokofiev never withdrew his original Concerto; although some aspects of the reworked version, such as the thematic material, are close to the original, both versions remain in the repertory as quite different works. Inspired by his work with Rostropovich on Op. 125, Prokofiev began composing a Concertino Op. 132, an altogether slighter piece whose finale is based on a theme derived from the finale of Op. 125. Complete only in short score at his death, it was edited by Rostropovich and orchestrated by Kabalevsky.[25]

The Communist party decree on music (1948) inspired Kabalevsky to cultivate a more lyrical idiom, as the elegiac central slow movement of his Concerto Op. 49 (1948–9) clearly demonstrates. His Second Concerto Op. 77 (1964) comprises three continuous movements, with two cadenzas acting as structural transitions to and from the central scherzo. Boundaries are further blurred by the dual tempo (slow–fast) of the first section and the outbursts of fast music in the concluding Andante, which uses a theme to which Prokofiev had recourse in his Concertino Op. 132.

The language of Glier's Concerto Op. 87 (1946) looks back to the previous century, while the interest of Shebalin (1950) and Knipper (1952; *Concerto-Monologue*, vc, 7 br, timp, 1962) in national musics is reflected in much of their later work. Similarly, Khachaturian draws upon his Armenian heritage for melodic and harmonic inspiration in his Concerto (1946), which combines lyricism and virtuosity – the cello was Khachaturian's own instrument – with solid workmanship. The second movement seems to derive directly from Armenian song, while the finale is based on 'a sabre-dance-like tune' and a contrasting, more expressive second idea. Khachaturian's *Concerto-Rhapsody* (1963) is more compact but of similar stock, its 'finale' owing much to Armenian folk-dance traditions. A single-movement structure in three sections, its material is derived from a lyrical melody in the central slow 'movement' which is itself built from various germinal ideas, such as the semitonal contours of the opening horn call (which also heralds the brilliant coda) and elements from the first section's substantial solo cadenza.

Shostakovich's two cello concertos stem from his mature years. The First Concerto (Op. 107, 1959), in four movements, begins with a tautly constructed Allegretto dominated by both the opening four-note cell (G, E, B, B♭), announced by the soloist, and a recurrent variant of the DSCH motif (C, B, E♭, D). A solo horn assumes a significant role in the development of material, loudly declaiming the four-note cell at several junctures. The lyrical Moderato adopts a modified three-part structure, its opening solo idea returning at the end in a most ethereal setting for solo cello (in harmonics) and celesta. A solo clarinet plays the central thematic material against a countermelody from the cello soloist. An unaccompanied bravura cadenza with a structural, developmental purpose serves as the third movement, ruminating on material from both the previous movements before launching the finale, a sonata-rondo with a strong Russian dance flavour. Towards the end, the first movement's opening idea is recalled (horn) and its various elements are ingeniously combined with the finale's principal theme. Shostakovich's Second Concerto (Op. 126, 1966) is less extrovert, its opening Largo meditative and withdrawn. Its other two movements are played without a break, the finale opening with an arresting fanfare for horns but incorporating moments of great tenderness and harrowing melancholy.

Tishchenko wrote his prize-winning First Concerto (1963), in one continuous movement, while pursuing postgraduate study with Shostakovich (1962–5). Like his Second Cello Concerto (1969, vc, 48vcs, 2dbs), it is a well-crafted work for unusual orchestral forces (ww, br, perc, org) and is a product of the freer Russian artistic climate for which Khrennikov (Op. 16; Op. 30), among others, had laboured. Denisov also enjoyed a new artistic freedom in his Concerto (1972), but without losing touch with the past. Apart from Agopov's single-movement Concerto Op. 10 (1984), the concertante works of Schnittke have captured most recent public attention. Schnittke's First Concerto (1985–6) comprises four movements in a fast–slow–fast–slow format, its final Largo featuring a beautiful melody based on Russian Orthodox chant which soars over bright, parallel-motion harmonies and an extensive sustained bass pedal. His Second Concerto (1989–90), in five movements, also reserves its emotional weight for the finale, a lengthy, concentrated passacaglia. Of very different intention is his Concerto Grosso No. 2 (vn, vc, orch), which is little short of an assault on the Baroque. A kaleidoscopic piece, by turns cacophonous, witty, plagiaristic, elegant and brutal, it offers little opportunity for solo display. When the soloists are not submerged by the large orchestra,[26] they play elegant Baroque pastiche or exchange simple melodic aphorisms.

Czechoslovakia

Martinů rediscovered his Czech nationalism during the 1930s, but, apart from certain melodic traits derived from Moravian folk song, patriotic sentiments are hard to find in his concertante works for cello. His Concertino (vc, ww, 1924), Concerto (str qt, orch, 1931), two Concertinos (pf trio, str, 1933) and First Cello Concerto (1930 rev. 1955) are essentially neo-Classical works from a composer who, nevertheless, constantly sought new modes of expression. His lyrical Second Cello Concerto (1944–5) perhaps comes closest to a patriotic gesture, its finale (bravura cadenza apart) being suggestive of a Czech landscape. The concertos of Kalabis (Op. 8, 1950–1) and Tich'y (1976–7) emphasise the virtuoso element, Tich'y's style often being reminiscent of Shostakovich, while Bázlik's *Epoché* ('Delay', vc, orch, tape, 1983) applies complex mathematical principles to electro-acoustic music.

Poland

Of Bacewicz's two neo-Classical concertos (1951, 1963) No. 1 is the more striking, its central Andante displaying influences of her studies in Paris with Nadia Boulanger. Penderecki's virtuosic First Concerto (1967–72), in one continuous movement, was originally written for the five-stringed *violino grande*, but its successor (1981–2), another large one-movement structure, has a more conventional history. Boguslaw Schäffer's *Concerto breve* (1959) is also noteworthy.

Lutosławski described his Concerto (1969–70) as a piece of 'collective ad libitum', his 'aleatory counterpoint' freeing performers to play assigned patterns or groups of pitches without fixed durations but in prescribed periods of time. The work marked for him a new direction, 'less brilliant in colour than in technique, with its synthesis of pure music-making and battle'.[27] 'The situation should be quite clear ... from the very first orchestral note', wrote Lutosławski, 'because the orchestra provides the element of intervention, interruption, even disruption. This is followed by attempts at reconciliation: dialogues. But these are in turn interrupted by a group of brass instruments, which in fact provide the element of intervention in the work. My aim was to find some justification for employing these two contradictory forces: the solo instrument and the orchestra. The relationship between these two forces undergoes a change in the course of the concerto. There is even a moment of complete harmony in the *cantilena*, but this provides the opportunity for the most violent of the interventions, this time from the whole brass section'.[28] Striking is the manner in which the overall structure builds from apparently disparate yet ultimately compatible episodes, which demand as much quasi-theatrical characterisation as technical brilliance from the soloist (e.g. the opening monologue). The orchestral contribution culminates in a nine-note chord played 'tutta forza' by all except the soloist, who registers his own individual triumph over adversity at the close.

Panufnik completed his Concerto (1991) only days before his death. Premièred in 1992, the tautness of its palindromic structure is impressive, its two movements, each in arch form, being a mirror-image of the other, slow then fast. Panufnik's geometrical source of inspiration for this work was the almond-shaped figure produced by the intersection of two circles. However, the result is not a dryly schematic work, but one characterised by a more open lyricism than might be expected of Panufnik.

Italy

Casella was one of the foremost champions of instrumental music in Italy at the beginning of the century. He composed his Triple Concerto Op. 56 (1933) for his own trio, the Trio Italiano; it uses the eighteenth-century concerto grosso as a model, the three soloists forming the contrasting concertino group to the orchestra's ripieno. Two years later, the Trio's cellist, Arturo Bonucci, was the recipient of Casella's Concerto Op. 58 (1934–5), a well-crafted work in three parts, comprising a central slow cantabile movement framed by a fast opening section and a lively, virtuoso finale.

Pizzetti concentrated his efforts in opera. His Cello Concerto (1933–4) is not as effective as the roughly contemporary works by Zandonai, Malipiero, Mannino (*Concerto lirico*, 1956, 1974) or Castelnuovo-Tedesco (1932–3). Zandonai's *Concerto Andaluso* (1934) presents quasi-Spanish material in a neo-Classical style enhanced by the use of a harpsichord, while Malipiero's Cello Concerto (1937) is remarkable for its rhapsodic nature, unusual orchestration and its extended cello solo, accompanied by bass and side drums, in the final Allegro. The last five years of Wolf-Ferrari's life yielded three concertos, including his *Invocazione* (Op. 32, 1945); but this is a retrospective work, its fantasy-like opening movement and tarantella finale framing a cello elegy with sparse accompaniment. More enterprising are the concertos of Fuga (1955), Zafred (1956) and Mainardi (four concertos; Concerto, 2vc, orch).

Spain

Gaspar Cassadó's compositions were influenced by Falla and Ravel, not least his D minor Concerto (1925), whose colourful orchestration includes a tambourine.[29] Rodrigo's style was similarly moulded by French and Spanish music. His neo-Classical *Concierto en modo galante* (1949), inspired by nineteenth-century Spanish dance, is characterised by its numerous bustling ostinatos and colourful orchestration, especially in the Zapateado rondo finale. His three-movement *Concierto como un divertimento* (1981–2) is similar in nationalist aims, orchestral texture and instrumental treatment. Its central slow movement is based on an old Castilian ballad 'There Sits King Ramiro', while its outer movements are high-spirited, the finale using celesta and xylophone to excellent effect.

Cristobal Halffter (1974) and José de Delás (1973) gradually progressed from their traditional Spanish roots to avant-garde techniques. Halffter's Concerto uses aleatoric devices and requires an enormous orchestra, including an almost soloistically treated sixty-piece string section and a wide range of percussion.

Scandinavia

Prominent among Norwegian composers of cello concertos were Sverre Jordan (Op. 51, 1947) and particularly Harald Saeverud, whose Op. 7 (1931) marks his development of an atonal, expressionist idiom. Klaus Egge composed his Op. 29 (1966) at a time when he was rejecting folk influences in favour of 'free serialism', in which he always preserved a feeling for melody and tonality.

Swedish composer Kurt Atterberg's dramatic Concerto Op. 21 (1917 rev. 1922) was founded on German and Scandinavian Romanticism, but his compatriots Rosenberg (1939, 1953), Nystroem (*Sinfonia Concertante,* 1940–4) and Pergament (1954) sought to progress from such a base, Nystreom and Pergament being influenced by early twentieth-century trends in French music. Rosenberg experimented widely and was regarded by his compatriots as an extreme radical, while the works of Wirén (Op. 10, 1936) and Larsson (1947, *Concertino* Op. 45 No. 10, 1956) demonstrate neo-Classical traits; Larsson also assimilated Hindemith's polytonal tendencies and technique of thematic metamorphosis in the late 1940s. Larsson-pupil Hans Eklund's concertante *Musica da camera* works (No. 1, 1955) are modelled directly on Hindemith's *Kammermusik* series, while Karkoff (Op. 31, 1957–60) and Linde (Op. 29, 1965) also adopted similar retrospective idioms. Rhythm is predominant in Bäck's Concerto (1965), which includes a prominent part for percussion and only minimal melodic interest.

One of the most prolific and individual Danish composers in recent years has been Niels Bentzon (1956, 1975), but the cello concertos of compatriots Koppel (Op. 56, 1952), Thybo (1959), Westergaard (1961), Holmboe (Op. 120, 1974) and Ruders (1988, 1993) are firmly rooted in the Nordic lyricism of Nielsen, combined with various other contemporary idioms (especially of Stravinsky and Bartók). Common to the formal structures of Bentzon, Westergaard and Holmboe is the unity attained through the subtle development of short motifs, often comprising small intervals.

Apart from the neo-Classical works of Merikanto (1919, 1941–4) and Englund (1954), Finnish composers appear to have been reluctant to cultivate the cello concerto. However, Merikanto's pupil Rautavaara (Op. 41, 1968) and Kokkonen (1969) triggered further interest in the genre, both emphasising virtuosity, often (and particularly in Rautavaara's case) at the expense of the orchestral contribution. More recently, Sallinen (Op. 44, 1976) and Aho (1983–4) have composed concertos for the instrument. Aho's work has been described as 'music of multi-dimensional time', referring to its multi-layered, disparate textures characterised by conflict between oblique combinations of timbrally remote instruments (notably the accordion, mandolin, saxophone, tuba and side-drum at the beginning of the second movement) and more traditional groupings.

Other countries

Hungarian interest in the genre is reflected in the works of Dohnányi (*Konzertstück* Op. 12, 1903–4), Moór (two cello concertos, 1905–6; Triple Concerto, 1907; Double Concerto, 2vc, orch), Hajdu (Concertino) and Kurtág (Concerto, vc, pf, orch), while Enesco's Symphonie Concertante

Op. 8 (1901), Golestan's Concerto (1935) and Vieru's Concerto (1962) and Double Concerto (vn, vc, orch, 1979) stand at the forefront of the Romanian cello literature. Other countries making notable contributions to the repertory include Belgium (Jongen: Op. 18, 1900; Absil: Concertino Op. 42, 1940), Yugoslavia (Kelemen: Concertino, 1958), Israel (Tal, 1961; Ben Haim, 1962), Iceland (Hallgrímsson), Latvia (Vasks, 1993–4) Estonia (Arvo Pärt, 1983) and Australia (Lumsdaine: *The Garden of Earthly Delights*, 1992), while the genre has blossomed in Japan and Korea. Particularly noteworthy Japanese concertos are those of Abe (1937), Otaka (1944), Yashiro (1960), Toyama (1966), Akutagawa (1969), Hirose (*Concerto Triste*, 1971, rev. 1974), Mamiya (1975), Shimoyama (1984), Yuasa (*Revealed Time*, 1986), Nishimura (1990) and Takemitsu (1991). Tokyo-trained Korean-German composer Isang Yun fulfils his aim of developing Korean music through the materials of Western music in his single-movement Cello Concerto (1976).

8 The sonata

ROBIN STOWELL

Introduction

The cello sonata forged three avenues of development in the eighteenth century. The late seventeenth-century form, for cello and continuo, involving a cello as the principal melodist, persisted well into the third quarter of the eighteenth century. Harmonic support in the form of semi-improvised chords or the realisation of a prescribed figured bass was provided by a keyboard instrument (normally an organ or harpsichord), which could be joined or replaced by a plucked instrument (chitarrone or archlute); in addition, the bass line could be sustained, normally by another cello or, possibly, a gamba. The nomenclature for such works ranged from 'sonata' to 'sinfonia', 'solo', 'trattenimento', 'divertimento', 'concertino' and other such terms.

The sonata's second avenue of development, the so-called 'accompanied sonata', involved the cellist in a subordinate role to an obbligato keyboard. This type, which challenged the dominance of the sonata with continuo and eventually superseded it, began and ended essentially with the early sonatas of Beethoven and his contemporaries, giving way to the third avenue, the true duo sonata for two equal protagonists.

The Baroque

The cello sonata evolved first in northern Italy towards the end of the seventeenth century. Two different types emerged: the *sonata da camera* ('chamber sonata'), which is essentially a suite of stylised dances; and the *sonata da chiesa* ('church sonata'), the movements of which have no dance allegiances.[1]

Italy
The cello was emancipated from its purely bass role towards the end of the seventeenth century when works for solo cello and for cello and continuo were composed by musicians in the basilica of San Petronio in Bologna. Violin music, as opposed to music for gamba, provided the models. Giuseppe Jacchini's *Sonate . . . per camera* Op. 1 (Bologna, *c.* 1695) and *Concerti per camera* Op. 3 (Modena, 1697) include the first known pub-

lished continuo sonatas for cello, two appearing in each publication;[2] but Domenico Gabrielli probably wrote his two *Sonate a Violoncello solo con B.C.*[3] in the late 1680s, and it is generally conceded that the composition of cello continuo sonatas starts unequivocally with Gabrielli's last four *Ricercari* in a manuscript of 1689. It may have commenced, however, with a *Sinfonia* for cello by Giovanni Battista Vitali or with a *Sonata . . . a Basso Solo, con B.C.* by Antonio Giannotti, if, indeed, this was intended for cello.[4] Other early examples of published cello sonatas appear in Luigi Taglietti's *Suonate da camera* Op. 1 (Bologna, 1697) and Angelo Maria Fiorè's *Trattenimenti da camera* (Lucca, 1698). Taglietti's publication comprises principally ten trio sonatas (2vn, bc), but it also incorporates eight 'Capriccios' (vc, bc), one of which requires scordatura (C–G–d–g). Fiorè's opus is a set of ten chamber sonatas (vn, bc), but it also includes three sonatas (vc, bc), a 'Minuet, a Violoncello solo', a 'Canone all 'Unisono a due Violoncelli' and an Allegro for two cellos, also in canon.

The cello sonata with continuo blossomed during the first half of the eighteenth century. Irrespective of where they worked, Italian composers contributed most to the evolution of the genre and to the development of a technical and musical language appropriate to it. Notable amongst a host of such composers are Giuseppe Valentini, Gaetano Boni, Antonio Vivaldi, Benedetto Marcello, Giorgio Antoniotto, Salvatore Lanzetti, Giovanni Somis and Giovanni Sammartini. Valentini's twelve *Allettamenti per camera* (vc/vn, bc; Rome, 1714) are essentially *da chiesa* sonatas with an additional final dance movement, while Boni's twelve *Sonate per camera* Op. 1 (Rome, 1717) show the influence of both Gabrielli and Corelli. Vivaldi's cello sonatas (RV39–47)[5] are mostly in a composite church-chamber style in which chamber elements are predominant; they have stylistic affinities with Marcello's six Sonatas Op. 1 (Amsterdam, *c.* 1732).

Antoniotto's Op. 1 (Amsterdam, *c.* 1735) comprises twelve sonatas (five for cello and continuo and seven for two cellos or gambas) of fairly conservative technical demand, but the technical requirements of Lanzetti's twelve three-movement *Sonate* Op. 1 (Amsterdam, 1736), his two unpublished collections Opp. 6 and 7, each comprising six sonatas, and various 'Solos' (vc, bc; 2vc/fl, bc) are advanced, especially as regards bow management. Somis made a significant contribution to the emergence of an abstract sonata genre. His numerous examples are principally for violin and continuo but include twelve sonatas for cello and continuo (Paris, *c.* 1740); these combine elements of church and chamber varieties, settle on a three-movement (usually slow–fast–fast) design and place emphasis on the first movement, which often resembles a skeletal sonata-form structure. Sammartini's six sonatas (Paris, 1742) generally support this trend, but his authorship of No. 6 in G is doubted, because it bears striking resemblances (but also some differences) to one of a set of twelve sonatas by Giuseppe Dall'Abaco.[6]

Dall'Abaco was one of several Italians who took advantage of the vibrant musical life of eighteenth-century London. Among them were a number of cellists, many of whom wrote continuo sonatas for cello, increasing its popularity as a solo instrument in England. Dall'Abaco contributed at least thirty-four such works, most of which look back to the style of his father. However, the sonatas of, for example, Giacobbe Cervetto (eighteen), Pasqualini (twelve), Stefano Galeotti (six), Giovanni Cirri (twenty) and Andrea Caporale (six) generally cultivate a fluent *galant* style, with clear-cut symmetrical melodies and numerous grace-notes, and comprise three movements (normally slow–fast–fast with the final movement commonly a minuet). However, all except the last of Francesco Geminiani's six *Sonates* Op. 5 (Paris, 1746) follow the Corellian four-movement format (slow–fast–slow–fast).

Elizabeth Cowling's invaluable research has also unearthed a lengthy list of cello continuo sonatas by Italian Baroque composers, much of whose work remains in manuscript in libraries around the world.[7] She reserves special mention for three sonatas by either Alessandro or Domenico Scarlatti,[8] two by Francesco Alborea (called Francischello), twelve by Giovanni Platti (1725), and one each by Nicola Porpora, Francesco Scipriani and Giovanni Pergolesi.[9] She also mentions a collection of *Six Solos For Two Violoncellos Compos'd by Sigr. Bononcini and other eminent Authors*; of these six sonatas, only the first is by Giovanni Bononcini, the 'eminent authors' Pasqualini, St Martini (probably Giuseppe Sammartini), Caporale, Spourni and Porta providing one each. However, a detailed study of these and other similar works is far beyond the scope of this chapter.

France

In France the cello sonata was cultivated by Italians living in Paris, such as Giovanni Pietro Ghignone,[10] Jean Baptiste Canavas *l'aîné*, and Giuseppe Fedeli Saggione, as well as by native Frenchmen. Boismortier's *Cinq Sonates* Op. 26 (Paris, 1729) is generally believed to be the first published French cello sonata collection. Another collection of six sonatas, Op. 50, by Boismortier followed in 1734. More musically and technically demanding, however, are the works of Michel Corrette (six sonatas; *Les délices de la solitude* Op. 20, Paris, *c.* 1739) and Jean Barrière. Barrière's first two books of sonatas (Paris, 1733), in four or five movements (generally slow–fast–slow–fast), demonstrate a mixture of church and chamber traditions, several movements bearing dance titles; they present a variety of technical challenges – passages in double thirds, arpeggiated chords, multiple stopping and brilliant passage-work in the higher registers of the instrument. His third and fourth books of sonatas, published following his visit to Italy (1736–9), are more technically challenging and comprise between three and five movements, some even including transitional Adagios between movements. Along with the work of composers such as François Martin (*Sonate da camera* Op. 1, Paris, 1748; six *Sonates* Op. 2, Paris, 1746) and Patouart (six *Sonates* Op. 1, Paris, 1749), they are significant precursors of the virtuoso sonatas of the French 'Classical' school.

Germany

Significant German composers of continuo sonatas were less numerous but include Jacob Klein *le jeune*'s *Sonates à une Basse de Violon e & Basse Continue* Op. 1 (*c.* 1720), of which Nos. 13–18 (Bk. 3) require the scordatura tuning D–A–e–b, Joseph Spourni's numerous sonatas, and Johann Triemer's six sonatas (Op. 1, *c.* 1745). Johann Ernst Galliard, who worked in London, composed a set of six sonatas for bassoon or cello (1733), at least two of which (those in F and in A minor) have withstood the test of time.

It should not be ignored that some cellists have adopted J. S. Bach's three Sonatas for viola da gamba and obbligato keyboard BWV1027–9 into their repertory. Recast in Leipzig from earlier works composed for other instrumental combinations, these sonatas were not conceived as a set and are mostly in the nature of trio sonatas, the harpsichord contribution being in two parts throughout, except for some occasional brief passages of figured bass. The individual movements display remarkable diversity of structure and character. The lyrical, quasi-pastoral opening Adagio of the G major Sonata (BWV1027) is followed by a jubilant concertante-like Allegro, a brief Andante and a powerful three-voice fugal Allegro moderato. The D major Sonata (BWV1028) adopts a similar external structure, but its short opening Adagio introduces a dance-like binary Allegro of *galant* character. The ensuing Andante is a siciliana in all but name, while the concluding Allegro incorporates two virtuoso solo passages at its climax. Both outer movements of the G minor Sonata (BWV1029) adopt ritornello structures which open in fugato vein, the melodies, rhythms and gestures (particularly of the first movement) suggesting those of a concerto rather than a sonata. The poignant central Adagio combines the Italian style of improvised ornamentation (here written out in full) with the slow triple metre and dignified style of the French sarabande.

Other countries

The publication of cello sonatas in other countries before *c.* 1750 was minimal, with no significant representation from British composers. One notable exception is the Dutchman, Willem de Fesch, whose early sonatas show allegiance to their seventeenth- and early eighteenth-century roots as well as certain virtuosic aspects (e.g. twelve *Sonate* Op. 4, Amsterdam, 1725),[11] but whose later style involves the simpler, more expressive idiom of the Italian *galant* (e.g. six sonatas each of Op. 8b (London, 1736) and Op. 13 (London, *c.* 1750)).

The continuo sonata from 1750 to 1800

The composition of continuo sonatas persisted in the second half of the eighteenth century, but there was an increasing trend towards leaving bass parts unfigured or incorporating in them more pertinent musical material; thus, the bass part gradually developed from its simple, harmonic supporting role to one of equal partnership. The three published sets of six sonatas each by Carlo Graziani (Opp. 1, 2 and 3, London, Paris and Berlin, *c.* 1760–70), Jean-Pierre Duport's predecessor as cello teacher to the then Crown Prince, Friedrich Wilhelm II, in Berlin, and the thirty-four sonatas of Luigi Boccherini reflect this trend to some extent. Most comprise three movements, exploit the higher registers of the instrument and mirror their composers' skills as executants.[12] However, Italian predominance in sonata composition was challenged by composers of various other European countries, particularly France and Germany.

Of French composers, the sonatas of Martin Berteau (Op. 2, Paris, 1767; four others in MS, 1759) foreshadow a more virtuosic trend in the genre, reaffirmed by the works of his pupils Jean-Pierre Duport, Joseph Tillière, Jean-Baptiste-Aimé Janson and François Cupis. Duport's twenty-four cello sonatas fully explore the cello's cantabile and technical possibilities throughout a range of almost five octaves. More virtuosic still are Tillière's numerous works in the genre, especially his minuet movements with variations and his brief written-out cadenzas, and the sonatas of Janson and Cupis similarly exploit the upper range of the instrument, the use of thumb-position and several intricate bowings. But the sonatas of Jean-Baptiste Bréval (e.g. Op. 12, Paris, 1783; Op. 28, Paris, 1787; Op. 40, Paris, *c.* 1795) herald the next generation in terms of style, craftsmanship and technical demand, even though they, like those of Triklir and others, still belong to the 'continuo sonata' genre.

German cellist Johann Schetky (the elder) composed various solos for his instrument and unfigured bass (six *Solos* Op. 13, London, *c.* 1795) as well as several sets of sonatas for harpsichord or piano 'with an arbitrary accompanyment [*sic*] of a violin and violoncello' or with violin only (e.g. his Op. 3, London, 1775), clearly showing the direction in which the genre was progressing.[13] However, the eighteenth-century continuo sonata reached its highest point of development in Germany in the works of Anton Kraft, although his two published sets (Op. 1, Amsterdam and Berlin, 1790; Op. 2, Offenbach, ?1790), each of three three-movement sonatas, fail to show the flair and imagination of Bréval and other members of the Classical French school.

In England, the sonatas of Raynor Taylor (*c*. 1780s) and Stephen Paxton (Op. 1, London, 1772) are noteworthy for their graceful melodies and expressive slow movements, but Paxton's six *Easy Solos* Op. 3 (London, *c*. 1778) adopt the simpler, more popular style characteristic of much English instrumental music of the time. Dutchman Pieter Hellendaal, resident in England from 1752, left a set of *Eight Solos* Op. 5 (Cambridge, *c*. 1780) that are retrospective in showing the influence of his teacher, Tartini. The Bohemian cellist Jan Stiastny also composed numerous sonatas and other works of merit for his instrument.

Beethoven and his contemporaries

Beethoven's first two sonatas 'for Harpsichord or Pianoforte and Violoncello Obbligato' Op. 5 (F major; G Minor) were products of his visit to Berlin in 1796. Dedicated to Friedrich Wilhelm II, they were composed for court cellist Jean-Pierre Duport. There were few precedents in the cello literature for these works,[14] which pre-date Beethoven's Violin Sonatas and derive not from the Baroque continuo sonata but from the so-called 'accompanied sonata', involving the cellist in a subordinate role to an obbligato keyboard. Formally, the Op. 5 sonatas are unusual in commencing with a slow introductory movement, leading to an Allegro; the finales are rondos. Beethoven's Sonata Op. 17 (1800), which Cowling claims appeared simultaneously in two versions – one for French horn and a more elaborate one by Beethoven himself for cello[15] – is of similar foundation but more concertante character.

Pianist and cellist are treated as equal protagonists in Beethoven's sonatas Opp. 69 (1807–8) and 102 Nos. 1 and 2 (1815). The A major Sonata Op. 69 was dedicated to Baron Ignaz von Gleichenstein, an amateur cellist and brother-in-law of Therese Malfati, one of the numerous objects of Beethoven's unrequited love. The most lyrical of his sonatas, its content is more serious and profound and more equally distributed between the instruments. Its noble Allegro ma non tanto begins with a long expressive melody for cello alone which spawns other thematic material both of the first group and later in the movement. A poetic and graceful Scherzo, with sonorous contrasting trio, and optimistic

Allegro vivace finale frame a brief lyrical and expressive Adagio cantabile.

The last two Sonatas Op. 102 (in C and in D) were composed in the summer of 1815 when Beethoven visited Countess Anna-Marie Erdödy at her Jedlersee estate near Vienna. They were written for the countess, who was an excellent pianist,[16] and Joseph Lincke and herald Beethoven's mature style in their terseness, concentration, texture and profundity. The first, which may have been inspired by Goethe's *Proserpina*, comprises two fast movements, each preceded by a slow introduction. The opening Andante leads into a Vivace sonata-form movement in the relative minor, its first idea comprising an inversion of the Andante's main theme and the second group showing rhythmic affinities with the first. The work's tight organisation continues, material from the opening Andante returning in the brief Adagio which prefaces the terse, sonata-form finale. Beethoven uses an unremarkable five-note rhythmic figure as the subject of his resourceful, sonata-form opening Allegro con brio of Op. 102 No. 2, while Schindler described the expressive, ternary Adagio as 'among the richest and most deeply sensitive inspirations of Beethoven's muse'.[17] The complex counterpoint of the final Allegro fugato, a challenging double fugue, was one of the principal reasons why this sonata failed to find favour with Beethoven's contemporaries.[18]

Foremost among the sonatas of Beethoven's contemporaries were the works of Ferdinand Ries (Opp. 20, 21, 125 and WoO2, 1799), Bonifazio Asioli (Sonata in C, *c.* 1801), Joseph Wölfl (*Grand Duo* Op. 31, *c.* 1805), Bernhard Romberg (numerous examples, of which the three sonatas of Op. 38 and the three of Op. 43 are most successful), Vincenz Hauschka (Opp. 1 and 2, Vienna, 1803) and Helène Liebmann, whose Sonata in B flat Op. 11 (Berlin, 1806) clearly displays the stylistic influence of Mozart, emphasised particularly in the finale – a set of seven variations on 'Là ci darem la mano' from *Don Giovanni*. More pianistically biased were the works of Franz Xaver Mozart (*Grande Sonate* Op. 19, Leipzig, 1820) and Johann Nepomuk Hummel, whose Sonata in A Op. 104 (1824) combines good craftsmanship, harmonic and melodic variety, brilliance and a wide expressive range. The three Sonatas Op. 16 of Georges Onslow, himself an amateur cellist, also reached a wide and appreciative audience, showing originality, harmonic interest, skilful instrumentation and a fairly equal treatment of the two instruments.[19]

Schubert wrote his Sonata in A minor (D821, 1824) for arpeggione and piano. A cross between a cello and a guitar, the arpeggione was invented in Vienna in 1824 by a friend of Schubert, Georg Staufer, but had a very brief existence; it was played with a bow, had six strings and twenty-four frets and was essentially a bass viol with guitar tuning. Promptly forgotten, the instrument was relegated to the museum; but Schubert's beautiful three-movement sonata has since become part of the cello repertory in an effective transcription.[20] The opening Allegro moderato combines a long, lugubrious principal idea with brilliant passage-work and much use of short repeated figures. A beautiful Adagio follows, with all the lyricism of one of Schubert's Lieder, and leads into the final Allegretto, a rondo in the tonic major with a vigorous 'East European' episode in D minor, and a much more urbanised one in E major. The vigorous episode returns (in A minor) prior to the reprise of the main rondo theme.

The Romantic era

The sonata played a secondary role to the concerto and other bravura genres in the Romantic era, owing to that period's emphasis on virtuosity and brilliance. Only a few nineteenth-century sonatas have withstood the test of time.

Germany and Austria

Mendelssohn composed his Sonata in B flat Op. 45 (1838) for his cellist brother Paul. Schumann praised it for its purity as abstract music. It comprises three movements, its melancholy, ternary Andante being framed by a sonata-form Allegro vivace and an Italianate final rondo especially notable for its dance-like episode in G minor. More interesting and of larger scale, however, is Mendelssohn's Second Sonata in D Op. 58 (1843), which comprises four movements and features the two instruments in equal partnership. The sonata-form opening movement is well argued, but fails to match for imagination the two middle movements, a typically light and humorous scherzo and a unique, tranquil Adagio. This latter alternates reflective passages of quasi-recitative (cello) with phrases of a chorale-like melody (piano), played in spread chords; chorale and recitative later overlap, and in the coda the pianist takes over the expressive recitative above a cello pedal punctuated with pizzicatos to form a moving conclusion. The sonata-form finale concludes the work in virtuoso style, showing affinities with the finale of Mendelssohn's D minor Piano Concerto.

Brahms, who played the cello as a child, composed an early sonata for piano and cello (unpublished and now lost), which was premièred at a private concert in Hamburg with the eighteen-year-old composer at the piano.[21] His first surviving essay in the genre (Op. 38 in E minor, 1862–5) is characterised by its exploitation of the cello's lower registers; this, together with the quality of its themes, accounts for its autumnal, elegiac character. Even the stormy 'second subject' of the opening movement soon reverts to the prevailing mood of elegy, illumined at the close of the exposition by a new, tender theme in the major mode. The lengthy development combines lyricism and drama and includes skilful use of contrapuntal devices; the recapitulation is rather exact, but the wonderful coda reharmonises the main theme in the major and extends it to bring the movement to a quiet and consolatory close. A charming folk-like Minuet (A minor) provides the centrepiece, with a pensive Trio in the unusually dark and distant key of F sharp minor, while the finale is a skilfully worked fugue, with a more lyrical (non-fugal but still very contrapuntal) middle section.[22] After some development of the main theme, the fugue returns in all its grandeur to bring the work to a climactic *più presto* conclusion.

Brahms's more profound Second Sonata Op. 99 (1886), composed for Robert Hausmann, comprises four movements. Its opening sonata-form Allegro vivace begins with a bold expressive cello melody, accompanied *tremolando* and then counterstated by the piano, and is eventually counterbalanced by an equally noble second theme for piano. The long development at first hovers over the vastly remote keys of F sharp minor and C sharp minor, and thence works its passage home. The recapitulation is fairly regular, but the first group is shorn of its counterstatement and the large coda takes a lingering farewell. The sustained opening melody (piano) and complementary pizzicato idea (cello) of the ternary Adagio, in the distant key of F sharp, are freely exchanged by the two protagonists; the middle section develops a third theme and the coda sums up all that has gone before. The third movement substitutes for a scherzo and trio but adopts a similar formal design, while the finale is a short sonata-rondo on a cheerful folk-like theme with two episodes of varied key and mood.

Some cellists like to think that they have a third *echt* Brahms sonata in their repertory, believing that Brahms himself transcribed (in D major) his First Violin Sonata Op. 78 for cello.[23] However, all documentary evidence and musical examination point to Paul Klengel as the arranger.[24]

Reinecke's three sonatas (Op. 42, *c.* 1855; Op. 89, *c.* 1869; Op. 238, *c.* 1896), written in a largely Brahmsian language, are of variable quality. The first, in A minor, is the most persuasive, but the second disappoints and the third, dedicated to Brahms, fades after a promising opening movement. More successful was Richard Strauss's early Sonata Op. 6 (1880–3), which testifies to his traditional training,[25] his admiration for Brahms and his own struggle for self-expression. Joachim complimented Strauss on the exuberant first movement's lyrical opening outburst. Despite overuse of motivic reiteration, this movement is otherwise well structured and confidently argued; the fughetta towards the close of the development is particularly inspired, along with the climactic coda. The cantilena of the central Andante smacks of Mendelssohn, while the finale is a brilliant rondo, mixing youthful vitality and humour with a certain Viennese charm. Strauss's student friend Ludwig Thuille also composed a creditable Cello Sonata, but its rhapsodic character affects adversely its proportions, particularly in respect of the prolix central slow movement.

Reger's four sonatas (Op. 5, 1892; Op. 28, 1898; Op. 78, 1904; Op. 116, 1910) demonstrate his development from a traditional Brahmsian stance, as in his serious, well-crafted but uninspiring Op. 5, to a more chromatic style influenced by contemporaries such as Wagner, Strauss and Busoni. With some justification, he considered his Third Sonata as his best chamber work – its third movement is a resourceful set of variations – but his complex chromatic and contrapuntal language has ensured that none is in the forefront of the repertory. Of lesser significance still are the sonatas of Georg Goltermann and Jean Nicodé (Opp. 23, 25, Leipzig, 1882), but Pfitzner's substantial, four-movement F sharp minor Sonata Op. 1 (1890), is quite Brahmsian, well-crafted, lyrical and surprisingly imaginative for a student work.

Austrians Heinrich von Herzogenberg (Op. 52, 1886; Op. 64, 1890; Op. 94, 1897), Ignaz Brüll (Op. 9, *c.* 1872) and Robert Fuchs (Op. 29, Leipzig, 1881; Op. 83, Vienna, 1908) were members of Brahms's circle in Vienna. Fuchs's works are especially rich in Schubertian lyricism and thematic invention and seem little affected by any of the radical musical innovations of their age. Brahms considered him 'a splendid musician; everything is so fine and skilful, so charmingly invented, that one is always pleased' – rare praise, indeed, from a composer who was often scathingly critical of the work of his contemporaries, whether friends or foes.

France and Belgium

Some parts of Lalo's Sonata in A minor (1856) and Alkan's *Grande Sonate de Concert* Op. 47 (1857) anticipate Brahms, Tchaikovsky, and in places even Fauré and Debussy. Alkan's work comprises four contrasting movements, its rhapsodic third movement (Adagio) being prefaced by a biblical quotation from the Old Testament prophet Micah. The confidently argued opening movement is followed by a siciliano, while a brilliant *rondo alla saltarello* concludes the sonata, its principal theme being enhanced by ingenious transformations at its every recurrence.

Saint-Saëns's First Sonata Op. 32 (1872) is set in C minor, aptly reflecting his grief following the death of a great-aunt who had cared for him in his infancy.[26] It is believed to have derived from some organ improvisation which actually provided Saint-Saëns with 'note-for-note the first and last pages' of the work.[27] More rewarding, however, is Op. 123 in F (1905). Its first movement opens majestically, its dramatic gestures being made all the more grandiose with double-dotted figures. A bustling scherzo follows, unusually cast as a set of eight variations, while the slow movement is an expressive 'Romanza', its somewhat hefty piano writing foreshadowing the pianist's role in the demanding finale.

Léon Boëllmann contributed a resourceful, if conservative, Sonata in A minor (Op. 40, 1897) in the final year of his brief career. Contrary to general belief, there is no documentary evidence to prove that Franck's cyclic Violin Sonata in A (1886) was originally intended for cello. No mention of the cello is made on the autograph or in the first edition, published by Hamelle (Paris, 1886).[28] Nevertheless, Delsart's arrangement of the work for cello and piano, also published by Hamelle (Paris, c. 1906), serves the instrument well.

Poland and Russia

Chopin's four-movement Sonata in G minor Op. 65 (1845–7) was the last publication of his lifetime; he played the last three movements at his last public concert, with the cellist Franchomme (to whom it is dedicated), in Paris in February 1848. The smaller forms of the two central movements, the Scherzo and Trio (D minor and major respectively) and the Largo, display Chopin at his best. The Scherzo combines grace and energy, its middle lyrical episode resembling a graceful waltz, while the brief, lyrical Largo is hardly more than an interlude. But the finale, of sonata-rondo design, is equally successful, showing some affinity with Chopin's own impromptus and sporting an optimistic major-mode coda. The opening Allegro moderato, however, demonstrates both Chopin's constant, ruminating and improvisational flow of rich, expressive ideas and his inability to organise them within a conventional sonata structure. The development, for example, is as much exposition as the exposition was development, incorporating towards its end a new, march-like theme, which is recalled in the coda following a greatly foreshortened recapitulation.

The principal nineteenth-century Russian contributor to the genre, Anton Rubinstein, came under Chopin's influence in Paris and developed a cosmopolitan style. He later composed two cello sonatas, Op. 18 in D (1852) and Op. 39 in G (1857), of which the second is the more lyrical and displays fewer Mendelssohnian traits, as well as showing a more individual creativity. A well-crafted Sonata in C minor (1825) by Ilya Lisogub is also noteworthy.

Scandinavia

The Swedish composer Franz Berwald left an interesting *Duo* in B flat major (1858), which typically combines the influence of Mendelssohn and Chopin with assured craftsmanship and numerous independent stylistic traits. Grieg also absorbed the influence of Schumann, Mendelssohn and

Chopin in his Leipzig years (1858–62), but his Sonata in A minor Op. 36 (1882–3), composed for his cellist brother Jon, displays more nationalistic elements, one reviewer unjustly criticising its 'ridiculous Scandinavianism, empty content, and unskilled development and form'.[29] Nevertheless, Grieg probably brought such criticism on himself, creatively self-borrowing thematic material from his *Trauermarsch zum Andenken an Richard Nordraak* (for the opening Allegro) and the 'Huldigungsmarsch' from the *Drei Orchesterstücke aus Sigurd Jorsalfar* (for the lyrical central movement) and persisting with the somewhat repetitious finale, inspired by Norwegian folk music.

Other countries

Dvořák's only essay in the genre was an unpublished Sonata in F (1870–1), of which the piano part has not survived, but cellists occasionally play a cello-piano transcription, not by the composer, of his Sonatina Op. 100 (vn, pf). Hungarian Károly Goldmark's Sonata in F Op. 39 (1892) shows some sparks of originality in the thematic ideas, rhythms and chromatic harmony of its three movements, but fails to sustain interest in the development of material. His compatriot Dohnányi's Op. 8 (1899) comprises a strange mixture of Brahmsian late Romanticism and more individual stylistic elements. The sonata-form first movement is followed by a lively scherzo and trio, while the lyrical Adagio, characterised by its rich, colourful harmony, leads into a set of variations which recalls material from previous movements.[30] The finale of Ethel Smyth's C minor Sonata, a student work also cast in the idiom of Brahms, has an Hungarian flavour, and her Sonata Op. 5 (1887) is even more heavily indebted to the German composer. Alfredo Piatti's four published sonatas (Opp. 28, 29, 30, 31 (Mainz, 1894–6)) failed to gain a permanent place in the repertory.

The twentieth century

Russia

Rachmaninov composed his lyrical, four-movement Sonata Op. 19 (1901) at the height of his creative inspiration in his late twenties. It has an affinity with his Second Piano Concerto, especially the first movement's second theme and the manner in which the pianist is the more technically active. The cellist has the lion's share of its wealth of melodies, some of which have close ties with one another and most of which are in melancholy vein. The outer movements are well-crafted sonata structures, the lento introduction of the first providing material for later development. The scherzo material of the second movement alternates with two slower sections, the more beautiful of which appears only once as the movement's centrepiece, but the rhapsodic third movement is less structurally taut, its opening theme predominating over a later subordinate idea.

Although he associated with a circle of progressive musicians, Myaskovsky's music was rooted firmly in the Russian tradition. That his style developed from complexity towards greater clarity is demonstrated by his revisions to his Sonata Op. 12 (1911), undertaken in 1945, three years before commencing work on his more tautly constructed Second Sonata Op. 81 (1948–9). By contrast, Alexander Tcherepnin (Op. 29, 1925; Op. 30 No. 1, 1925; Op. 30 No. 2, 1928) and Grechaninov (Op. 113, 1927; Op. 129, 1931) developed a more cosmopolitan existence and style, their cello sonatas dating from their respective periods of residence in Paris. Myaskovsky's teaching and compositional style were the formative influences on Kabalevsky's Sonata Op. 2 (1927), but his Second Sonata Op. 71 (1962), though preserving his essential lyricism, is of more individual inspiration. Shebalin, another Myaskovsky pupil, has much in common with his teacher's style in his Sonata Op. 51 No. 3 (1960), notably the influence of Russian folk song and the ability to structure and integrate large-scale movements.

Shostakovich's Sonata in D minor Op. 40 (1934) shows him moving towards a more contained and reflective style – the predominant tone is lyrical and inturned, notably in the sonata-form opening Moderato. Even the typical wit of the scherzo, a waltz with a middle section picked out by cello harmonic glissandi, is partly softened by moderate tempo and restrained texture. The intensely slow and somewhat enigmatic Largo restores the primacy of line, the piano's contribution being limited mainly to long chords and soft repeated quavers, but the thematic material is once again shared in the rondo finale. The dry simplicity of the main theme is deceptive and ironic, leading to the work's most violent incidents and concluding it abruptly and unexpectedly.[31]

Prokofiev began to sketch his Sonata Op. 119 in 1946, but the final version was not completed until the spring of 1949, with the editorial assistance of Rostropovich, who gave the first performance later that year. Though stylistically comparable to other of his late works, notably the Seventh Symphony and the Ninth Piano Sonata, this sonata is no simple essay in valedictory nostalgia; only an occasional lack of memorable themes and rhythmic flexibility gives an air of self-parody to music which, from harmonic and structural standpoints, is full of vitality. The long opening melody of the first movement is, for all its diatonic blandness, situated in the cello's most sombre register, and the brief hint of chromatic acid in the third bar is a carefully placed portent. The exposition then grows into an eloquent duet, with several important additional themes (the 'second subject' is a lively, good-natured folk tune) which gain prominence in the development, notable for its numerous changes of speed. The recapitulation is resourcefully rescored, and the extended coda is itself a reshaping of the development, building the main climax of the movement before concluding quietly. The sprightly outer sections of the ternary Moderato have as a contrasting central section a lyrical Andante, while the finale comprises a wealth of different ideas, clearly establishing that ironic, slightly bitter air which characterised Prokofiev's musical sense of humour. Instead of development, a new theme even more artless in character than the four-square first subject is introduced, first by the cello with a simple piano accompaniment and then by the piano with a complicated cello accompaniment, but the work ends with a grandiose coda in which the opening theme of the first movement is triumphantly recalled.

More recent works have ranged in mood and content from the harsh technical demands and subsequent introspection of Galina Ustvol'skaya's *Grand Duet* (1952), which displays the influence of her teacher Shostakovich, to Karen Khachaturian's Sonata (1966) and the rhythmic complexities (Recitative), microtones and technical challenges (Toccata) of Denisov's Sonata (1971).[32] Gubaydulina's *Sonata, Rejoice!* (vn, vc, 1981) and Schnittke's two works in the genre (1978, 1994) deserve mention. Schnittke's First Sonata subdivides into three continuous sections: a scurrying Presto is framed by the brooding, chorale-like opening section, which sets out the work's themes, and a powerfully desolate Largo finale. This latter is a dignified lament which develops thematic material from the opening movement and recalls phrases from the Presto in slow motion.

France

The sonatas of Ropartz (1904, 1918), Huré (1907, 1913, 1920), Vierne (1910), Pierné (1919) and Magnard (Op. 20, 1910) are creditable works, Huré's First Sonata embodying cyclical principles within a continuous single-movement structure; but the essays of Debussy and Fauré are arguably the most significant French cello sonatas of the century. Debussy's Sonata (1915) in D (with modal and whole-tone inflections) is the first of three completed works of a projected set of six.[33] Although the structure of the *Prologue* is derived from the development of cellular ideas, the rough outline of a sonata form is discernible. The cellular approach is clearly evident in the relationship between the forceful opening idea (stated at the outset by the piano and elaborated by the cello) and its tranquil development as the secondary idea. The middle section is as much elaboration as development and it culminates in a much-lengthened restatement of the main themes, ending with a short coda. The central *Sérénade* is in three sections, the material developing from motifs introduced by the cello at the outset. The brief third section leads into the animated, multi-sectional finale, whose central Lento (*molto rubato con morbidezza*), according to the theory that this sonata reflects Debussy's preoccupation with the symbolic figure of Harlequin,[34] represents Harlequin's final unmasking, the final disillusionment.

Fauré's two late sonatas (Op. 109, 1917; Op. 117, 1921) were written during a particularly fertile period of song and chamber music composition. Op. 109 in D minor is a complex, three-movement work in which the first movement's powerful rhythmic impetus, intensive exploitation of motifs and accomplished counterpoint often overshadow melodic elements. The modal tendencies of Fauré's melodic style are evident in the central Andante, while the final Allegro commodo (D major) unites the whole by featuring melodic intervals and rhythmic patterns from both earlier movements. Op. 117 in G minor is more relaxed, yet equally expressive and tautly structured, the restrained first movement eventually building to a major-mode climax towards its close. The expressive slow movement, a direct descendant of Fauré's own *Elégie*, again introduces modal inflections in its second theme, but the finale, with the syncopations of its two complementary melodies, its toccata-like accompanying figuration and its central chorale-like melody seems somewhat contrived in both its internal organisation and its final exuberant flourish.

D'Indy reacted strongly against the musical novelties of the 1920s such that his Sonata Op. 84 (1924–5) is virtually a suite, its four movements (Entrée, Gavotte en rondeau, Air and Gigue) adopting titles and styles of the French Baroque. Marcel Rubin's Sonata (1928) takes after the colourful contemporary style of Poulenc, while Tortelier's (1944) looks back to Fauré, but with some echoes of Stravinsky in its bucolic finale. Poulenc freely admitted his discontent at his own writing for solo strings[35] and, as Roger Nicholls observes, 'many sections of the Cello Sonata [1948] would sound better on a bassoon'.[36] But Milhaud's Sonata Op. 377 (1959) is a bright and jazzy work written in his typically breezy and technically accomplished style.

The Americas
The cello sonatas of Leo Sowerby (1921) and Barber (Op. 6, 1932) adopt a conservative, lyrical and strongly Romantic approach to the genre, Barber's often being likened variously to the styles of Brahms (first movement), Rachmaninov or the young Scriabin.[37] Cowell's Sonata (1915) dates from a period of experiment and innovation, while Diamond's (1936–8) demonstrates the broadening of his artistic horizons during his sojourn and study (with Nadia Boulanger) in Paris. Other significant contributions came from Norman Dello Joio (Sonatina, 1943; *Duo*

Concertato, 1945), Weber (Op. 17), Foss (*Duo*, 1941), Carter (1948) and Finney (Sonata No. 2, 1950).[38]

Finney's Second Sonata comprises five movements cast in the form of an arch; the finale includes elements of the opening movement, the second and fourth movements are both fast and an Adagio arioso forms the peak. However, Carter's work is more experimental, particularly with regard to rhythm. Dissatisfied with the limited range of rhythm in Western as opposed to some Indian, African and other musics, Carter devised a technique called 'metrical modulation' – 'a means of going smoothly, but with complete accuracy, from one absolute metronomic speed to another, by lengthening or shortening the value of the basic note unit'.[39] This technique is most apparent in the third movement, an expressive Adagio which incorporates elements of American-Negro melody, but the rondo-like finale also features complex rhythms and frequently changing metre. The opening Moderato juxtaposes a free-flowing lyrical cello melody and regular staccato piano punctuation imitative of a clock ticking, presenting a contrast between psychological time (in the cello) and chronometric time (in the piano). The light, vivacious second movement is a quasi-parody of some contemporary American idioms; it features syncopated rhythms and, like the finale, incorporates elements of jazz.

Like Carter, John Lessard, a composer of 'French-orientated neo-Classical pieces'[40] wrote his energetic three-movement Sonata (1962) for the cellist Bernard Greenhouse. Other notable American contributions to the repertory include works by John Bavicchi (No. 2, Op. 25, 1956), Roy Harris (*Duo*, 1964),[41] John Dawney (1966), Alan Stout (1966) and Canadian Sophie Eckhardt-Gramatté (*Duo Concertante*, 1959). Bavicchi's Second Sonata ends with a fugue, while Harris's *Duo* combines a fantasy-like opening movement, an expressive elegy and a formally adventurous finale. Elements of aleatoric technique infiltrate Dawney's three-movement sonata, which includes in its finale a unifying cello cadenza, recalling previous thematic material, but Eckhardt-Gramatté's *Duo* is remarkably terse in its organisation, focusing especially on three notes in the first movement and in much of the last, in which a twelve-note theme provides the climax. The central movement, inspired by a mobile of Calder, tries to create a parallel freedom of motion in music through omission of bar-lines.

American citizen Leo Ornstein's impassioned Sonata Op. 52 (*c.* 1918) betrays his Russian heritage and shows affinities with Rachmaninov's Op. 19, while Kurt Weill's Sonata (1920) is an early work of cyclical design which displays Busoni's idiom before Weill actually received instruction from the German-Italian composer. Among other notable contributors were Nikolai Lopatnikoff (Op. 11, 1928), Ernst Toch (Op. 50, 1929), Canadian Jean Coulthard (1947), Ingolf Dahl (*Duo*, 1946, rev. 1948),

Alex Haieff (1963), Henri Lazarof (*Duo*, 1973) and André Previn, the latter's four-movement Sonata (1993) combining jazz pizzicato riffs, angular, introspective melodies and artful cadenzas to create a work whose varied textures create an emotional bridge between Shostakovich and Thelonius Monk.

Composers from Latin America also left a rich legacy of sonatas, notably Mexicans Manuel Ponce (1922), Carlos Chávez (Sonatina, 1924), Luis Sandi (Sonatina), and Blas Galindo Dimas (*c.* 1953), Argentinians Alberto Williams (Op. 52), José Mariá Castro (Sonata; Sonata, 2vc) and Alberto Ginastera (Op. 49, 1979), Colombian Uribe-Holguín (two Sonatas), Chilean Enrique Soro and Brazilians Heitor Villa-Lobos (1915; 1916), Mozart Camargo Guarnieri (1931; 1955) and Cláudio Santoro (No. 2, 1947; No. 3, 1951). Villa-Lobos' Second Sonata, in four movements, is arguably the pick of the bunch; remarkable for its French influence, its first two movements resemble the work of Franck and Fauré respectively, while the finale recalls the first movement's principal theme (cello in diminution) accompanied by *très sec* piano chords (in imitation of a tambourine) in the manner of Debussy's Cello Sonata.

Great Britain

In the wake of sonatas by Tovey (Op. 4, 1900), Hurlstone (published posthumously: London, 1909), Holbrooke (*Fantasie-Sonate*, Op. 19, 1904) and John Foulds (Op. 6, 1905, rev. 1907) came a rich vein of British contributions to the genre. Delius's Sonata (1916) is unusual for his flexible, expansive melodies and the subtleties of their accompaniments and includes some self-borrowing from his earlier *Romance* (vc, pf). Frank Bridge wrote his two-movement Sonata mostly during the First World War, completing it in 1917. Its first movement, broadly in sonata form, combines free-flowing lyricism with a lucid sense of architecture, and fluid harmonic and tonal idioms. Tonal freedom is even more marked in the episodic finale, which culminates in a broad D major return of the first movement's principal theme.

Rebecca Clarke arranged her Viola Sonata (1919) for cello in 1921, while 1923 welcomed substantial sonatas by Ireland, Bax and York Bowen. Ireland's Sonata in G minor, though harmonically complex and even at times tonally ambiguous, is candidly rhapsodic and lyrical in mood. Its rhapsodic tendencies often cloud the formal outlines, confused by Ireland's fondness for cyclical recurrence of themes. The outer movements in particular are thematically linked, with the cello's musing first-movement theme returning in more vigorous form to supply material for the finale. The theme itself is typical of Ireland in its apparently untiring ability to spin new melodic thoughts from old ones, so that when the second subject emerges *con grazia* in a modal B flat it still sounds like an outgrowth from material already introduced. This quality is even more marked in the slow movement, which weaves an almost unbroken thread of melody from the succulent piano theme that follows the brief transitional introduction. York Bowen's Sonata Op. 64 (1923) and Bax's three essays in the genre share the lyrical, rhapsodic qualities of Ireland's work. The final Epilogue and the sensuous slow movement – the central section using the 'Woodland Love' theme from his *Spring Fire* – provide the highlights of Bax's dramatic, uneven Sonata (1923). His Sonatina (1933)[42] and *Legend Sonata* (1943) are also of variable quality, the latter also using self-borrowed material – a quotation from 'Fand's song of immortal love' – in the central slow movement.

The English 'Hindemithians' Arnold Cooke (1926, 1941) and Franz Reizenstein (Op. 22, 1947) contributed significant works to the genre, while Rawsthorne's harmonic idiom often possesses the austere qualities of Hindemith's style. However, some of the slower sections of Rawsthorne's Sonata (1948) exude a striking, pensive lyricism, also common to much of the work of Bantock (1940, 1945), Scott (1950), Rubbra (Op. 60, 1946) and Moeran (1947). Rubbra's three-movement Sonata concludes with a set of variations rounded off by a fugue, while the concentration of structural thought in Moeran's sombre Sonata is such that most of its three movements' thematic material shares common intervals of a major/minor third and/or perfect fifth.

Peter Racine Fricker (Op. 28, 1956) and Iain Hamilton became increasingly interested in serialism, Hamilton occasionally going beyond Fricker's essentially tonal application of such principles in his Sonata (Op. 39, 1958–9), which is characterised by its cello cadenzas and its toccata-like piano figuration, and Sonata No. 2 (1974). Schoenberg's pupil Roberto Gerhard described his work in the mid-1950s as 'athematic'; his Sonata (1956), a free recomposition of his Viola Sonata (1946), illustrates the greater reliance on rhythmic texture and instrumental colour than on melody that such a description implies.

Britten's Sonata in C (Op. 65, 1961) was the first fruit of his friendship with Rostropovich, each of its five short movements exploiting the cello's capacity for urgent eloquence. The first movement, 'Dialogo', is a tautly constructed quasi-monothematic sonata design, while the scherzo, in which the cellist plays pizzicato throughout, is reminiscent of Bartók. The beautiful central 'Elegia' builds to an impassioned climax, the dramatic significance of which is strengthened by its continued reliance on the narrow intervals of the work's basic motif. A bizarre, energetic 'Marcia', exploiting ponticello and harmonics, and a driving final 'Moto perpetuo' conclude this extraordinary work of contrasts.

Lennox Berkeley's *Duo* (1971) is a well-crafted, single-movement work of contrasting sections. Alun Hoddinott's First Sonata (Op. 73 No. 2, 1970) is also through-composed, its intense opening nocturne and brilliant concluding scherzo-toccata being linked by a cadenza. Hoddinott's second essay (Op. 96 No. 1, 1977), however, comprises three movements and is more lyrical, particularly the central Adagio. The opening Moderato is essentially a dialogue between the two protagonists and the finale is an energetic *moto perpetuo*, which nevertheless makes way for some lyrical episodes. A third sonata appeared in 1997.

More recent British additions to the repertory include George Benjamin's virtuosic *Duo* (*c.* 1980), striking in its imaginative colours and textures, and works by Anthony Hedges (1986), Priaulx Rainier (*Grand Duo*, 1980–2) and Alexander Goehr (Op. 45, 1986). Goehr's Sonata is a well-wrought, economical four-in-one movement structure, its various sections contrasting in character, tempo and texture. It exploits a wide range of string techniques, sonorities and colour effects, perhaps most notably in its second main section, a brief 'recitando' for solo cello.

Germany and Austria

German composers made a comparatively small contribution to the genre. Günther Raphael's early Sonata (Op. 14, 1925) perpetuates the idiom of Brahms and Reger, while Blacher's (1940) cultivates a lyrical approach, keeping well within the bounds of tonality. More academic were Hessenberg (Op. 23, 1942), Fortner (1948) and Hindemith, whose Sonata Op. 11 No. 3 (1948) is somewhat relentless and lacking in true inspiration. Harald Genzmer perpetuated the Hindemith tradition, notably in his Sonata (1953), but his later works, among them a Sonatina (1967) and a Sonata (vc, harp, 1963), are more individual and ambitious in scope. Hermann Reutter was also influenced by the Hindemith school, but later adopted a retrogressive late Romantic style, his *Sonata Monotematica* (1970) confirming in its title its closely integrated construction. Bertold Hummel's Sonatina No. 2 (*c.* 1977) is rather lightweight, but his three-movement *Sonata Brevis* (*c.* 1969) is concisely crafted, its finale recalling previous motifs to provide overall unity.

Webern's short Sonata (1914), in one movement, was among the manuscripts and sketches retrieved by Hans Moldenhauer from the former house of Webern's daughter-in-law Hermine in the Viennese suburb of Perchtoldsdorf in 1965. It seems that Webern, responding to a suggestion from Schoenberg, set out with the specific aim of writing, at last, a substantial and extended work for the cello. After a time, however (as he told Schoenberg in a letter of July 1914), he felt a compelling urge to leave this sonata and write what became the Op. 11 pieces. The surviving

movement of the two planned is a fully worked piece in Webern's mature
pre-serial idiom – basically an expressionist style with steep melodic and
dynamic gradients, but, as always with Webern, very brief, elliptical gestures and a concentrated motivic scheme.

Italy

Apart from Pizzetti's dramatic Sonata in F (1921), twentieth-century
Italian composers have made few outstanding additions to the sonata
repertory. Malipiero's uneven early Sonata (1907–8) is barely surpassed by
his more mature Sonatina (1942), while Casella's neo-Classical C minor
Sonata (Op. 8, 1906)[43] is disappointingly derivative. His later C major
Sonata (Op. 45, 1926), however, benefits from a more advanced harmonic
style. Castelnuovo-Tedesco's Sonata (Op. 50, 1928) dates from a period of
gradual decline in his output, confirmed by later works in the genre (Op.
144, va, vc, 1950; Op. 148, vn, vc, 1950; Op. 208, vc, harp, 1967), and Wolf-
Ferrari's Sonata (1945) is disappointingly retrospective. Quite the opposite is Chailly's *Sonata tritemetica No. 5* (1954), one of his 'Twelve
three-theme Sonatas'; a continuous single-movement work with clearly
contrasted sections, its introductory Largo provides the thematic material
of the other sections, which include elements of jazz influence, fairly free
use of metre and recitative. A dramatic declamatory recitative opens
Enrico Mainardi's four-movement Sonata (1958), the best of his works in
the genre (including his Sonatina, 1939; *Sonata quasi fantasia*, 1962) with
its expressive slow movement (Nocturne), stormy tripartite finale and
with the dramatic Grave at its heart.

Czechoslovakia

Apart from Ervín Schulhoff's Sonata (Op. 17, 1914), the Czech contribution is dominated by Martinů, whose three sonatas (1940, 1941, 1952)
were composed at a particularly difficult period in his career, after he was
blacklisted by the Nazis. His Second Sonata is the most successful. Its outer
movements have remarkable rhythmic and contrapuntal vitality and the
moto perpetuo finale incorporates a demanding cello cadenza. The central
slow movement comes closest to expressing in musical terms Martinů's
dedicated patriotism.

Hungary

Emanuel Moór's seven sonatas straddle the two centuries. They are not
especially distinguished for their thematic material, but some of the later
ones, such as Op. 76, are notable for their 'freer applications of standard-
ised forms'.[44] Moór's principal successor, Kodály, left two essays in the
genre; his Sonatina (1921–2) has never attained the success of his earlier

Sonata Op. 4 (1909–10), even though both works demonstrate his structural expertise and rich melodic vein. Op. 4 comprises just two movements, the second reflecting his interest in traditional folk dances and recalling material from the opening movement, a fantasia in a quasi-improvisatory and episodic style.

Other countries

Romanian Georges Enesco's First Sonata (Op. 26 No. 1, 1898) is a large-scale Brahmsian work in four movements; but his Second Sonata (Op. 26 No. 2, 1935) adopts a more progressive angular language, notably in its relatively dissonant second movement and its folk-influenced 'Final à la roumaine', which incorporates quarter-tones and piano writing imitative of the cymbalom. Also nationalistic is Cassadó's *Sonata, nello stile antico spagnolo* (1925),[45] which is steeped in Spanish colour from its opening recitative and ensuing Allegro to its final set of variations on a Spanish dance theme. Rodolfo Halffter's Sonata Op. 26 (1960) is another notable Spanish work, combining the tradition of Falla with more contemporary idioms, while Rodrigo's *Sonata a la Breve* (1978) displays his unmistakable lyrical and colourful Spanish ambience.

Other significant contributions to the repertory came from Holland (Willem Pijper: 1919, 1924; Hendrik Andriessen: 1926; Henk Badings: 1927, 1929, 1934; Sem Dresden: 1916, 1942; and Léon Orthel: two sonatas), Belgium (Joseph Jongen: Op. 39, 1912), Portugal (Luiz de Frietas Branco: 1913), Switzerland (Arthur Honegger: 1920; Conrad Beck: Sonatina, 1928; Sonata, 1954), Turkey (Ahmet Saygun: 1935), Australia (Arthur Benjamin: *Sonatina*, 1938), Scandinavia (Hilding Rosenberg: 1923; Kurt Atterberg: Op. 27, 1925; Erkki Salmenhaara: 1960; and Lars-Erik Larsson: *Sonatina* Op. 60, 1969), Greece (Nikolaos Skalkottas: Sonatina, 1949; Dimitris Tertsakis (*Duo*, vc, perc, 1973) and from the Korean-German composer Isang Yun (*Duo*, vc, harp, 1984).

9 Other solo repertory

ROBIN STOWELL

In addition to the sonata and concerto, the cellist's concert repertory comprises four further principal areas: music for unaccompanied cello; short genre pieces for cello with orchestra or keyboard; variations; and transcriptions and fantasias. Many nineteenth-century solo works for the cello were composed by cellists, who were strongly influenced, particularly in the first half of the century, by the violin repertory. Travelling virtuosos such as Duport, Romberg, Servais, Franchomme, Piatti, Goltermann, Grützmacher, Davidoff, Popper, Fitzenhagen, Klengel and Becker wrote for their own use and also to meet the rapidly growing demands of flourishing middle-class audiences; their aim was both to satisfy the public's taste, to entertain and to demonstrate their own technical prowess. Writing for solo cello was only a peripheral interest for most of the 'front-line' nineteenth-century composers, probably because of the perceived problems of balance between the cello, with its tenor range, and the expanding orchestra or developing piano.

Music for unaccompanied cello

Among the first to compose for unaccompanied cello were the Italians Giovanni Degli Antoni, Domenico Gabrielli and Domenico Galli. Degli Antoni's *Ricercate* Op. 1 (Bologna, 1687) comprises twelve unaccompanied ricercari, pedagogical works for the instrument which might also be used as a bass for harpsichord improvisation – seven include figured bass with this option clearly in mind. Although perfectly playable on the conventional four-stringed cello, Kinney's recommended use of a six-stringed instrument tuned like the bass viol, with the alternate tuning for the lowest string depending on the key, C (or D)–G–c–e–a–d^1, has its advocates.[1] Gabrielli wrote his seven *Ricercarj per violoncello solo* (1689) for a four-stringed cello tuned C–G–d–g. In keeping with his own reputation as a virtuoso cellist, they incorporate florid passage-work and double- and multiple-stopping, and demonstrate an acute awareness of the technical potential and sonority of the instrument. Galli's only known work, *Trattenimento musicale sopra il violoncello a' solo* (Modena, 1691), was probably inspired by his association with Gabrielli at the Este court at

Modena. Written for a solo cello tuned B♭¹–F–c–g, its twelve sonatas (literally 'entertainments') lack structural and tonal coherence.

Three further composers associated with Modena, G. B. Vitali,
Giuseppe Colombi and Antonio Giannotti, played some part in developing the unaccompanied cello literature. Although their works prefer either
'basso' or 'violone' to 'violoncello' in their titles or prefaces, their musical
content seems most suited to the cello and probably anticipated the works
of Antoni and Gabrielli. Vitali's *Partite sopra diverse sonate* includes ten
pieces of variable length and title for an instrument tuned B♭¹–F–c–g, all
except the opening toccata being variations. Colombi left manuscripts of a
chaconne, a toccata and eighty-one *Balli Diversi*, these latter comprising
mainly short dances, but the intentions of Giannotti's legacy are ambiguous, his manuscript describing the four-movement sonata as one for
'basso solo' and continuo in its title but as *Sonata a violon solo* internally.[2]

J. S. Bach's six Suites BWV1007–12 represent the culmination of the
medium in the Baroque. Written *c.* 1720 probably for the Cöthen gambist
and cellist Christian Abel,[3] the earliest surviving manuscript is by Bach's
second wife, Anna Magdalena (*c.* 1727–1731), but the first published
edition did not appear until 1825. Each suite shares a similar overall
format – Prelude, Allemande, Courante, Sarabande, a pair of lighter
dances, and Gigue – and all the movements are of binary design save the
Preludes, which are of variable constitution; that of No. 5 is modelled on
the French overture, its stately opening section followed by a fugue, while
No. 6 commences with a brilliant virtuoso movement. Two Menuets constitute the pair of dances in the first two suites, with two Bourrées fulfilling
that role in Nos. 3 and 4, and two Gavottes in Nos. 5 and 6. Most of the
movements adopt the key of their parent suite, but the second of the pair of
dances in the first three suites takes the parallel major/minor key. Suites
1–5 are written for a conventional four-stringed cello, No. 5 requiring the
A string to be lowered a tone to accommodate some otherwise unplayable
chords and provide contrast of timbre. The Sixth Suite is written for a five-
stringed cello tuned C–G–d–a–e¹.

Apart from contributions from composers such as Julius Klengel
(*Caprice in the form of a chaconne* Op. 43; *Suite* Op. 56), Offenbach (at least
thirteen operatic fantasies) and Sibelius (*Theme and Variations*, *c.* 1887)
nearly two hundred years elapsed before the appearance of the next significant works for the medium by Reger, often nicknamed 'the second
Bach', and Kodály. But Reger's three *Suites* Op. 131c (1915) are no mere
imitations of Bach; dedicated in turn to Klengel, Becker and Grümmer,
they marry Bach's technical rigour with Wagner's rich harmonic language
and other more Classical traits. They have in common a certain melancholy vein, especially No. 3 in A minor, whose Andante with five variations

is the jewel of the trio, culminating in virtuoso passage-work. But they may justly be viewed as the fuse that linked Bach with the explosion in the repertory for solo cello in the twentieth century.[4]

Of Reger's compatriots, Hindemith and Fortner have been among the foremost influences as composers and pedagogues. Hindemith's concise Sonata Op. 25 No. 3 (1923) is an arch structure in five contrasting movements, while Fortner's liking for variation form is reflected in his quasi-Brahmsian *Suite* (1932), which includes some 'Variations on the song of an old French Troubadour' and his *Thema und Variationen* (1975) for Paul Sacher (see p. 144). Fortner's pupils Günther Becker (*Studie zu Aphierosis*, 1970) and Hans Engelmann (*Mini-Music to Siegfried Palm*, 1970) both responded to commissions from Siegfried Palm, while Henze contributed to Sacher's celebrations (*Capriccio per Paul Sacher*, 1976–81) some years after his successful *Serenade* (1949), which shows the influence of René Leibowitz, then one of the leading champions of the theories of the Second Viennese School. It is a collection of nine short but distinctive movements which differ widely in character and style. More challenging are Zimmermann's Sonata (1959–60), comprising three individual strands each notated on a separate staff, and Lachenmann's very distinctive sound-world in his *Pression*. Austrians Wellesz (Sonata Op. 31; Suite Op. 39) and Schnabel (Sonata, 1931) were influenced by Schoenberg and his school, while the musical roots of Gál (Sonata Op. 109a; Suite Op. 109b) lay in late Romanticism, his Suite even recalling Baroque and Classical models.

Kodály's Sonata Op. 8 (1915) is one of his most individual and, for all the limitations of the medium, one of his most ambitious works. Among other effects it requires the lowest two strings to be tuned down a semitone to B^1 and F♯ respectively. Its three movements, linked by various recurrent motifs, incorporate melodic and rhythmic elements of Hungarian folk music and exploit fully the technical and emotional range of the instrument. Despite the careful construction of the music along cyclic lines, the effect is very much that of an expansive, lyrical improvisation with memories, perhaps, of the type of singing Kodály had heard on his folk-song collecting trips before the First World War with Bartók.

British works in the medium were many and varied. Following Tovey's Sonata Op. 30 came sonatas from composers such as Bantock, Wilfred Josephs, Leighton (Op. 52) and Judith Weir (1980), Partitas from McCabe (Op. 44) and Roxburgh, and rhapsodic pieces by Ireland, Bax and Rubbra. But Britten's three Suites (Op. 72, 1964; Op. 80, 1968; Op. 87, 1972), inspired by Rostropovich's playing of Bach's unaccompanied works, represent the kernel of the British contribution. The First Suite comprises six movements – 'Fuga', 'Lamento' (with its e–e♭ conflict), 'Serenata' (entirely in pizzicato), 'Marcia' (with its military ostinato), 'Bordone' (with appropriate drone effect) and 'Moto perpetuo'; it is played without a break and is enclosed and divided by 'Cantos', sustained chorale-like sections which, as the source of the work's cell-shapes, provide unity. The Second Suite explores new ground but is less successful overall. Its five movements include a declamatory opening section, a witty, resourceful 'Fuga', an 'Andante lento' which brings into conflict major and minor thirds, and, typically, a 'Ciaconna'. Britten's Third Suite is usually considered his most attractive, its nine movements finding unity in their derivation from Russian themes, three of Tchaikovsky's folk-song arrangements ('The Grey Eagle', 'Autumn' and 'Under the Little Apple Tree') and the 'Kontakion' (Hymn for the Dead). However, variants of these melodies contribute most of the thematic interest; not until the end of the finale do the melodies themselves appear, one after another, in their original forms. Thus the solemn opening Lento derives from the 'Kontakion', the 'Marcia' is based on 'The Grey Eagle' and 'Autumn' and the 'Canto' on 'Under the Little Apple Tree'. The elaborate 'Barcarolla' incorporates elements of three of these themes, while the 'Fuga', 'Recitativo' and 'Moto perpetuo' are interlinked and the ground of the final Passacaglia is derived from the 'Kontakion'.

Britten-collaborator Imogen Holst's *Fall of the Leaf*, three short studies on a sixteenth-century tune, is a cold, bleak essay, but Walton's Passacaglia (1979–80) is a resourceful attempt to match Britten's inspiration in the genre. Arnold's seven-movement *Fantasy* Op. 130 (1987) is mildly Waltonesque in style, while the outline and certain thematic ideas of Hoddinott's *Nocturnes and Cadenzas* Op. 101 (1979) are derived from his own similarly titled Op. 62 (vc/orch). David Blake's three *Scenes* comprise a variety of styles, particularly the extensive final piece, which provides sharp contrast from the central tango. More experimental are Finnissy's *Andimironnai*, arranged into 'clausulae' of varying duration, and *Doves Figary* (1976–7), an elaboration of a tune from Playford's *English Dancing Master* with microtonal inflections and drones. Swayne's *Canto*, with its recurrent ostinatos, was inspired by Amadu Bansang Jobate's playing of the African *kora*, while Tavener's *Thrinos* (1990) and palindromic *Chant* (1995) confirm the influence of his conversion to the Russian arm of the Orthodox Church. Jonathan Harvey's *Curve with Plateaux* (1982) incorporates microtones and percussive effects and its central section exploits the highest registers of the cello, culminating in sonorities representative of bells, with the heavy blows on the lower string like the tolling of a bell. Bell-like sonorities also feature in Harvey's *Three Sketches* (1989), which require a second D string to be substituted for the G string.

Ibert's *Etude-Caprice, pour un Tombeau de Chopin* (1949), a UNESCO

commission to commemorate the centenary of Chopin's death, incorpo-
rates several melodies from the Polish composer's oeuvre, and his
Ghirlarzana (1950), literally 'wreath', is a memorial tribute to Vera
Koussevitzky. Apart from these pieces and works by Tortelier (Suite, 1945;
Mon Cirque, 1986), Sauguet (Sonata, 1956), Jolivet (*Suite en concert*, 1965),
Boulez (*Explosantefixe*, 1973) and Jolas (*Scion*, 1973),[5] French music for
solo cello is dominated by Xenakis, whose diverse interests led him to
apply his knowledge of mathematics and architecture to composition. His
Nomos Alpha (1965–6) is, in his words, 'a thorough exploration of the
structure of groups and of structures beyond time'. In his foreword, he
explains that he uses a 'special melody (Nomos), variantly played up' as the
basis for this 'symbolic music', built on 'offtime architectonics'.[6] He
employs traditional notation on one, two or three parallel staves but
includes some compelling effects, such as knocking and whistling noises,
extreme dynamic contrasts, senza vibrato, microtones and acoustical
beating, all indicated by specific symbols. Xenakis' *Kottos* (1977) is named
after one of the multi-armed giants conquered by Zeus and its extra-
musical content prompts some interesting experiments in cello technique
and sonority (see chapter 13, pp. 219–20).

Belgian violinist Ysaÿe's Sonata Op. 28 (*c.* 1924) is vastly inferior to his
six Solo Violin Sonatas (Op. 27), but it demonstrates some Bachian
polyphony in the finale, whose middle section includes a four-voice
fugato. Dutchman Henk Badings's continuous three-movement Second
Sonata (1951) has some affinity with Kodály's Sonata. More progressive is
the work of Hendrik Andriessen (Sonata, 1951) and Heinz Holliger
(*Chaconne*, 1975; *Trema*, 1981), and Andriessen's son Louis, whose *La Voce*
(1981) requires the cellist to sing and to substitute a second A string for the
D string. The principal Spanish contribution to the genre is Cassadó's
Suite (1925), based on national melodies and rhythms, but Benguerel's
Estructura III (1964), Luis de Pablo's *Ofrenda* (1980) and Guinjoán's
Cadenza (1981) are in more individual and progressive styles. Maltese
composer Charles Camilleri's *Fantasia concertanti* (1969–70) is one of
eight similarly titled works with a common structure; the first movements
are rooted in a pulse of ten, while the slower middle movements employ
dramatic use of silence in a sea of harmonics, and the finales blossom into
elaborate improvisation.

Apart from Berio's tribute to Sacher (*Les mots sont allés*, 1976–8) and
Nono's *Diario Polacco* (1982), Italy is represented by cellist Enrico
Mainardi's unaccompanied works for his instrument and, more impor-
tantly, those of Dallapiccola and Scelsi. Dallapiccola's *Ciaccona,
Intermezzo e Adagio* (1945) combines serial and tonal principles and
reflects on the tragic events of the war, the cello depicting the horrors of

the conflict in the *Ciaccona* before becoming more reflective in the central section of the *Intermezzo* and concluding with gestures of peace in the expressive Adagio. Scelsi's *Trilogia* (1957–64), is an amalgamation of three works (*Triphon*, 1957; *Diathome*, 1957; *Yggur*, 1961–4) which depict the three ages of man. It comes midway between his Bartókian gestural expressionism and his later concentration on the dramatic tension realisable from the relationship of as few as two adjacent notes, modified by rhythmic and textural variation. This latter style is demonstrated in the final section of *Yggur* ('Old Age – Memories – Catharsis'), which explores by means of scordatura the micro-intervals between B♭ and the sharpside of B♮ in a manner suggestive of meditation or mysticism. Scelsi's *Ko-Tha* (1978) is for a six-stringed instrument, while his *Sauh* (1979) is based around one note but requires the use of a double-bow technique (two bows clasped together) also exploited in *Il Funerale di Carlo Magno*; however, *Voyages*, while maintaining the fascination with micro-intervallic writing, subdivides into two sections. The first, 'La Fleuve Magique', focuses on two D's in harmonics played on two strings one octave apart, the upper part being modified by using a metallic thimble to produce percussive sounds on the higher harmonic. The second part, 'Il allait seul', concentrates on the pitches B♭ and middle C, played simultaneously and modified by quarter-tones.

The most prolific Scandinavian composer in the medium was Niels Bentzon, who wrote four well-crafted Sonatas (1956, and three in 1974) and various other works of quality. Sallinen's two-movement Sonata (1971) and *Elegy for Sebastian Knight* (1964) are sombre, melancholy pieces, but Rautavaara's Sonata Op. 46 (1969) is more virtuosic, especially the molto allegro finale. Bjorn Fongaard's Five Sonatas Op. 125 (1973) revive in a modern idiom Louis Couperin's *Préludes non mesurés*, while Nordheim's *Clamavi* (1980) is said to show affinity with Hindemith's Viola Sonata Op. 25 No. 1. Finally, Icelander Haflidi Hallgrímsson, himself a cellist, explores a full tessitura and a wide range of left-hand and bowing techniques in his *Solitaire* (1970), comprising five challenging and eloquent monologues, and Finnish composer Kalevi Aho's *Solo IV* (1997) is a rewarding, virtuosic competition piece.

The American solo cello literature includes sonatas by Persichetti (1952), Crumb (1955), Diamond (1956–9), Halsey Stevens (1958, 1967) and Adler (1966). Crumb's work is often singled out for special praise, its three tautly structured movements comprising an often elegiac opening Fantasia, a short set of variations on a pastoral theme and a dramatic, bravura Toccata, in which some jazz influence is in evidence. Stevens's work is a suite of five movements, of which the second, a demanding Chaconne, and fourth, a meditative Nocturne, are highlights. Other notable works for the medium include Robert Gross's *Epod* (1955), 'a very free lyric poem in the nature of an incantation'; Rózsa's *Toccata Capricciosa*, a rhapsodic display-piece based on a popular Magyar motif; Rorem's beautiful suite of musical sketches *After Reading Shakespeare* (1981); Fantasies by Schuller (1951), Finney (1957) and Siegmeister (1965); and various titles by Wuorinen, Sessions, Carter, Perle, Schulman, Hovhaness, Gehlhaar, Vainberg, Cage, Earle Brown, Harbison, Feldman and Frances-Marie Uitti. Feldman's *Projection I* (1950) is one of a demanding series of timbre studies which introduce complex graph notation with pitches and rhythms annotated in very general terms, while Uitti's *Xantrum* (1977), *Oaxano* (1979) and *Ricercare* (1984) use scordatura and require the use of two bows.

Of those composers who took American citizenship, the suites of Bloch and Krenek are most significant. Bloch's three examples (two in 1956, and one from 1957) are simple and rhapsodic in style, while Krenek's (Op. 84, 1939) is a serial work, its five movements based on the same note-row. Mexican Julián Carrillo exploits microtones in his six solo sonatas, while Argentinian Mauricio Kagel's dramatic approach to music is demonstrated in *General Bass* (1971–2) and *Siegfriedp* (1971), both composed for a concert of 'Gespräche mit Kammermusik' in Cologne (May 1972). *Siegfriedp*, for example, is written entirely in harmonics and involves a vocal part for the cellist, incorporating sounds ranging from audible breathing to humming, singing, groaning and shrieking.

Apart from Martinů's *Etudes rhythmiques* (1931) and Benes's Sonata (1985), the Czech solo cello literature is dominated by Alois Hába, whose microtonal experiments spawned his *Fantazie in Quarter-tones* Op. 18 (1924) and his two complex *Suites in Sixth-tone System* (1955). Ligeti's dramatic Sonata is the most substantial Polish contribution, supported by Penderecki's virtuosic *Capriccio per Siegfried Palm* (1968), with its detailed performance instructions, and competition piece *Per Slava* (1986) and Lutosławski's *Sacher-Variationen* (1975). Regrettably, Prokofiev was unable to complete even the first movement of his projected Sonata Op. 133 before his death,[7] but notable Russian contributions include Tcherepnin's Suite (1945), Vasks's hauntingly beautful *Ein Buch* (1978), which requires wordless singing of the cellist, Gubaydulina's *Ten Preludes* (1974) and three works by Schnittke: *Klingende Buchstaben* (1988), a 40th birthday present to cellist Alexander Ivashkin which uses as its principal theme the monogram of their two names; his deeply moving *Madrigal in Memoriam Oleg Kagan* (1991); and his dramatic *Improvisation*, written for the 1993 Rostropovich International Cello Competition. Japanese composers such as Shin Matsushita (*Repère mobile*), Toshiro Mayuzumi (*Bunraku*, 1960), Takekuni Hirayoshi (*Epitaph*), Mao Yamagishi (*Metamorphosis*), Hifumi

Shimoyama (*Ceremony No. 2*), Michio Mamiya (Sonata, 1971), Toshio Hosokawa (*Sen II*, 1986) and Toshinao Sato (*Bandori-No-Uta*) have all played a part in broadening the solo cello repertory. Mayuzumi's work re-creates the polyphonic conversation between a narrator and the shamisen player[8] in the Bunraku puppet show popular during the Edo period, while Mamiya's Sonata demonstrates his interest in Japanese folk music. Hosokawa requires the use of two bows and the lowering of the C string by a minor third.

The 70th birthday of Swiss conductor Paul Sacher in 1976 prompted *12 Hommages à Paul Sacher*, composed at the suggestion of Rostropovich. Holliger, Boulez, Henze, Britten, Berio, Lutosławski, Halffter, Ginastera, Beck, Fortner, Dutilleux and Huber each wrote a piece using the six letters of Sacher's name as a musical motif. For some, the motivic orientation of their task became central to the work, while others employed the motif less obviously, disguising it, for example, in chordal arpeggios. Many of these works have since become established repertory in their own right, such as Dutilleux's *Trois Strophes sur le Nom de Paul Sacher*, Henze's *Capriccio* and Boulez's *Messagesquisse*, in which six additional cellos join forces with the soloist. Lutosławski's *Sacher-Variation* comprises two motifs of contrasting character, the first (B♭–A♭–G–F♯–F) contemplative and the other (E♭–A–C–B–E–D, derived from Sacher's name)[9] more demonstrative, in that it is distinguished by its bold melodic contour and *fortissimo* dynamic and gradually increases in prominence as the music proceeds. At the very end it is heard, for the first time, at a lower dynamic, ending with two soft chords which spell out the Sacher hexachord.

Some composers have been attracted in recent years to the additional possibilities offered by amplification and the general application of electronic devices to the medium. Like John Harbison (*The Bermuda Triangle*, amp vc, sax, elec org, 1970), Australian Peter Sculthorpe writes for amplified cello in his *Requiem for Cello Alone* (1979), an intensely devotional work which uses the original plainchant as the point of departure for its six movements. Mario Davidovsky (*Synchronisms No. 3*, 1964), Kenneth Heller (*Labyrinth*), Roger Smalley (*Echo II*, 1979), Peter Schuback (*The Sunset*, 1982; *Roten Ur*, 1983), Lucien Bertolina (*Vorticosamente*, 1984) and Jonathan Harvey (*Ricercare una melodia*, 1985; *Advaya*, 1994) are among those who have successfully combined live instrumental performance with recorded electronic sounds. Harvey's *Philia's Dream* (1992) is described as 'an improvisation for cello and synthesiser following mutually determined directives' and requires the use of two bows and special tunings. Pioneered by Frances-Marie Uitti, the polyphonic potential of the double-bow technique has been exploited by numerous other composers since the mid-1970s, notably Scelsi, Nono, Kurtág and Richard Barrett.

Meanwhile, Rolf Gehlhaar (*Solipse*, 1974), Schuback (*Comportamenti*, 1984), Saariaho (*Amers*), Behrman (*Figure in Clearing*, 1972; *Cello with Melody-driven Electronics*, 1975), Machover (*Electric Etudes*) and Brian Ferneyhough are among those who have experimented with electronic music. Ferneyhough's *Time and Motion Study II* (1973–6) requires 'electronics, computer and three "electric performers"', while Machover's *'Begin Again Again'* aims to mix performed music with stored sound by linking an electro-acoustical cello to 'real time' computers and requiring the cellist's right hand to be strapped into an electronic hook-up to facilitate computer-monitored bow movement.

Genre pieces for cello and orchestra

The nineteenth-century explosion in the composition of short genre (or 'character') pieces for violin and orchestra or keyboard, including romances, elegies, legends or national dances as well as abstract pieces with serious artistic intent, was only partially matched in the cello repertory. However, the appearance of such works increased in the twentieth century, a concertante orchestral setting often serving as a less formal substitute for the traditional concerto concept.

Russia

Apart from pieces such as Davidoff's *Allegro de concert* Op. 11 (1862) and *Ballade* Op. 25 (1875), much of the Russian repertory has a melancholy character often belied by its title, as in Tchaikovky's *Pezzo capriccioso* Op. 62 (1887). This latter begins as a melancholy Andante con moto in B minor with expansive melodies and largely subdued accompaniment. The piece's capriciousness is evident in the alternation of this opening character with a lighter, scherzando vein, which wins through in the end. Glazunov absorbed Tchaikovsky's lyricism, evident in his *Two Pieces* Op. 20 (1887–8) and particularly in his *Chant du ménestrel* Op. 71 (1900), but Tcherepnin's quasi-nomadic existence prior to taking American citizenship contributed to a cosmopolitan musical language which could embrace equally well evocative works such as *Mystère* Op. 37 No. 2 (vc, ch orch, 1926) and pieces based on Georgian folklore such as his *Rhapsodie Géorgienne* Op. 25 (1922). The melancholic vein is continued in Grechaninov's *Syuita* Op. 86 (1929), Mosolov's *Elegiac Poem* (1961), Despic's *Recitative and Passacaglia funèbre* Op. 52a, Sil'vestrov's *Meditatsiya* (1972), Gubaydulina's *Seven Words* (vc, bayan(accordion), strgs, 1982) and to a certain extent in Gubaydulina's *Detto II* (1972) and Schnittke's *Dialog* (vc, ch ens, 1965) and *Four Hymns* (1974–7).

France

Neither D'Indy's *Lied* Op. 19 (1885) nor Saint-Saëns's *Allegro appassionato* Op. 43 (1875) lay claim to being profound, but both works are melodious and imaginatively scored. Fauré's orchestral writing has often provoked criticism, but most commentators agree that his popular, moving *Elégie* Op. 24 (1880, orchd 1901) works best in its orchestral guise. Massenet's rhapsodic, three-movement *Fantaisie* (1897) is somewhat short on inspiration, but André Caplet's *Epiphanie d'après une légende Ethiopienne* (1923) is much underrated, exploiting a wide range of technical resource (e.g. pizzicato glissandos, harmonics and double-stopping) in its lyrical cadenza and including some original touches, not least in the final 'Danse des petits nègres'. Florent Schmitt, a pupil of Massenet and Fauré, was inspired by the latter's *Elégie* to compose a *Chant élégiaque* Op. 24 (1899–1903, orchd 1911), but the jazz-influenced *Final* Op. 77 (1926) and especially the through-composed *Introit, Récit et Congé* Op. 113 (1951–2), in which the 'Congé' section develops motifs sketched earlier in the 'Introit', have created a more lasting impression. Ropartz abandoned his conservatoire studies with Massenet in order to study composition with Franck, an association which is evident in his *Adagio* and *Rapsodie* (1928). Another Franck pupil, Georges-Adolphe Hüe (*Andante et Scherzo*) was most prolific in vocal music, a genre in which Koechlin made a late start to his composing career, inspiring his twenty *Chansons bretonnes sur d'anciennes chansons populaires* Op. 115 (vc, pf, 1931–2, orchd 1934). Milhaud's response to folk cultures extends beyond France in his *Suite Cisalpine* Op. 332 (1954), based on various Piedmont melodies, while Françaix's *Fantaisie* (1955) and Sauguet's *Mélodie concertante* (1963) offer a range of contrasting moods. Sauguet's work is predominantly lyrical, but Françaix's runs the gamut from its opening Prelude (Andantino) and brief cadenza through its brilliant, rhythmic *écossaise*, melancholy *élégie*, and lively scherzo to its multi-faceted finale, with its internal waltz section, bravura cadenza and witty conclusion. Xenakis's *Epicycles* (1991) has attracted recent public attention.

Germany

Max Bruch's works for cello and orchestra include his ternary *Canzone* Op. 55 (1890), the *Adagio nach keltischen Melodien* Op. 56 (1890), actually based on one Scottish and one Irish melody, and *Ave Maria* Op. 61 (1892), virtually a transcription of an aria from a secular choral work *Das Feuerkreuz*; but *Kol Nidrei* Op. 47 (1880), a slow one-movement piece of a devotional character based on traditional Hebrew themes, has proved his most enduring.[10]

Although strictly speaking a symphonic poem, Strauss's *Don Quixote:*

Fantastic Variations on a Theme of a Knightly Character Op. 35 (1896–7) has a double identity as a concertante work, featuring a cello (Don Quixote) and viola (Sancho Panza) soloist in its depiction of the adventures of Cervantes's immortal figure.[11] After an elaborate introduction outlining the gradual deterioration of the Don's mental state through his preoccupation with archaic books on Knight Errantry, ten free variations retell some of the pair's adventures, incorporating striking musical pictorialism, particularly in the portrayal of windmills, sheep and the flying horse. A sad, meditative section, dealing with Quixote's death and incorporating motivic recall, concludes this technically challenging, humorous and highly inventive work. Also extra-musically inspired is Henze's *Ode an den Westwind* (1953), in which a solo cellist reflects the natural imagery of Shelley's poem. Comprising five separate movements, the work follows Shelley's descriptive verse closely, Henze annotating the score at various appropriate junctures. The first movement is largely of introductory function, but the lively second movement depicts the oncoming storm and is followed by a delicate *tranquillo*, which takes its lead from Shelley's poem. A solemn march precedes the finale ('Apotheosis'), featuring tubular bells and glockenspiels and directed to be played like a hymn. Henze's *Sieben Liebeslieder* (1984–5) adopt a simpler, more lyrical style encased within a shifting polyphonic texture, while Fortner's *Zyklus* (vc, wind, harp, perc, 1969) reflects his liking for counterpoint and clarity of formal structure in its six movements.

Great Britain

The British musical renaissance prompted a variety of works for the medium. Bantock's various 'Poems' – 'Elegiac' (1909), 'Sapphic' (1909) 'Celtic' (1914) and 'Dramatic' (1941) – his *Hamabdil* (1919) and Delius's *Caprice and Elegy* (1930) are well conceived and richly melodious, whereas Holst's *Invocation* Op. 19 No. 2 (1911) anticipates the mood and atmosphere of his *Egdon Heath*. Vaughan Williams withdrew his *Fantasia on [five] Sussex Folk Tunes* (1929), written for Casals, but Howells's *Fantasia* (1936–7), the remains of a once-planned concerto, thrives on its contrasts of mood, which shift from genial optimism to the profound melancholy and Elgarian nostalgia of his *Threnody* (1936). The 1940s and 1950s yielded little of British significance in the medium save Rubbra's *Soliloquy* Op. 57 (1943), Alan Bush's *Concert Suite* Op. 37 (1952) and Leighton's *Veris Gratia* (vc, ob, str, 1950). Of larger scale are Howard Blake's *Diversions* (1989) and Lennox Berkeley's three-movement *Dialogue* (1971), the latter bearing similarities in the central *più vivo* section of its second movement with parts of the finale of Shostakovich's Second Cello Concerto; its jaunty finale eventually incorporates reminiscences of the opening movement. The background of impressionistic woodwind calls against which the cellist operates in Alexander Goehr's melancholic *Romanza* Op. 24 (1968) suggests the influence of Janáček.

Maxwell Davies's *Vesalii Icones* (1969), inspired by anatomical drawings by Vesalius, is a music-theatre work in fourteen linked sections which trace a pilgrimage round the Stations of the Cross. The function of the soloist in Gordon Crosse's *Ceremony* Op. 19 (1966) is to provide tonal contrast to the full orchestra. Derived from his opera *Purgatory* Op. 18, it is an accessible set of fantasias or free variations, framed by a prologue and epilogue. By contrast, Maconchy's *Epyllion* (1974–5) explores the character of the solo cello 'in melodic coloratura of a fantastic, semi-improvisatory sort'.[12] Somewhat clearer in design is Hoddinott's *Nocturnes and Cadenzas* Op. 62 (1969), which takes the form of a symmetrical arch. The two outer sections – slow, brooding meditations – are each linked to the central scherzo by solo cello cadenzas, the first growing in intensity, but the second subsiding gently to lead to the tranquil concluding nocturne. It has elements in common with Hoddinott's *Scena: Noctis Equi* (1989), inspired by Marlowe's Dr Faustus crying out to prolong the dark so that the fateful hour in which he is judged may never approach: 'Stay night, and run not thus'. The resultant intense, dramatic work in one continuous movement subdivides into a nocturne (Andante), a scherzo (Presto), an intensified reprise of the Andante with cadenza, a second Presto, a second, impassioned cadenza and a moving final Adagio.

Tavener's *The Protecting Veil* (1989), written for Steven Isserlis, is a single-movement work in eight continuous sections with programmatic superscriptions (e.g. 'the Anunciation', Lament at the Cross', 'Tears of the Mother of God'). The title refers to 'The Feast of the Protecting Veil' of the Greek Orthodox Church, which commemorates the Greek's victory over the Saracen invasion in the tenth century. Tavener uses the Byzantine system of eight modes both for the background structure which underpins contrasting sections, and for his melodic material. The cello sings almost throughout, and predominantly in its upper register, representing the Mother of God's unending song, but the climactic fifth section is a solo cadenza. Following this work, Tavener became increasingly attracted to the cello as an instrument with which to express his spiritual thoughts. The prominent cello part in the string quartet *The Hidden Treasure* (1989) exemplifies this attraction, as does his *Eternal Memory* (vc, str orch, 1991), which makes partial reference to *The Protecting Veil* and is in itself an expanded version of his *Thrinos* for unaccompanied cello. He describes *Eternal Memory* as 'the remembrance of death' – the remembrance of Paradise Lost. The serene opening section represents the remembrance of Paradise Lost from which man has fallen, and comprises a simple

Byzantine-like chant in verse-and-response form from the cello with a gentle chordal string support. The more agitated central section reflects the transient nature of life, but the return to the serenity of the opening 'looks forward to unknown paradise promised to us, yet to come'.[13]

Among other notable British contributions to the medium are Gavin Bryars's *The North Shore* (1995) and Mark-Anthony Turnage's *Kai* (1989–90), the latter scored for a jazz-based ensemble and incorporating a slow final movement as a requiem for the German cellist Kai Scheffler, a former member of the Ensemble Modern.

The Americas

Apart from Victor Herbert's *Suite* Op. 3 (1894), Henry Hadley's *Concert Piece* (1907), Frederick Jacobi's *Psalms* (1932), Ben Weber's *Ballade* and *Sinfonia* Op. 21 and Porter's *Fantasy* (1950), William Schuman's *Fantasy: Song of Orpheus* (1960–1) is one of the foremost American works in the medium. Derived from his song 'Orpheus with his lute', composed in 1944 for a production of *Henry VIII*, the graceful lyricism of its outer sections is contrasted by the two cadenzas that link them to the central scherzo, in which fragments of the song are developed. However, Bloch's *Schelomo* (1915–16) has overshadowed the works of his adopted countrymen. A declamatory work in a free, one-movement design with strong Hebraic melodic and rhythmic characteristics (hence the subtitle 'A Hebrew Rhapsody'), it is an emotional portrait of King Solomon, represented by the solo cello. An opening cello cadenza introduces most of the important motifs of the work, which alternates passages of monologue and narrative with vehement outbursts. Also noteworthy are Bloch's *Voice in the Wilderness* (1936), an orchestral poem with cello obbligato, Krenek's *Capriccio* (1955), Feldman's *Cello and Orchestra* (1972), Diamond's *Kaddish* (1987–8) and Kirchner's *Music for Cello and Orchestra* (1992). The *Fantasia* (1945) of Villa-Lobos dates from the beginning of his last phase of creative activity, when an interest in instrumental virtuosity pre-dominated over his affiliation to Brazilian popular music, while Camargo Guarnieri's *Shoro* (1961) is also noteworthy.

Czechoslovakia

Dvořák's Schumannesque *Silent Woods* (1893) is a beautiful arrangement of the fifth of a collection of piano duets, *From the Bohemian Forest* Op. 68 (1883–4), while the jolly Rondo Op. 94, composed for Wihan in a cello-piano version in two days over Christmas 1891, was orchestrated two years later. Martinů's charming *Sonata da camera* (1940) belies the particularly difficult period of political unrest in which it was conceived, while Vitazoslav Kubicka's dramatic Fantasia (1986) is dedicated to the memory of Líbor Pavlicek, a student whose death was due to fascist imprisonment. Jan Novák's *Capriccio* (1958) is a truly virtuoso work which incorporates jazz elements; in its central movement, 'Circulus vicioso', Novák uses a twelve-note series as thematic material for the first time.

Other countries

Hungarian Emanuel Moór is justly remembered for his two nationalistic Rhapsodies (1907, 1911), a *Ballade* (1914) and his Largo Op. 105, while Cassadó's *Catalonian Rhapsody* (1928) and Casals's *Sardana* (1927) and *El cant dels ocells* (vc, strg, 1972), an arrangement of a Catalan folk song, are the principal Spanish contributions. Henriëtte Bosmans's late Romantic, almost palindromic *Poème* (1926) is a notable Dutch essay, while Swiss composer Frank Martin wrote ballades for a number of instruments with piano or orchestra, orchestrating his original *Ballade* for cello and piano in the same year of its composition (1949). Popper composed numerous character pieces, of which his programmatic, six-movement *Suite Im Walde* Op. 50 (Hamburg, 1882) and folk-orientated *Ungarischer Rhapsodie* Op. 68 (Leipzig, 1894) are the most significant for cello and orchestra; nevertheless, his *Requiem* (Hamburg, 1892), a moving funeral ode for a trio of cellists and orchestra, remains one of his best-known compositions.

Malipiero's *Ariona* (1912), Dallapiccola's skilfully scored *Dialoghi* (1959–60), Zandonai's *Serenata Medioevale* (1909) and *Spleen* (1934), Petrassi's *Prelude, Aria and Finale* (1939) and Berio's *Il Ritorno degli Snovidenia* (1976–7) are the principal Italian examples and Penderecki's *Sonata* (1964) and Baird's *Scene* (vc, harp, orch, 1967) the major Polish essays. The title of Penderecki's work alludes not to the Classical form but to its intent as an exercise in instrumental sonority. Penderecki's select orchestral forces emphasise darker instrumental sonorities that mix well with the solo cello timbre, but include a large battery of percussion and the work involves the soloist in microtonal passages and various unusual effects, such as hitting the strings with the palm of his right hand, beating the fingerboard with his finger-tips, playing below the bridge and making grinding sounds with the bow against the string.

In Scandinavia, Sibelius's *Two Pieces* Op. 77 (1914) for violin or cello and orchestra are of limited substance, but Pergament's *Kol Nidre* (1949), Rautio's folk-influenced *Divertimento* (1965), with its central lullaby and final Offenbachian can-can, Nordheim's *Tenebrae* and Eklund's *Pezzo elegiaco* (1969) have been popular, while Sallinen's *Chamber Music III*, subtitled 'The Nocturnal Dances of Don Juanquixote' (1986), and Hans Abrahamsen's *Lied in Fall* (1988) have attracted more recent interest. Supposedly portraying an 'aged composer's farewell to youth', Sallinen's beguiling piece comprises a series of short, light-hearted movements which recall nostalgically the dance music of the mid-twentieth century. Significant among other countries' contributions to the genre were Belgians Ysaÿe (*Méditation* Op. 16; *Sérénade* Op. 22; *Poème nocturne*, vn, vc, orch, Op. 29) and Jongen (*Second Poème*, 1914–16), Austrian Wolfgang Rihm (*Erster Doppelgesang*, vla, vc, orch, 1980; *Monodram*, 1982–3), Estonian Arvo Pärt (*Pro et contra*, 1966), Indian Naresh Sohal (*Dhyan I*, 1974), the Yugoslav Milko Kelemen (*Changeant*, 1968) and the Japanese composer Toru Takemitsu (*Scene*, 1959; *Orion and Pleiades*, 1984).

Genre pieces for cello and piano/organ

The nineteenth century

Several composers contributed to broadening the literature for cello and keyboard in the nineteenth century. In Germany, Schumann's *Adagio and Allegro* Op. 70 (hn/vn/vc, pf), *Fünf Stücke im Volkston* Op. 102 (vc/vn, pf) and *Phantasiestücke* Op. 73 (cl/vn/vc, pf) were composed in 1849 and are characteristic products of his later years – the piano writing, often featuring persistent, restless arpeggio movement, is typical of a certain anxiety over effects of texture which crept into Schumann's music in the mid-1840s. The three *Phantasiestücke* are the pick of the bunch, although all are in A (minor, major, major, respectively), in ternary form, and are rather similar in mood and movement. In the first piece the middle section grows organically out of the main material, in the manner of song-form as understood by Schumann himself. But the other two pieces have contrasting central sections, in F (No. 2) and A minor (No. 3), not, however, without thematic links with the main material. Indeed, a sort of cyclicism pervades the whole group, perhaps more because of a consistent quality in the melodic invention than because of any conscious aim at unity. Three of Max Bruch's *Four Pieces* Op. 70 (1896), all in ternary form, are based on national melodies, movements entitled respectively 'Finnländisch', 'Tanz (Schwedisch)' and 'Schottisch' following the opening 'Aria'.

Prominent among the French contribution was Jacques Offenbach, who was a cellist in the orchestra of the Opéra-Comique in Paris in the late 1830s long before his success in operetta. Leaving that orchestra in 1838, he made the acquaintance of Flotow, through whom he gained entry to Paris salons, performing with him jointly composed pieces for cello and piano. Among these collaborative ventures were collections entitled *Rêveries* (1839) and *Chants du Soir* (1839), but Offenbach also composed individual pieces and collections of his own, notably the *Introduction et valse mélancolique* Op. 14 (1839), *Deux âmes au ciel, élégie* Op. 25 (1843),

Chants du crépuscule Op. 29 (1846), *Rêverie au bord de la mer* (1849) and the étude-caprice *La course en traîneau* (1849), as well as works for several cellos (e.g. *Adagio et scherzo*, 4vc, 1845) or for cello and other instruments (e.g. *Las campanillas*, vc, bells, 1847).

Saint-Saëns parodied Offenbach, amongst others, in his *Le Carnaval des Animaux* (1886), of which by far the most popular movement is 'Le Cygne', a beautiful cello-piano miniature. However, his attractive earlier *Suite* Op. 16 (1862), in five short movements, contains some vigorous idiomatic writing for the cello, while his *Romance* Op. 51 (1877), *Chant saphique* Op. 91 (1892) and *Prière* Op. 158 (org, vn/vc, 1919) are, by contrast, more tender and lyrical. A ternary *Intermezzo* (*c.* 1880) was discovered by Piatigorsky in Paris in 1938, but far more significant are Fauré's eight works for cello and piano. The two late Sonatas (Opp. 109, 117) apart, these are short simple movements characteristic of their composer's mode of thought and innate lyricism. The *Elégie* in C minor Op. 24 (1880, orchd 1901), in a straightforward ternary form, has a certain stillness and serenity created by the falling sequences of the main melody, which is only briefly disturbed by the more restless and impassioned middle section. Fauré's *Petite Pièce* (*c.* 1888) has remained unpublished, but his *Romance* Op. 69 (1894) is a lyrical ternary movement and *Papillon* Op. 77 (*c.* 1885) combines *moto perpetuo* outer sections – containing some characteristic twists and turns – with a more relaxed lyrical central episode. The *Sicilienne* Op. 78 (1898), originally written for cello and piano, has become better known as the third movement of Fauré's incidental music for *Pelléas et Mélisande* Op. 80,[14] but the *Sérénade* in B minor Op. 98 (1908), dedicated to Casals, has failed to withstand the test of time.

Apart from Glazunov (*Elegie* Op. 17, 1887) and Rachmaninov (*Romance*, 1890; *Two Pieces* Op. 2, 1892), the principal Russian contributor was Carl Davidoff, whose numerous cello-piano pieces include a *Romance*, *Acht Stücke*, and a *Waltz* Op. 41 No. 2. Sibelius's early, passionate *Malinconia* Op. 20 (1901) is justifiably his best-known cello piece, much of the remainder of his output such as the *Tempo di Valse 'Lulu Waltz'* (1889) and *Andantino* (*c.* 1884) being little more than well-crafted salon music. Nevertheless, his *Andante molto* (*c.* 1887), written for his brother Christian, is more substantial, incorporating a solo cadenza, and his *Four Pieces* Op. 78 (1915–19) are of more mature cast. Busoni's *Kleine Suite* Op. 23 (1886), in four movements, is a relatively early work in the spirit of the Rococo but with rich Romantic harmony, while Liszt's two *Elegies* (1874, 1877) and *Romance oublieé* (1880) are of minor significance, but *La lugubre gondola* (1882) is an imaginative, lyrical piece which is essentially an experiment in impressionism.

Among those who acknowledged their national heritage were Chopin

(*Introduction and Polonaise* Op. 3, 1829–30) and Suk, whose melancholic
Op. 3 *Balada* (1890) and *Serenade* (*c.* 1898) incorporate, unusually for this
composer, certain features characteristic of Czech folk song. Dvořák, who
developed a national style without a conscious effort, also acknowledged
the heritage of foreign nations, notably in his *Polonaise* (1879); but
Austrian David Popper composed music with varied nationalistic leanings
(e.g. *Mazurka* Op. 11; *Polonaise de concert* Op. 14; *Tarantelle* Op. 33; and
five *Spanish Dances* Op. 54), probably to curry favour with his audiences
on tour. He also enriched the repertory with a whole variety of other
works, ranging from his *Serenade* Op. 54 to his sentimental *Wie einst in
schöneren Tagen* or *Devotion* Op. 50 and to pieces with extra-musical
associations such as his *Papillon* (from his six *Characterstücke* Op. 3),
Elfentanz Op. 39 (with its uninterrupted spiccato demands), and his
Concert Etudes Op. 55 (e.g. No. 1 'Spinning Song').

The twentieth century

The twentieth century witnessed a marked increase of examples in the
genre such that only a small and select proportion can be reviewed here.
These works drew upon an even greater diversity of musical styles, especially with the onset of that so-called musical revolution – the atonality
and serial composition of Schoenberg and the Second Viennese School.

Schoenberg wrote nothing for cello and keyboard, but his pupil,
Webern, himself a cellist, left his *Two Pieces* (1899), a student work discovered in 1965 which provides a fascinating index to the late romantic
origins of Webern's terse, yet precise and intense style; this is shown at its
most obsessive in the *Three Pieces* Op. 11 (1914), in which twelve-note (or
nearly) groupings seem to occur almost as a matter of course, though not
yet systematically or, perhaps, consciously. A contemporary in Vienna,
Hans Gál, was uninfluenced by such developments and remained faithful
to his musical roots in Brahms and Strauss in his attractive four-movement *Suite* Op. 6 (1920).

The work of Reger, a fervent admirer of Brahms, spanned the two centuries in Germany, and his *Zwei Stücke* Op. 79e (*Caprice* and *Kleine
Romanze*, 1904) bear witness to a close stylistic affinity. By contrast,
Hindemith demonstrated his continuing enthusiasm for composing for
amateur performers in his *Three Pieces* Op. 8 (1917) and *Drei leichte Stücke*
(1938), while Zimmermann's *Intercomunicazione* (1967) and Isang Yun's
Nore have justly earned their places in the professional repertory in more
recent times.

Early twentieth-century British composers latched on to the character
piece with some zeal. Delius's ternary *Romance* (1896) was later followed
by his *Caprice* and *Elegy*, completed from sketches in 1930 with Eric

Fenby's assistance. Among Frank Bridge's large quantity of chamber music in the first decade or so were numerous short, worthwhile pieces (*Moto perpetuo*, 1900 rev. 1911; *Cradle Song*, 1902; *Scherzetto, c.* 1902; *Serenade*, 1906; *Elégie*, 1911; *Mélodie*, 1911; *Meditation*, 1912; *Spring Song*, 1912; *Morning Song*, 1919; *Souvenir*, 1919), some for either violin or cello and piano. The output of composers such as Cyril Scott (including *Pierrot amoureux* (1912); *Pastoral and Reel* (1930); *Andante languido*; and various other pieces), Hurlstone (*Lullaby*), Wordsworth (*Nocturne* Op. 29; *Scherzo* Op. 42), Hamilton Harty (*Irish Prelude*; *Humoresque*; *Scherzo-Fantasy*) and Moeran (*Irish Lament*; *Prelude*, 1948) was in similar vein, while Vaughan Williams's *Six Studies in English Folksong* (1927) is one of the finest examples of his treatment of folk-song material. Reizenstein's expressive *Elegy* Op. 7 No. 2 and *Cantilena* Op. 18 are attractive, lyrical additions, as are Lennox Berkeley's *Andantino* (*c.* 1955), Frankel's *Elégie Juive* and *3 Poems* Op. 23 and Kenneth Leighton's haunting *Elegy* Op. 5 (1949), *Partita* Op. 35 and *Alleluia pascha nostrum* (Op. 85, 1981), the latter inspired by plainchant. Similarly, John Joubert's *Kontakion* Op. 69 is based on the Russian Orthodox chant for the dead, while James Macmillan has arranged for cello-piano his violin-piano piece *Kiss on Wood*, the serene simplicity of which reflects the composer's devotional intention.

Dance provides the inspiration for works by Seiber (*Dance Suite*), Christopher Bunting (*Dance-Caprice* and the second of his pair, *Elegie and Scherzo*) and Philip Cashian (*Dancing with Venus*), while the theme of sleep is common to Mark-Anthony Turnage's three lullabies of moderate difficulty *Sleep On* (1992) and Richard Rodney Bennett's charming, if saccharine, *Dream Sequences*. Bennett's *Sonnets to Orpheus* (1979) is more challenging, as are Jonathan Harvey's *Dialogue* (1965), Nigel Osborne's sombre, concise *Remembering Esenin* (1974) and John Buller's avant-garde *Scribenery*, inspired by the character Glugg in *Finnegan's Wake*. Some of William Lloyd Webber's music has been brought to the fore in recent years by his cellist son Julian, notably his *Lyric Suite* and *Two Pieces* (1950); also noteworthy are Giles Swayne's *Four Lyrical Pieces*, Colin Matthews' *Three Enigmas* (1985), and Caroline Bosanquet's tender, eloquent *Elegy (In Memoriam Joan Dickson)*.

Lukas Foss' *Capriccio* (1946) is one of his pieces of 'American popularism' and has been likened to cowboy music in a Classical framework, while Porter's *Poem*, Carter's *Elegy* (1943) and Rorem's *Mountain Song* (1949) are of more serious intent. More progressive impulses came via the experiments of Feldman, whose *Durations II* (1960) is an example of chance music applied to note-durations, Cowell (*Hymn and Fuguing Tune No. 9*, 1950; *Four Declamations with Return*), Rochberg (*Ricordanza*) and Wuorinen (*Adapting to the Times*, 1970; *Duuiensela*). Bernstein arranged as *Two Meditations* (1977) two excerpts from a theatre work entitled *Mass* (1971), while Miklós Rózsa's spirited *Toccata capricciosa* Op. 36 is a worthy tribute to Piatigorsky. Bloch's three sketches *From Jewish Life* (1924), of which the celebrated 'Prayer' comes first, and *Méditation Hébraïque* (1924) belong to his celebrated 'Jewish cycle', intensely emotional pieces in which Oriental or quasi-Hebrew traits are never far from the surface. Significant contributions from Latin America include Villa-Lobos's attractive *Little Suite* (1913) and Ginastera's *Pampeana No. 2* (1950).

Reyngol'd Glier was a direct heir to the Russian Romantic tradition and his *Ballad* Op. 4 (1902) and *Twelve Pieces* Op. 51 (1910) admirably demonstrate his gift for expressive melody. Prokofiev's *Ballade* Op. 15 (1912), with its noble tunes and pungent harmonies, comes into a similar category, while Tcherepnin's *Ode* (1919) and *Mystere* Op. 37 are somewhat more anguished, the latter written in commemoration of the untimely death of cellist Umberto Benedetti's nine-year-old son. Shostakovich's *Three Pieces* Op. 9 (1923–4) were unpublished and have not survived, but a lyrical Moderato, discovered in 1986, and an arrangement of a dance from his early ballet *The Golden Age* have entered the repertory. Shostakovich's-pupil Sofiya Gubaydulina, 'a Russian Messiaen', has contributed an effective cello-organ piece, *In Croce* (1983), which forms a kind of musical cross, with the organ beginning in the high register, the cello in the low, and the two crossing in the middle. Denisov's *Three Pieces* (1967) date from a period in which he exploited serial procedures and unconventional instrumental techniques, while Schnittke's *Epilogue from the Ballet Peer Gynt* involves experiments in electronic music.

Of the French contribution, the first two of Nadia Boulanger's *Trois Pièces* (1915) are predominantly of rhythmic interest, but the third piece, in three sections (with a coda derivative of the opening section), is more lyrically inspired, as are Chaminade's *Serenade*, Alain's ternary *Largo assai ma molto* (1935), Jolivet's *Nocturne* (1943), Milhaud's *Elégie* (1945), Gaubert's *Poème romanesque* and Sauguet's *Ballade* (1960). Immediately attractive are the various pieces of Françaix (*Berceuse; Rondino staccato; Nocturne; Sérénade; Mouvement perpétuel*, 1944) and Tortelier, most notably *Spirales* (1943) and some of his short encores; of these, the burlesque *Le Pitre* and *Pishnetto* (1975), pizzicato throughout and demanding a kind of strumming with both hands during its course, have been firm favourites. Auric's imaginative series of *Imaginées* includes one work for cello and piano (1969); Ohana's *Syrtes* (1970) and *Noctuaire* (1975) are also noteworthy, the latter being an evocative study designed as a test piece for final-year students at the Ecole Nationale de Musique de Boulogne-Billancourt. Notable among the Belgian contribution is Jongen's *Humoresque* Op. 92 (vc, org, 1930).

Some composers have shown strong nationalistic tendencies in their work, notably Kodály (*Magyar Rondo*, 1917), Falla (*Suite populaire espagnole*) and Cassadó, most of whose original compositions are extra-musically inspired and imbued with Spanish colour and particularly Catalan intonations and rhythms. Principal among these are the poetic *Serenade*, the popular *Requiebros* and the virtuosic *Danse du diable vert*. Janáček's *Pohádka* (Fairy Tale, 1910), a kind of love duet inspired by a Romantic poem by the Russian author V. A. Zhukovsky, and various pieces by Martinů (four *Nocturnes*, 1930; six *Pastorales*, 1930; *Suite miniature*, 1930; seven *Arabesques*, 1931) comprise the main Czech contribution to the genre, while Swede Ingvar Lidholm's *Quatro Pezzi* (1955) exploit serialism. Pizzetti's *Tre Canti* (first version, 1924) demonstrate the vocal nature of his thematic material, while his Italian compatriot, Scelsi, searching for a style in *Dialogo* (1932), reverts to a neo-Romantic idiom in his *Ballata* (1945).

Variations

Towards the end of the eighteenth century the *air varié* (commonly based on a popular operatic aria or national folk tune) became increasingly popular as a vehicle for bravura display, notably by virtuosos such as Bernard Romberg (Op. 50, Op. 61). However, Beethoven was most significant among the early contributors to the medium; inspired by the questing technique of Jean-Louis Duport in Berlin, he composed for the French cellist the two Sonatas Op. 5 and two sets of variations, one (WoO45, 1796) on 'See the Conqu'ring Hero Comes' from Handel's *Judas Maccabeus* and the other (Op. 66, 1796) on 'Ein Mädchen oder Weibchen' from Mozart's *Magic Flute*. Most of the latter set of twelve variations and coda are in a Mozartean vein of comedy; but the tenth and eleventh, in the minor mode and a slower tempo, wear a more Beethovenian aspect. Beethoven's later set of seven variations on (WoO46, 1801) 'Bei Männern, welche Liebe fühlen' from the same Mozart opera and Danzi's *Variations on a theme from Mozart's 'Don Giovanni'* are somewhat less ambitious.

Although sets of variations were not as plentiful in the cello repertory as, for example, in the violin literature, the genre was at the height of its popularity in the nineteenth century with notable contributions from Mendelssohn (*Variations concertantes* Op. 17, 1829), Weber (*Variations*, 1810, on a theme from his own *Grand Pot-pourri*, 1808),[15] Dancla (*Theme and Variations*), Joseph Merk (*Variations* Op. 4), Busoni (*Kultaselle, variations on a Finnish Folksong, c.* 1890) and Boëllmann (*Symphonic Variations* Op. 23, 1893), as well as cellist-composers such as Servais, Popper and

Klengel. Even some of Paganini's variations for violin (e.g. *Introduction and Variations on 'Dal tuo stellato soglio' from Rossini's 'Mosè'*) were adapted for the cello by virtuosos such as Silva, and later Fournier and Gendron. But Tchaikovsky's *Variations on a Rococo Theme* Op. 33 (1876) is arguably the most popular set for cello and orchestra. The binary 'Rococo' theme, introduced by the cellist after a brief, Schumannesque orchestral introduction, is well suited to variation treatment: sufficiently simple in outline for elaboration and clear in structure for instant recognition in disguise. Tchaikovsky's eight variations (with coda) are relatively freely treated, the second featuring a lightning exchange of short phrases between soloist and orchestra and the fourth comprising a light-hearted Allegro vivo which develops the material extensively. The orchestra has the theme in the sixth variation, with various trills and cadential embellishments in the solo part, but the seventh variation masquerades as a graceful Andante sostenuto. The eighth variation leads directly into the coda and reverts to the Rococo mood of the opening.[16]

The term 'variation' has been interpreted in diverse ways by composers of the current century. While there has been no lack of works that exploit variation technique, the number of independent compositions for cello is comparatively few. Most enduring have been the works of Respighi (*Adagio con Variazioni*, vc, pf, *c.* 1907), Françaix (*Variations de concert*, vc, strg, 1950), Hindemith (*Variationen über ein altenglisches Kinderlied 'A frog he went a-courting'*, vc, pf, 1941), Martinů (*Variations on a theme of Rossini*, vc, pf, 1942; *Variations on a Slovak Folksong*, vc, pf, 1959) and Lutosławski (*Grave*, vc, pf, 1981),[17] but worthy contributions have also been made by Tovey (*Elegiac Variations* Op. 25, 1909), Piatigorsky (*Variations on a Theme of Paganini*, vc, pf/orch), Gnesin (*Theme and Variations* Op. 67), Lopatnikoff (*Variations and Epilogue*, 1946), Malcolm Williamson (*Variations*, vc, pf, 1964), Jórunn Vidar (*Variations on an Icelandic Song*), Piston (*Variations*, vc, orch, 1966), David Amram (*Honor Song for Sitting Bull*) and Henze (*Introduktion, Thema und Variationen*, 1992).

Transcriptions and fantasias

The vogue for transcriptions started in the nineteenth century when itinerant virtuosos such as Alfredo Piatti transcribed for cello popular works from other repertories to supplement and enhance their own concert programmes with worthwhile pieces. Piatti, for example, arranged a selection of Mendelssohn's *Songs Without Words* for cello and piano and between 1881 and 1898 published arrangements for cello of works by composers as diverse as Ariosti, Boccherini, Brahms (e.g. *Hungarian*

Dances), Porpora, Christopher Simpson, Valentini and Veracini. He also arranged J. S. Bach's First Cello Suite for cello and piano. Julius Klengel also adapted many works for his instrument, as well as making creditable editions of Classical cello sonatas and concertos. His pupil, Piatigorsky (who also studied with Alfred von Glehn), also published some skilful transcriptions, notably of Weber's *Adagio and Rondo* (originally written for harmonichord), and he collaborated with Stravinsky on the cello version (1954) of the *Suite Italienne* (from *Pulcinella*). Popper also made arrangements of Baroque compositions and some Schubert songs (e.g. 'Du bist die Ruh'; 'Frühlingslaube'), twenty-five of his transcriptions being published (*c.* 1878–1911) by Johann André in a collection entitled *Perles Musicales-from the Concert Repertoire of David Popper*. Cassadó produced many workman-like transcriptions for cello, notably of concertos by Mozart (horn) and Weber (clarinet), piano pieces (Op. 72) by Tchaikovsky and works by a wide variety of other composers. In typical Kreisler fashion, the Allegretto grazioso, supposedly by Schubert, is evidently a piece of Cassadó's own composition.

Various other songs by Schubert, as well as by Brahms, Rachmaninov and others, have been transcribed for the instrument. Daniil Shafran even arranged Brahms's *Vier ernste Gesänge* Op. 121 for cello and piano, and works by Liszt (e.g. *Consolation* No. 3, Rachmaninov (e.g. *Vocalise* Op. 34 No. 14) and Falla (e.g. dances from *El Amor Brujo* or *La Vie Brève*), among others, have appeared for the cello-piano combination. Composers such as Dvořák (*Silent Woods* Op. 68 No. 5 and two *Slavonic Dances*), Rheinberger (Six Pieces Op. 150), Elgar (*Romance* Op. 62) and Bartók (Rhapsody No. 1) have made successful transcriptions of their works for cello and keyboard.

Fantasias (often in the form of variations) on well-known themes, mostly taken from opera, also became an indispensable part of musical entertainment in the nineteenth century, although examples for the violin far outweigh those for cello. Offenbach's numerous unaccompanied operatic fantasias are worthy of a second mention, but more significant are Belgian cellist Adrien Servais' sixteen Fantasias (vc, orch, Mainz, n.d.), including *Souvenir de Spa* Op. 2, *Souvenir de St Petersburg* Op. 15, and *O Cara memoria* Op. 17, countless duos (vc, pf) on opera themes, including fourteen in collaboration with pianist Jacques Gregoir, and duos (vn, vc) on opera themes in collaboration with violinists Hubert Léonard and Henri Vieuxtemps (e.g. *Grand Duo . . . sur des motifs de l'opéra 'Les Huguenots' de Meyerbeer*). Dotzauer also composed duos on themes from Auber's *La Muette de Portici*, Rossini's *Guillaume Tell* and Bellini's *Le Pirate*, and cellists such as Franchomme, Kummer and Goltermann added to the repertory of transcriptions, fantasias and potpourris on popular songs and operatic melodies.[18] Romberg seems to have preferred national songs on which to base his numerous works in the genre, generally entitled 'capriccio' or 'divertissement', while Piatti wrote several fantasias on themes from the operas of Bellini, Donizetti and Piccini, as well as on folk songs from Russia, Sweden and elsewhere. Popper's *Russian Phantasy* Op. 43 and *Scotch Fantasia* Op. 71 were also motivated by his travels, while Davidoff's *Fantasie über russische Lieder* Op. 7 (*c.* 1860) is a genuine nationalistic gesture.

10 Ensemble music: in the chamber and the orchestra

PETER ALLSOP

Any attempt to chart the early history of the cello, in whatever genre, inevitably founders on ambiguity of terminology. We accept that bass violins were widespread in Italy throughout the seventeenth century and that they existed in various sizes, the smallest tuned a fifth higher than the modern cello,[1] but when was a violone, violoncino, basso da brazzo, bassetto di viola, violone piccolo or whatever a cello?[2] This problem is inevitably aired elsewhere in this volume, but its most direct relevance is to the ensemble sonata for two or more melodic instruments, since by the time collections of solo compositions for a stringed bass and continuo appeared in print, composers (or at least publishers) had mainly settled on 'violoncello'; there are no solo collections for violoncino.[3] It would seem that 'violoncello' was first used with some frequency by Bolognese composers from Giulio Cesare Arresti's *Sonate a 2, & a Tre. con la parte del violoncello a beneplacido* (1665),[4] but others in his immediate circle were still far from consistent. Giovanni Battista Vitali described himself as 'suonatore di violone da brazzo' on the title-pages of his publications but is referred to variously as a player of the 'violoncino' and 'violonlino' in the records of the Bolognese basilica of San Petronio; yet, after his appointment to the Court of Modena in 1674, the Church authorities advertised for a replacement, 'being vacant the position of violoncello through the departure of Gio. Batt. Vitali'.[5] Ten years later, the title-page of Domenico Gabrielli's *Balletti* reveals that he was 'Sonatore di Violoncello in S. Petronio di Bologna', even though the part-book is labelled 'violone'. Conversely, the *Arie, e correnti a tre, due violini e violone* (1678) of another of Vitali's associates, Giovanni Maria Bononcini, labels the bass part-book as 'violoncello', while a manuscript copy in Modena, where he worked, gives 'violoncino'.[6] It would seem that these composers either wrote for a variety of different instruments virtually identical in range and designed to play the same parts, or for one instrument whose nomenclature was still fluid.

During the 1680s, while the new term achieved some currency in Bologna, other nomenclatures still prevailed elsewhere. At San Marco in Venice 'violoncini' are mentioned as late as 1694,[7] while the change began in Rome only *c.* 1694 and older composers such as Corelli still used 'violone' into the next century.[8] One school of thought suggests that this did not signal the introduction of a new instrument but merely the adoption of a more fashionable terminology,[9] but Alfred Planyavsky argues that the violone remained distinct from the violoncello, basing his conclusions on the not inconsiderable number of title-pages which mention both instruments, notably Bartolomeo Bernardi's *Sonate da camera a tre, due violini e violoncello col violone o cembalo* (1692) and Giovanni Reali's *Suonate e capricci a due violini, e basso, con una folia a due, violini, e violoncello con violone obligatti* (1709).[10] Of particular significance are the several collections of Giulio Taglietti, one of the most important composers of early cello sonatas, whose Op. 3 calls for 'violoncello e spinetta o violone', Op. 8 'violone, violoncello e B. C'., Opp. 9 and 10 'violoncello, violone o claveceno'. The Op. 1 (1704) of Corelli's pupil, Michele Mascitti, contains six sonatas for 'violino solo col violone o cembalo', and six 'a due violini, violoncello, e basso continuo', surely a strange choice of wording if the distinction were meaningless. Such instances counsel at least a degree of caution in the hasty assumption that violone by this time meant cello, even if one feels instinctively that the instrument specified by such composers as Corelli was, indeed, the equivalent of the modern cello.[11] After all, the bass player in his ensemble at the court of Cardinal Ottoboni can be identified as the internationally renowned cellist Giovanni Lorenzo Lulier.

Similarly, 'violoncino', first listed as one of the options in Giovanni Battista Fontana's posthumous *Sonate* (1641), must have been constructionally so close to the violoncello as to make little difference. There is no doubt of its novelty, for the Venetian publisher Alessandro Vincenti thought it necessary to advise the purchasers of Cavalli's *Musiche Sacre* (1656) that 'the part named violoncino, should be placed next to the violins, which compete together, but may be replaced by a chitarrone, bassoon, or other similar instrument capable of the same speed, or it can be left out at one's discretion'. From these brief references it may be deduced that the instrument was new, that it blended well with the violins and that it was capable of some agility. The advent of these smaller bass violins has often been seen as a response to the increasingly florid parts in ensemble sonatas, but timbre and blend must have been the overriding factors. Bass parts in the 1650s, or indeed the 1680s, were no more difficult than that of the *Sonata per il violone* of Cima's *Concerti ecclesiastici* (1610), and as to size, Bottesini, Dittersdorf and even Haydn considered the double bass perfectly capable of the most dexterous playing.[12]

Only nine years after Cavalli's collection, Arresti's *Sonate* appeared in Venice, but was his 'violoncello' another instrument so remote from the violoncino as to warrant a change of nomenclature, or did the publisher simply adopt Arresti's Bolognese usage? After all, even today both cities preserve vibrant local dialects, and in the seventeenth century Venetians often retained their own idiosyncratic nomenclatures, preferring violetta to viola (the latter term being applied to the melodic *bass* instrument). It has been proposed, however, that there was a substantial difference between the violoncino and the violoncello relating to the lowest string: while the former still used gut, the latter was wire-wound; but in every other respect the instruments were virtually identical.[13] The decisive change to wire-wound strings was most relevant to the bass violin since the resulting increase in tension for a given string-length made possible the construction of a smaller, more manageable instrument, while at the same time increasing the resonance and sonority of the lowest string. Nevertheless, it seems somewhat far-fetched that a player would suddenly decide to rename his instrument after a visit to the string maker to replace his bottom string. We can only speculate as to what instrument violinists would be playing today had luthiers in the 1920s displayed such pedantry over the adoption of the steel 'E' string! A more plausible conjecture is surely that in response to the development of this new instrument, string makers were prompted to overcome the deficiencies inherent in the gut lowest string.

In this early development it is also necessary to discard the age-old myth that, until the time of Haydn and Mozart, the cello was languishing in its own Dark Ages, condemned to the servitude of reinforcing the bass of the continuo. Such a belief reveals a profound misunderstanding of the role of the melodic bass instrument in the early sonata.[14] There is no evidence that at this time the keyboard continuo was normally doubled by a melodic instrument in ensembles.[15] This may have been the case in eighteenth-century Germany if C. P. E. Bach is to be believed,[16] but in Italy, the home of both the cello and the sonata, whenever a melodic bass is mentioned on the title-page its function is always as an essential melodic voice and never as a continuo instrument. This principle is already established in the *Sonata a 3* from Cavalli's *Musiche sacre.* In the opening fugal section the violoncino participates in the imitation of the subject on equal terms with the violins, sharing in the animated dialogues of semiquavers in later sections, while in the lovely ground-bass finale (so redolent of the operatic composer), it again provides the melodic imitation above the bass tetrachord, where it is quite clear that the 'cello' is not doubling the continuo but providing the thematic part (see Ex. 10.1). The same may be said of Arresti's sonatas of 1665, and both composers may have conspired with the publishers in a discrete deception, for in neither case is the cello part optional as claimed. From the mid-seventeenth century the cello, however labelled, was considered to be an independent voice on a par with the other melodic instruments in the ensemble.

Ex. 10.1 F. Cavalli, *Musiche sacre* (1656), Sonata a 3

Nor is it commonly recognised that many *da camera* sonatas of this period are intended in the first instance for *unaccompanied* performance with an option of *replacing* the melodic bass with a keyboard. In the case of the 'Passemezo' from Giovanni Battista Vitali's *Varie partite* (1682) for two violins and violone there can be little doubt that the composer was intending a *tour de force* for his own instrument, the cello (see Ex. 10.2). The last quarter of the seventeenth century also saw the rise of a major new genre – the unaccompanied duo for violin and 'cello'. The earliest of these was

164 Peter Allsop

Ex. 10.2 G. B. Vitali, *Passemezo* (1682)

Ex. 10.3(a) B. Laurenti, *Sonate per camera* (1691), Sonata 9
(b) A. Corelli, *La Follìa*, Op. 5 (1700)

Giovanni Maria Bononcini's *Arie . . . a violino e violone, over spinetta* (1671), in the 'violone o spinetta' part-book of which the composer noted that 'one should bear in mind that the violone will produce a better effect than the spinet since the basses are more appropriate to the former than to the latter instrument'. The fate of this medium was sealed after the spectacular success of Corelli's Op. 5, for many years the most popular set of duo sonatas ever published. Even as late as 1700, Corelli still refers to 'violone', but his co-pupil in Bologna, Bartolomeo Laurenti, had already made the change in terminology by 1691 in his *Sonate da camera a violino, e violoncello*. It is worth noting that a figured bass is not included in Laurenti's collection, since he does not offer the option of keyboard accompaniment. This undermines the rather tenuous theory that in such sonatas the cello was to provide chords.[17] Many passages in both Laurenti and Corelli are decidedly unidiomatic for the keyboard (see Ex. 10.3), and, as late as Tartini and Veracini, such unaccompanied duos were perfectly normal, remaining one of the most popular mediums throughout the eighteenth century, extensively cultivated by Perti, Montanari, Manfredini, Dall'Abaco, Vivaldi, Valentini, Platti, Tessarini, Somis, Pugnani, Giardini and many others.[18]

Trading on Corelli's success, the early eighteenth century saw an exodus of Italian virtuosi, who were now able to capitalise on the mass markets created by the burgeoning northern European publishers. These cellists provided a common basis for the formation of the national schools which were soon to flourish throughout Europe. London was particularly favoured in its roster of famous cellists, among them Nicola Francesco Haim, Salvatore Lanzetti (the author of an important cello tutor and a collection of sonatas offering six compositions for two cellos or a German flute) and Giacobbe Cervetto, whose output includes a set of sonatas for three cellos, again with the cautious option of two violins. In Paris, despite the spectacular Indian summer of the bass viol, the Italians made their mark in the hands of Giuseppe Fedeli and Giovanni Pietro Ghignone, a master of both cello and violin and associate of Mondonville and Gaviniès. Ghignone's Op. 2 (1737) contributed to the small literature for two cellos alone – a combination particularly favoured by Jean-Baptiste Joseph Masse, who left four sets between 1736 and 1744. In Germany and Austria, too, the long-standing susceptibility to Italian fashion was fostered by Evaristo Dall'Abaco in Munich and his son in Bonn, and Carlo Graziani in Berlin, while Antonio Vandini and Tartini carried out the same mission in Prague. After the rise of the Parisian school, French cellists became some-what in vogue; the Duport brothers spent much of their lives at the Prussian Court of Friedrich Wilhelm II, who was himself a cellist.

The activities of these erstwhile virtuosi may have been extensive, but their contributions have largely been eclipsed by the fecundity of the cellist Luigi Boccherini, who also worked for Friedrich Wilhelm II but spent much of his life in Madrid. Among the six hundred works accredited to him are an abundance of trios, quartets, sextets, and combinations with piano, but the largest single category comprises over a hundred quintets, scored mainly for two violins, viola and two cellos.[19] These follow fairly standard-ised forms of three or four movements, the most consistent overall struc-ture being fast binary, slow binary or ternary, minuet and trio, and rondo or binary finale, although the ordering of the inner movements may be reversed. Both the first violin and first cello are allotted parts of consider-able brilliance, and the latter is often set in a very high tessitura (see Ex. 10.4). The 'concertante' element is therefore very pronounced and takes precedence over equality of part-writing, although predominantly chordal textures may often be enlivened by some measure of independent figura-tion in the parts. Boccherini's concern was not for elaborate working out of

Ex. 10.4 L. Boccherini, Quintet No. 6, Op. 29 (1779) G.318, Cello I

Ex. 10.5 L. Boccherini, Quintet No. 3, Op. 39 (1787) G.339

thematic germs but in the quality and originality of the ideas themselves, and his melodic orientation is emphasised by the presentation of material doubled in octaves or in thirds or both (see Ex. 10.5). Nevertheless, his works display great originality, combining features from his Italian background with Spanish elements such as the *seguidilla spagnola* and *fandango*, and incorporate a wealth of colouristic devices such as harmonics, *sul ponticello, con sordino, flautato* and pizzicato. The essential disparity with the Viennese Classicists is neatly summarised by Amsterdam: 'in much music of Haydn, Mozart and, later, Beethoven, one experiences organic growth of the subject matter; in Boccherini the effect is that of a musical still-life, complete and perfect all at once'.[20] This seemed of little concern to contemporaries such as Charles Burney who considered Boccherini's music to be 'bold, masterly and elegant, second only to Haydn'.[21]

Boccherini was not alone in cultivating the quintet with two cellos; Giuseppe Maria Cambini produced more than one hundred during his years in Paris, while his rival in Madrid, Gaetano Brunetti, accounts for at least sixty-three. This period is of course associated with the rise of the string quartet to its 'classic' position of authority numerically overshadowing all other combinations, at least within the Austro-German tradition. It has long been accepted that the 'emancipation of the cello' was crucial to this development, leading to the 'radical equality of parts' so lauded by Sandberger.[22] If, in Haydn's early quartets, the bass part is indeed subservient to the first violin, this does not stem from any functional relationship to the basso continuo – there is no evidence that a keyboard was used even in his earliest quartets.[23] Haydn is particularly guilty of this censure in his early quartets, since he favoured melody and accompaniment textures more than many of his contemporaries, such as Franz Xaver Richter.[24] The limitations inherent in this style were perfectly evident to amateur chamber musicians such as John Marsh, who lamented the lack of interest in the lower parts, extolling the virtues of the 'Ancient Music':

> The Bass sometimes (particularly in Corelli) is of as much or more consequence than of either of the violins, consequently, although a first-violin performer may find less air in the ancient than in the modern music, yet the other performers will find more; and to an audience, who judge of the effect from the whole, there will, perhaps (in many pieces that may be selected) seem to be as much air in the ancient style as in the modern.[25]

Perhaps Marsh had not yet experienced Haydn's Op. 20 quartets. Tovey, seizing on the momentous significance of these works to the future development of the string quartet, singled out the cello for special note in the first quartet (see Ex. 10.6):

> A deep, quiet chuckle from the 'cello at the end of the fourth bar of Op. 20, No. 1 then comes as a warning that a new element is entering into Haydn's quartet style; and eight bars have not passed before the cello is singing in its tenor regions, not as a solo, nor with any new technique, but nevertheless with an effect which instantly shows that Haydn's imagination has now awakened to the sound of the cello as something more than a mere amenable bass to the harmony.[26]

Haydn may well have been influenced by his pupil Anton Kraft, for whom he composed his Cello Concerto in D, and for whom Beethoven wrote the solo cello part of the Triple Concerto. It is a tenet of the Classical string quartet that each instrument is allotted its fair share of the important material of the movement, although admitedly, the first violin frequently steals the limelight in compositions such as the 'Tost' Quartets, which Haydn wrote for an amateur violinist. He seems less generous in his treatment of the cello in the Op. 50 quartets dedicated to Friedrich Wilhelm, rarely offering it special treatment – apart, perhaps, from the 'dolce' theme announced to a light accompaniment of the viola alone in the third quartet (see Ex. 10.7).

The same cannot be said of Mozart's 'Cello Quartets' (K.575, 589, 590)

Ex. 10.6 J. Haydn, Quartet No. 1, Op. 20

also dedicated to Friedrich Wilhelm. On Mozart's own admission, Haydn's 'Russian' Quartets Op. 33 (1781), 'written in a new and special manner', had come as a complete revelation to him, which led him to strive for some fairer distribution of labour among the parts; the fruits of this 'long and arduous endeavour' are immediately apparent in the six quartets dedicated to Haydn.[27] By the time of his visit to Berlin in 1789, however, Mozart was in dire need of patronage and the chance to ingratiate himself with Friedrich Wilhelm was doubtless the decisive factor in his abandonment of the textures which he had sought so painfully to acquire. Subject material is continually allotted to the cello, and equally prominent are the extensive sections of 'exchange dialogue' between first violin and cello (see Ex. 10.8). On such occasions it falls to the viola, or even the second violin, to supply the bass. As it happened, these works were all published without dedication after Mozart's death, and were advertised as 'Concertante Quartets', placing them within a genre much favoured at the time. Dittersdorf, too, contributed to the medium of concertante cello quartet, but most works of this kind favour the first violin, even those of Boccherini. Much of this output was written to serve a particular purpose; Gaetano Brunetti, for instance, reflects the limited violinistic abilities of his patron, Carlos IV of

Ex. 10.7 J. Haydn, Quartet No. 3, Op. 50

Ex. 10.8 W. A. Mozart, Quartet K. 590

Spain, with the dullest of accompaniments in the other parts. Concertante textures were still not uncommon in orchestral music late in the century, for besides Haydn's well-known early symphonies 'Le Matin', 'Le Midi' and 'Le Soir', Symphony No. 95 also exhibits vestiges of these traits.

With Beethoven, the process of equalisation of parts is so advanced that

Ex. 10.9 L. van Beethoven, String Quartet in F major, Op. 59 No. 1

it would almost seem an impertinence to focus on any one instrument in his chamber music, except to re-echo Klaus Marx's statement that in the late quartets 'the absolute priority of the musical intention over instrumental exigencies created cello parts of unusual difficulty'.[28] Yet it is surely the spacious opening melody presented without preamble by the cello that makes the F major Razumovsky Quartet (Op. 59 No. 1) the most memorable of the set; nor is the cello prepared to relinquish its lead, supplying the second subject, initiating the scherzando with its monotone rhythm and presenting the 'Thème Russe' of the finale (see Ex. 10.9). In none of his earlier quartets is the cello so consistently called upon to initiate. It is no coincidence that Op. 59 followed on immediately from the 'Eroica' Symphony, with its careful discrimination of bass and cello – among the earliest instances of a cello melody above the bass in orchestral writing. Such differentiation was a *fait accompli* in large-scale chamber music with cello and double bass, whether Beethoven's Septet Op. 20 or the octets of Schubert and Spohr. The exploitation of the upper-middle register in cantabile lines often of great expressiveness characterises much of the best writing for cello throughout the nineteenth century, not only in chamber music but also in the symphonic repertory, from Schubert's Eighth Symphony through to the works of Brahms, Dvořák and Bruckner.

In chamber music for strings alone the string quartet held its own from the late eighteenth century onwards, massively outweighing all other combinations. Of the memorable exceptions that immediately spring to mind, Mozart's E flat Divertimento K.563 (vn, va, vc, 1778) is especially gracious in its treatment of the cello, and Beethoven's five string trios add to a repertory which Dunhill remarks 'has never exercised a very great fascination for composers'—the unaccompanied trio sonata excepted![29] The string quintet, of course, has its fair share of masterworks – Mozart's G minor (K.516) and the F and G major quintets (Opp. 88, 111) of Brahms – but it is remarkable how few of these call for two cellos, most preferring the 'standard' scoring of two violas.[30] This is perhaps even more surprising given the extraordinary warmth and richness achieved in Schubert's Quintet in C (D956) by pairing the two instruments, often way above the viola (see Ex. 10.10). This combination found another devotee in the French composer of English descent Georges Onslow, a keen cellist who wrote over thirty quintets. The string sextet, on the other hand, requires two cellos in most instances, claiming works as diverse as Tchaikovsky's *Souvenir de Florence* Op. 70, Brahms's two masterpieces (Opp. 18, 36) and, as a valediction to nineteenth-century Romanticism, Schoenberg's effulgent sextet *Verklärte Nacht* (1899) on a poem by Dehmel.

Of the larger string ensembles, the octet has fared best, especially in the wake of Mendelssohn's exuberant Octet Op. 20 (1825). Its 'symphonic orchestral style' differs fundamentally from the antiphonal treatment of Spohr's Double Quartet Op. 65, which he claimed inaugurated 'a wholly new kind of instrumental work which, so far as I know, I am the first to attempt. It is most like a piece for double chorus, for the two quartets which cooperate here work against one another in about the same proportions as the two choirs do'.[31] As Brown points out, earlier examples do exist, such as Albrechtsberger's *Trois Sonates à deux choeurs* (1804), while a late survival of the principle is discernible in Milhaud's Quartets Nos. 14 and 15, which may be played either separately or together. The arrangement in two equal

Ex. 10.10 F. Schubert, Quintet in C, D956

bodies may seem obvious in the octet, but the string nonet is not so readily divisible. Aaron Copland's solution in his Nonet for Solo Strings is to divide the strings into threes, and the entire composition has its genesis in the three chords of the three cellos announced at the outset.[32]

If the string quartet had no real challenger for supremacy from other combinations of strings, it was forced to yield ground to the piano. Over many generations the most prolific composers of chamber music were, in fact, pianists, notably Mozart, Beethoven, Hummel, Schumann, Mendelssohn, Brahms, Saint-Saëns, Franck, Fauré, Debussy and Ravel. The piano trio had already achieved considerable popularity by the end of the eighteenth century as demonstrated by Beethoven's Op. 1 and the fifteen works in this medium by Dussek. Piano quartets and quintets became increasingly common in Mannheim and Vienna from the 1760s, to be popularised in Paris by Cambini and Johann Schobert and in London by Tommaso Giordani. Of particular note from the cellist's point of view are the 'Three Favourite Quartets' of J. C. Bach (1785), since they are scored for the unusual combination of keyboard, violin and two obbligato cellos, each of which maintains considerable independence.[33] It would seem that these were more to the taste of the general public than the gloomy complexity of Mozart's G minor Piano Quartet K.478 or even the less emotionally demanding K.493. At the turn of the nineteenth century, quartets and quintets with piano had their adherents in the works of Dussek and Ferdinand David, and between 1821 and 1825 Mendelssohn could count three piano quartets and a piano sextet among his juvenilia. It was Schumann's contributions to both media which seemed most to capture the Romantic imagination – especially the Piano Quintet in E flat, Op. 44 (the direct influence of which can be seen on Dvořák's Op. 81) – and with the two piano quartets and quintet of Brahms, these works established a formidable mainstream orthodoxy. The dominance of pianist-composers was equally evident in France, as fostered in Parisian music societies from the mid-nineteenth century. Twenty years before his Piano Quartet in B flat, Op. 41 (1875), Saint-Saëns had produced a piano quartet and quintet, a line which continued into the twentieth century with major contributions from Fauré, Franck, Chausson, D'Indy and Milhaud. On the whole, these two media have not been the vehicle for radical experimentation, but the First Piano Quintet Op. 80 of Charles Koechlin is remarkable for its intense dissonance and Ernest Bloch's Piano Quintet (1923) uses quarter-tones.

Any combination of cello with piano poses inherent problems of duplication of function. It may fairly be said of Haydn's trios that, for all their power and vitality, the cello is still very much tied to the bass of the piano,[34] and the degree of liberation in Mozart's mature works does not disguise the concertante nature of the piano writing. The piano trio in particular posed enormous problems of balance, especially in the hands of pianist-composers such as Mendelssohn and Schumann, who seemed unable to resist the temptation for pianistic display at the inevitable expense of the cello. Coupled to this, all these ensembles were greatly affected by the piano's enormous increase in volume over the hundred years of its development, culminating in the introduction of the iron frame in 1856. The effect on the cello is aptly summarised by Basil Smallman in respect of the piano trio:

> increasingly the principal provision of a firm bass-line fell to the piano, leaving the cello either to double ineffectively, in a manner alien to an advanced chamber style, or to move to the tenor range and to the presentation of interior counterthemes or cantabile melodic passages. As a

result the overall sonority of the trio combination began to change, the high-pitched cello parts imparting a richly emotive character to the scoring which, if not treated carefully, led rather too easily to turgid or sentimental modes of expression.[35]

Even with those composers who were more concerned with the integrity of the parts or had a special affinity for the instrument, the cello is more often called upon to initiate in slow movements, as in the wonderfully evocative B flat Trio (D898) of Schubert, and this prejudice is still shared at the end of the century in the 'Dumky' Trio Op. 90, where Dvořák exploits the rich tones of the cello to encapsulate the melancholy mood of the work. There is no more telling testimony to these inherent problems and their solution than the cello part of the revision of Brahms's Trio in B major Op. 8 (1854) after a period of thirty-five years.[36]

All these considerations elevate the 'emancipation' of the cello, as exemplified by the Viennese string quartet, almost to the position of a moral imperative, but throughout its entire history one of its main functions has been to provide accompaniments to the thematic material presented in the violins, a task it achieves with ever-increasing ingenuity through arpeggios, pizzicati, chords and the like. At the same time, itinerant virtuosi such as Romberg, Dotzauer, Kummer and Popper needed a large repertory of show-pieces. None of these famous virtuoso cellists was an equally fine composer, although works for unusual combinations, such as David Popper's *Requiem* Op. 66 for three cellos, are noteworthy.

Nineteenth-century opera composers also exploited the incomparable vein of lyrical melody of which the cello was supremely capable. Rossini's decision to score the opening of *Guillaume Tell* for five solo cellos inaugurated a particular vogue for such choirs. It was certainly much admired by Berlioz:

> The first movement depicts most successfully in our opinion, the calm of profound solitude, the solemn silence of nature when the elements and the human passions are at rest. It is a poetic beginning to which the animated scenes that are to follow form a most striking contrast – a contrast in expression, even a contrast in instrumentation, this first part being written for five solo violoncellos, accompanied by the rest of the basses, while the entire orchestra is brought into play in the next movement, 'The Storm'.[37]

Other composers of grand opera seemed just as impressed, for the introduction to the second scene of Act 3 of Meyerbeer's *L'Etoile du Nord* (1854) employs four cellos; the practice was taken up by Verdi in *Nabucco*, *Aida* and *Otello*, while Puccini could not have better captured Cavaradossi's mood of desperation and longing while awaiting his execution in the final act of *Tosca*. Wagner, who was never averse to taking a lead from Parisian

Ex. 10.11 R. Strauss, *Also Sprach Zarathustra*

Ex. 10.12 B. Bartók, Quartet No. 3

grand opera, also scored for cellos in the first act of *Die Walküre* (1856). Aside from opera, the cello section in Richard Strauss's *Also Sprach Zarathustra* is divided into eight parts (see Ex. 10.11), while in *Don Quixote* the hero is portrayed principally by a solo cellist in a concertante role.

Even within a traditional medium such as the string quartet, the twentieth century presents a tapestry of bewildering diversity. The demands of expressionism, impressionism, serialism, etc., have created new sound-worlds for the cellist, as even a cursory glance at the range of pizzicati required in Bartók's Fourth Quartet reveals – snap, brush, *sul ponticello*, glissando – and the cello actually presents, in pizzicato chords, the theme for the Third Quartet's variations (see Ex. 10.12). If this treatment appears exhaustive, subsequent possibilities have been endless, with pizzicato over the entire string length, above and below the fingerboard, with different parts of the finger. Besides the string quartet, other traditional combinations have provided notable classics. The duo for violin and cello includes Ravel's *Sonate*, Kodály's *Duo* Op. 7, Honegger's *Sonatine*, and Martinů's *Duo* (1927) and *Duet* (1958). Nor has the cello choir been neglected, from Julius Klengel's *Hymnus* Op. 57 for twelve cellos[38] to Villa-Lobos's *Bachianas brasileiras* Nos. 1 and 5 (1930, 1938–45) for eight or more cellos and *Fantasia*

Ex. 10.13 M. Kagel, *The Match*

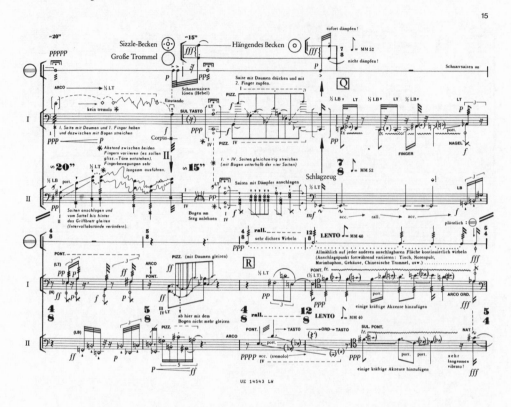

UE 14543 LW

Concertante (1958) for at least thirty-two cellos, Robert Linn's *Dithyramb* (1964–5) for eight cellos, Blacher's *Blues and Rumba Philharmonica* (1972) for twelve cellos, Boulez's *Messagesquisse* (1977) for one solo and six other cellos, Xenakis's *Retours-Windungen* (1976) for twelve cellos, and Lukas Foss's *200 Cellos: A Celebration* (1982; commissioned for the First American Cello Congress). Perhaps fortuitously, the cello has often found itself in company with a host of wind instruments – clarinet, oboe, flute and horn – in works such as Schubert's Octet and Dvořák's *Serenade*. In recent times, especially in the post-war period, uniformity of sound has given way to mixed groupings, often including voice, after the manner of such twentieth-century classics as Schoenberg's *Pierrot Lunaire* and Stravinsky's *Soldier's Tale*. These have created new uniformities favouring small mixed ensembles such as in Peter Maxwell Davies's *Versalii Icones*, in which the role of the cello is central. Most of these works tax the abilities of professionals, let alone amateur chamber musicians whose needs have long been disregarded. The apotheosis of virtuosity has been entertainingly satirised in Mauricio Kagel's *The Match* (2vc, perc, 1964), in which the two cellists are dressed as table-tennis players and the percussionist acts as umpire as they endeavour to outdo each other in outrageous acts of bravado (see Ex. 10.13).

Such new challenges, where they relate specifically to the cello, cannot be ignored.[39] Scordatura retuning of the bottom string is common enough (Ravel, Honneger, Respighi, Strauss, Stravinsky) but Xenakis's String Quartet instructs the player to alter every note ('entornant la cheville à chaque note'). In *Eidesis II*, Alcides Lanza requires one cello to tune a quarter-tone high, and the other a quarter-tone low. Quarter-tones were used systematically as early as Hába's String Quartet No. 1 (1919), while his Fifth Quartet (1923) employs sixth-tones. The range of bow placings seems boundless. In *Match*, Kagel requires bowing as close as possible to the left-hand fingers, while Fortner's Quartet places the bow above the fingers, and in the Nonet of J. B. Childs the player must bow underneath the string just in front of the bridge. Michael von Biel's Quartet No. 1 presents an amazing compendium of these devices, even requiring the cellist to place a double bass mute on the strings between bridge and fingerboard and play alternately above and below it. Even Gardner Read departs from his usual impartial codification in his mention of Xenakis's *Charisma*, where the cellist is directed 'to "grind on the bridge with the bow," which produces a "brutal" sound according to the composer, a description one is not inclined to question'.[40] Perhaps the cellist may be forgiven if he questions where it will all end.

11 Technique, style and performing practice to *c.* 1900

VALERIE WALDEN

The Violoncello is an Excellent instrument, not only in concert, but also for playing Lessons &c.
This instrument may be Consider'd as a Large Fiddle only held the contrary way ...

ROBERT CROME, 1765[1]

The prevailing idea about the 'cello is that it does very well in a quartet, or trio, or in orchestra
work, but that as a solo instrument it has no charm. This is very odd indeed, if you stop a
moment to consider the violoncello for what it really is – just a big violin with a bass voice.

RAY G. EDWARDS, 1913[2]

This instrument is not recognisable in his hands; it speaks, expresses, it renders all of the charm
that was heretofore believed to be exclusively reserved for the violin.

REVIEW OF JEAN-PIERRE DUPORT, 1762[3]

Well it is true that extraordinary artists, as for instance Servais, manage the violoncello so that
one might believe one is listening to a violin concerto ...

ALLGEMEINE WIENER MUSIK-ZEITUNG, 1842[4]

Violinists alone, of all string players, have been able to attain the popularity of singers or pianists
... but in the last few years an artist has come to the fore, whose accomplishments have gone far
toward changing traditional beliefs. Pablo Casals, the Spanish cellist, is now not only considered
the greatest exponent of his instrument, but eminent musicians have pronounced him the
greatest of all living interpreters.   *CURRENT OPINION*, 1918[5]

The preceding evaluations speak to the ever-present issue faced by those eighteenth- and nineteenth-century cellists who sought recognition as virtuosos: could their performances be as pleasing and acceptable to audiences as those of violinists? The accomplishments of such artists as Lanzetti, Jean-Pierre and Jean-Louis Duport, Romberg, Servais, Davidoff and Casals repeatedly proved that, indeed, the cello could easily match its smaller confrère in providing musical gratification. Yet to do so they, and other innovative and artistically creative players, had continually to recast themselves as the architects of modernisation as they searched for idiomatic performance techniques which allowed their music, in tandem with that of violinists, to be stretched, moulded, and refitted to conform with ever-changing stylistic requirements and regional preferences.

The development of idiomatic performance practices, however, also required the fundamentals of cello technique to be disengaged from those of the violin and, for pre-nineteenth-century players, the viola da gamba. Concomitantly, as cellists reached for parity with violinists in the display of technical complexities, the quest for excellence and effectiveness before audiences of differing ranks and localities led players to assume diverse, and sometimes contradictory, performance styles and technical manner-

isms. The panorama of cello performance history thus yields two perspectives: (1) a broad overview of how the instrument's technical methodology developed; (2) particular information about individual musicians,
their music-making and, of no less influence upon twentieth-century
players, the gradual codification of national schools of playing.

Among the primary source materials for the study of historical cello
procedures are instructional tutors. As listed in Appendix I, over eighty
cello methods were published before 1900, excluding anonymous
methods, translations and edited republications. The orientation of these
methods changed by time-period. The earliest tutors emphasised the
viability of the cello, the specified or implied comparison being to the viola
da gamba, which continued to be cultivated to the end of the eighteenth
century. The methods of Corrette, Crome, Azais, Baumgartner, Hardy and
Kauer focused on the merit of the cello for playing simple tunes and
accompaniments, their instructions being intended for students without
professional ambitions. Solo skills, with greater detail being given to the
refined bowing skills of Berteau, are found in the methods of Tillière and
Cupis, while fingering patterns were prescribed in a short work by Lanzetti.

The next group of instructional works reflects the advent of the cello as
a suitable concert instrument for all musical genres and attempts to define
systematic rules for fingering and bowing. French practices are illustrated
in the methods of Aubert, Bideau, Raoul, Müntzberger, Bréval, Duport
and the Paris Conservatoire; German traits are propounded in the
methods of Schetky, Alexander and Fröhlich; while Schetky's principles
are reiterated in the English tutors of Gunn and Reinagle.

It was not until the late 1820s that the changes in style occasioned by
the advent of the Tourte-design bow and musical Romanticism were
reflected in study material. The influence of Romberg is also a strong presence in the lessons of Baudiot, Hus-Desforges, Dotzauer, Kummer and
Lee. Methods detailing other regional practices from the first half of the
nineteenth century include those of Rachelle and Stiastny. By the second
half of the nineteenth century cello pedagogy was firmly established,
through both the esteem granted to virtuoso teachers and the syllabuses of
national conservatories and lesser schools of music. The numerous
methods published after 1850 attest to the popularity of cello study by
both amateurs and aspiring professional musicians.

Regional variations are also discernible in the notation used to write
cello music, especially among eighteenth-century composers and publishers who grappled with the instrument's quickly expanding range. The bass
clef was commonly used to write notes within the first two octaves, C to c^1.
During the early part of the eighteenth century pitches of the third octave
were notated with moveable C clefs; Corrette stated that Italian players

wrote in tenor clef, while French players preferred alto clef.[6] For accompanists, the Italian system of bass and tenor clefs became, and remained, the norm: the tenor clef was instituted when pitch reached e^1 or f^1, or when the cello part separated from that of the double bass.[7]

Among soloists, use of all moveable C clefs, as well as the treble clef read at pitch, was fashionable until about 1760. A trend was then instigated by French players and publishers who sought to make cello music accessible to violinists: they restricted notation to the bass and G clefs, with the notes written in the violin clef being played one octave lower on the cello unless designated *8va*, in which case the notes were played at pitch.[8]

The Italian and French systems were both used during the later years of the eighteenth century, but some players came to view them as flawed. Boccherini simplified the Italian system by eventually limiting himself to bass, tenor and treble clefs read at pitch.[9] Tricklir adopted such notation in the 1780s, as did Romberg in the following decade. Romberg became the most vocal and influential advocate for notating cello music at pitch, and the international popularity of his compositions led to the eventual abandonment of the French system during the nineteenth century. Romberg was also responsible for codifying the following notational indicators: the thumb sign ϙ; o for the open string; and ₒ placed above the finger number, e.g. $\overset{\circ}{3}$, to indicate a natural harmonic.[10] Romberg adopted the directional markings for down-bow (⊓) and up-bow (∨) introduced by Parisian violinists.

The position at the instrument

The manner of holding the instrument for solo playing remained consistent until the final decades of the nineteenth century: playing without an endpin was the most common attitude. Piatti, Grützmacher, Hausmann, Rabaud and Whitehouse were among the last players to advocate this hold, described by Arthur Broadley:

> The player to sit on the front part of the chair with the feet advanced, the left a little more forward than the right. The 'cello to be held with the legs, the lower part of the front edge [table] of the instrument being held in position by the right calf – the edge of the back being supported by the left calf – the legs of the player not to cover the ribs of the instrument so that the vibration is not impeded. The upper part of the back to the right of where the neck of the instrument is fitted should rest against the chest of the performer, this will throw the scroll of the instrument a little to the left of the face. The instrument to be held high enough for the bowing to clear the knees of the player.[11]

The endpin gradually came into fashion among solo players during the second half of the nineteenth century.[12] For those who adopted the device – Servais, Davidoff and De Swert were among the earliest advocates – the height of the cello from the ground remained about the same as when the endpin was not used. According to Broadley, 'the legs are not required to hold the 'cello, the left knee alone being brought into use as a slight support – not to hold the instrument from the ground, but to prevent it from rocking backwards and forwards'.[13] De Swert's portrayal is shown in Figure 11.1.

The cello hold varied to a greater degree among accompanists. Eighteenth-century players frequently played larger cellos, the girth of these instruments requiring the cello to be placed on the floor, either on the left foot, or resting on some type of lifting and holding device such as a short endpin. Resting the cello on the left foot remained traditional among French cellists through to the beginning of the nineteenth century[14] and Lamare was noted for using this hold, even for solo playing.[15]

Until the end of the Victorian period, the practice of women playing the cello was considered to be socially unacceptable. For those who wished to defy decorum, the cello could be held in the usual manner; an endpin was a decided convenience or, according to Van der Straeten, there were two other methods

> which are more graceful, and therefore more frequently followed. The first and best is to turn both legs to the left, bending the right knee and placing it under the left one. The left edge of the back should rest against the left knee, and the instrument against the chest, in a slanting position.
> The second is, to rest the right knee on a cushion or stool concealed by the back of the instrument, the latter leaning against the left knee.[16]

A third position, disliked by Van der Straeten, involved crossing the right leg over the left, the instrument resting against the right leg.

Basic left-hand placement took one of two forms. Influenced by violin posture, and represented by Romberg (see Fig. 11.2), the oblique hand-setting brought the thumb around to the C-string side of the neck, with the fingers falling at a slant upon the fingerboard. This position was com-monplace among eighteenth-century players, many of whom found it convenient for an instrument with a thick neck joint and held low to the floor; it was the hand-position advocated by Janson, Romberg and Vaslin. Both Romberg and Vaslin stated that it created more reliable strength in their neck-position fingerings.[17] The other hand-setting, shown in the illustration of De Swert (see Fig. 11.1), placed the thumb in the centre of the neck, with the rounded fingers lying perpendicular to the fingerboard. This was the positioning taught by the majority of cellists who published

Fig. 11.1 The manner of holding the cello and bow as illustrated in the tutor of Jules de Swert

Fig. 11.2 The manner of holding the cello and bow as illustrated in the tutor of Bernhard Romberg

tutors, John Gunn and Jean-Louis Duport being especially vociferous on the subject.[18] Generally, only one position was advocated for the thumb: it was placed perpendicularly across two strings, the palm of the hand was rounded, and the fingers placed on their tips.[19]

Holding the bow

Conventional bow-holds of the eighteenth and nineteenth centuries generally fall into three categories: over-hand above the frog, over-hand at the frog and under-hand at the frog. The under-hand grip duplicated that of gambists and, as exemplified by Johann Schetky, was employed throughout the early years of the nineteenth century.[20] Over-hand holds followed violin practice. According to Muffat and Corrette, some French players of the early eighteenth century placed their fingers on top of the stick, with the thumb underneath the hair.[21] The prevailing method was to place the little finger in front of the frog, and the thumb on the stick between the second or third finger. The slant of the knuckles towards the tip varied somewhat between players, although all agreed that the leverage of the forefinger was most important in achieving the various nuances of bowing. This hand-position – with minor variations as to distance from the frog, placement of the little finger on or over the stick, and finger proximity to the hair – remained acceptable throughout the nineteenth century, especially among French and Belgian players (see again Fig. 11.1).

French violinists led the way in altering eighteenth-century bow-holds: an over-hand grip at the frog was an important component of their methodology. Although French cellists did not, in this instance, follow suit, Romberg (Fig. 11.2), using Tourte-design bows, appreciated the increased leverage against the strings which resulted from a bow-grip at the frog, and he is the first cellist documented as advocating this playing method.[22] Dotzauer, Kummer and Lee followed Romberg's lead, as did later nineteenth-century German and Russian cellists, but the wrist and fingers were held in a more relaxed and rounded position. Both French and German practices were influential throughout the period on players of other schools: Casals, for instance, used a grip above the frog in his early career.[23]

The development of fingering technique

The principles of neck-position fingerings were devised according to two stratagems. As cellists of the early eighteenth century gradually extended

Ex. 11.1 Common eighteenth-century finger assignments

A. Corrette's fingerings
B. Lanzetti's fingerings
C. Baumgartner's fingerings

Ex. 11.2 The finger assignments of Jean-Louis Duport

A. Diatonic fingerings
B. Extended fingerings

their range beyond first position, one system adapted violin fingerings to the larger instrument, with intervals of both semitones and whole tones being executed with the same finger. According to Corrette's instructions (see Ex. 11.1), the fingers required for first and second positions were the first, second or fourth, while the first, second and third fingers were used in third and fourth positions.[24] Third and fourth positions were also frequently compressed with whole tones being taken sequentially with the first, second, third and fourth fingers.

Later eighteenth-century tutors designated a finger for each semitone in half, first and second position, and necessary extensions were taken most frequently, although not exclusively, with the second finger. Distinctions between third and fourth positions were made according to note patterns and, as demonstrated in the fingerings of Lanzetti and Baumgartner (see Ex. 11.1), compression of the third and fourth positions continued; such fingerings were also permissible for sequences above fourth position.

The second method, eventually considered to be more idiomatic to the instrument, fingered each semitone with a separate digit throughout the first four positions, with no compression of third and fourth position (see Ex. 11.2). Extensions, which were necessary when intervals were changed from a minor to a major third, were limited to the second finger, with rare exceptions allowing an extension with the fourth finger. Pitches above fourth position were assigned the first, second and third fingers. This system

Ex. 11.3 B. Romberg, *A Complete Theoretical and Practical School*, p. 47

Ex. 11.4 N. Baudiot, *Méthode*, vol. I, p. 21 (treble clef one octave higher than played)

became the hallmark of those cellists who were influenced by Berteau, the treatise of Jean-Louis Duport being the definitive work on the subject.

By the nineteenth century, the practicality of the French system led to the general codification of diatonic fingerings within the first four positions, but variations in shifting practices persisted. Many players of the late eighteenth and early nineteenth centuries sought to organise shifting methodology as a strict adjunct to regulated fingering patterns; the key issue was continuity of phrasing uninterrupted by shifting. Jean-Louis Duport achieved this by using sequential fingerings, the shift always being performed from one finger to another. In his words this was because

> everyone knows that the delicacy of touch of the fingers is what makes a pearl, and for certain, one does not have this touch when one slides one finger from one semitone to another, because if the timing of the bow has not caught the moment when the finger has slid to attack the string, a disagreeable sound follows.[25]

While many French and English cellists of the first half of the nineteenth century followed Duport's strictures, others found that same-finger shifting, especially between semitones or whole tones, made intonation more reliable as the shifts remained small, especially when lengthy slurs were added to the equation. This method of shifting, illustrated by Corrette, was customary among earlier players and remained popular among cellists with German associations, including Alexander, Bideau and Romberg (see Ex. 11.3). Another more widely accepted skill was the finger-replacement shift, a technique illustrated as early as Corrette's tutor. This method of changing position came to be used with articulated slurs; Baudiot noted that players of his era found that combination of bowing and fingering to be very expressive (see Ex. 11.4).[26]

Ex. 11.5 H. Rabaud, *Méthode*, p. 23

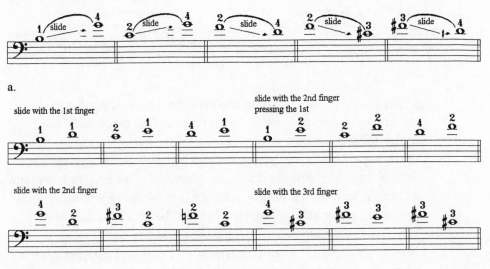

a.

b.

Shifting methodology for those players who followed the generation of Duport, Baudiot and Romberg was formulated with differing priorities. As the nature of melody and use of timbre transmuted into Romantic forms, players, instead of using shifts primarily to expand range, increasingly employed shifting to add colour and expression to music, or for visual, virtuoso effect. While sequential patterns and finger-replacement shifts remained a part of performance practice – sequential fingerings being especially favoured for scales – same-finger shifting became the most common means of moving from one interval to another in differing positions. Rabaud and Davidoff each presented an in-depth discussion of the rules which accompanied changes of position, their shifting practices being reduced to two basic principles: shifts were either (1) taken with the finger that has just been used (see Ex. 11.5a), or (2) executed with the finger that is about to be used (see Ex. 11.5b). Either formula may necessitate the use of a grace-note to guide the hand to its new setting.

The expansion of the solo cellist's range presented an early quandary that was only partially solved by imitating violinists' shifting practices. While players and luthiers also experimented with an increased range by including a higher-tuned string, during the 1730s virtuosos determined that the most practical way of expanding their technical repertory was to employ the thumb as a playing digit. The thumb is used as a moveable nut, with an octave span created by the placement of the thumb and third finger on adjacent strings. Historically, integration of the fourth finger and the C string into upper-register fingering patterns are the only issues for which guidelines were markedly varied.

Ex. 11.6 S. Lee, *Méthode*, p. 49

Instructions from Corrette and Lanzetti demonstrate that players of the mid-eighteenth century commonly added the fourth finger to upper-register or thumb-position patterns, starting with the thumb placed on e^1 (see Ex. 11.1).[27] Fingerings using all four fingers developed into a stylistic attribute for such players as Tricklir, Schetky and Romberg. In contrast, Berteau's French school did not consider use of the fourth finger to be appropriate beyond the occasional addition of an extra note to a scale pattern lying on the A string, and it was only after Romberg's technical mannerisms were incorporated into French technique by Baudiot that the fourth finger was prominently used by Conservatoire-trained players.

Before the 1820s the usual method of playing in thumb-position was to set the hand in stationary, block hand-positions, playing as many notes as possible within the horizontally placed octaves before moving to the next hand-setting. According to Romberg, Boccherini used clef changes to indicate his hand-positions, while notated fingerings to this effect are found in works by Filtz, Tricklir, Schetky, Jan Stiastny, Anton Kraft and Romberg.[28] This procedure allowed for speed, precision and clarity within a wide range of notes. Tricklir and Romberg in particular marked their expansion of the hand-setting to include the C string, Romberg exploiting the leveraged, lower bow grip to make playing in the upper registers of the lower strings his idiosyncratic hallmark.[29] Again, it was only after Baudiot integrated this feature of Romberg's playing into nineteenth-century French methodology that French cellists consistently incorporated the C string into their own solo literature.[30]

The next generation of virtuosos considered block, stationary hand-settings to be too confining, especially with regard to the development of sentimental phrasing. While such thumb-position fingerings remained familiar, players continued to devise different methods of fingering upper-register passages: one method maintains the thumb in one setting while the fingers move outward into consecutive positions. This concept is found in French technique as early as Jean-Louis Duport's *Essai* (Etude 20) and was later illustrated by Lee (see Ex. 11.6). However, Davidoff, who gave precedence to the sonority of the upper strings for his melodies, is credited with codifying these fingerings into a universally accepted principle (Davidoff's hinge).[31]

Elements of colour

While the basic sounds of the violin family are generated by a simple vibrating string and fingered pitches, additional complexity is achieved through the application of varied bowing techniques and special effects. Although pre-twentieth-century cellists universally agreed that they were incapable of executing all of the many violin bowing idioms on their larger instrument, they nevertheless successfully adapted numerous bow-strokes and bowing patterns, together with various special effects, to the cello. Some of these techniques became standard to all violoncellists, regardless of time-period or geographic location, while others began as the provenance of one group of musicians and were eventually disseminated and adapted to regional preferences or stylistic trends.

Bowing patterns and varied strokes were first devised by Italian players; Lanzetti, for instance, achieved distinction for his abilities with slurred staccato.[32] However, the use of varied bowings as a virtuoso device became especially attractive to French performers who, at least from the time of Lully, were indoctrinated with a national sense of bowing uniformity and precision structured in accordance with the rule of down-bow. In addition to the fundamentals of *détaché*, slurs, slur/*détaché* combinations and arpeggios, favoured techniques included *bariolage, batteries, brisure, piqué,* slurred staccato and natural harmonics. As outlined in the methods of Tillière and Cupis, eighteenth-century French teachers regulated the string-crossing patterns of *batteries* and *brisure* into precise formulas, these tutors being the first to apply reversed bowings (starting with an up-bow rather than a down-bow) to patterns which alternate between a low string and a high string. Duport provided specific instructions for dotted-rhythm *piqué* bowings, preferring separate strokes to the linking of the long and short note-values.[33]

Berteau is credited with incorporating natural harmonics into solo literature; this feature of his playing was remarked on by Rousseau and notated in Berteau's extant sonatas.[34] The French school integrated both natural and artificial harmonics into their teaching and solo works, and Jean-Louis Duport apparently developed a third species of harmonic: described as 'something between a firm note and an Harmonic', this effect was produced 'not by pressing the finger tightly against the Finger-board, but by bending the string sideways from right to left'.[35]

Slurred staccato was also favoured by Berteau and his students. This bowing was specifically differentiated from separate staccato, which, until the beginning of the nineteenth century, was defined as a separate, dry stroke of Italian origin.[36] At this time, the most common method of executing slurred staccato (designated 'the Feather' by Robert Crome) was to

Ex. 11.7 Articulation for *détaché* bowing

keep the bow on the string and articulate each note with a short bite.[37] The first and last notes were played louder than the interior notes, and slurred staccato could be executed with both down- and up-strokes. It should be noted that, despite frequent use, French players such as Jean-Louis Duport considered it to be a most difficult stroke to execute.[38]

Austro-German performers of the eighteenth century, excluding the French-born Tricklir, did not have the same appreciation of defined bow-strokes as their French contemporaries, and regulated bowing patterns, slurred staccato and natural harmonics were little used by these players until the beginning of the nineteenth century. Instead, Austro-German cellists generated musical interest through contrasting sonorities and variable dynamics. The timbre of the C string's full range was significant to Austro-German cello playing, as attested by the concertos of Haydn, Anton Kraft, Tricklir, Romberg and Beethoven, and the sonatas of Beethoven and Jan Stiastny. Other works which demonstrate interesting variations of sonority are the concertos of Ritter, who often used scordatura and who was described as performing slow movements with a heavy mute, thus altering the cello's timbre.[39] *Sul ponticello*, also designated *alla gamba*, was another colouring technique applied by German performers to solo passages. French practice, in comparison, limited the technique to accompaniment figures of rapidly played notes.

Alterations to instrument and bow design, as well as the interaction of violinists and cellists who toured during the years of the French Revolution and following wars, greatly expanded the repertory of bowing techniques, special effects, and the universality of their application to the cello. In the years around the turn of the nineteenth century, the execution of *détaché*, separate staccato and *martelé* strokes remained consistent with previously established practices. Separation was required between each articulated note, the part of the bow used being determined by the tempo of execution. According to the teachers of the Paris Conservatoire, *détaché* notes of moderate tempo (see Ex. 11.7) were played in the middle of the bow, and separation was achieved by pulling a fast stroke, quickly stopped. *Détaché* notes of a fast tempo were played similarly, but in the upper third of the bow. Notes assigned a *martelé* wedge were a little longer than *détaché* notes, and also longer than notes marked with dots (which were to be short), but were played with the bow removed far enough from the bridge for the sound to be round and sweet.[40]

The most obvious changes in bow management generated by the Tourte-design bow concerned the systematic lengthening of slur group-ings and the continued widening of dynamic variations. Following Romberg's practices, German performers of the Dresden school devel-oped an especially broad legato style of playing: power of sound through-out the instrument's full range was the focus. However, Romberg also integrated all forms of harmonics into standard technique. Perhaps because of the lower, leveraged bow grip, this school remained conserva-tive in its use of slurred staccato and the evolving forms of off-the-string bowings. This conservatism did not extend to other cellists of the Austro-Hungarian empire, as numerous examples of slurred staccato exist in the works of Alexander, the Stiastnys and Joseph Merk.

Virtuoso proficiency with different bowings remained a focal point of the French cello school. Bowings in which the hair leaves the string, such as *spiccato* and *sautillé*, began appearing in French teaching and solo works in the late 1820s. Emulating the showmanship of virtuoso violinists, Servais made *sautillé*, *spiccato* and other forms of 'springing' bow-strokes a promi-nent feature of Belgian technique by the mid-point of the century. Familiarity with these bowings was subsequently expected of every late-nineteenth century player.

Several other colouring devices underwent changes between the early years of the eighteenth century and the final years of the nineteenth century. Vibrato, for instance, fluctuated in popularity according to time-period, region and individual taste. Dotzauer commented that vibrato was especially favoured by Italian players, indeed the violinist Geminiani is the primary eighteenth-century source for information regarding vibrato for cellists.[41] Recommending that 'it should be made use of as often as possi-ble', Geminiani considered that variable rates of width and speed were necessary according to the 'affect' of the music.[42]

The popularity of vibrato among eighteenth-century cellists is affirmed by Romberg, who remarked that 'an improved taste has at length exploded the abuse of this embellishment'.[43] He recommended that vibrato be limited to the enhancement of a strong bow stroke. Dotzauer and Kummer, while continuing to caution against over-use, also consid-ered vibrato a positive addition to long, sustained notes.

Injunctions against exaggerated vibrato usage continued throughout the nineteenth century, although such warnings suggest that players applied the technique to disparate degrees. In 1884 Vaslin complained that 'the constant vibration of the left hand' becomes monotonous.[44] At the turn of the century, opposing viewpoints were offered by Broadley and

Van der Straeten. Broadley counselled that vibrato was especially necessary in sustained passages, its speed being adjusted to suit dynamic levels
and sonority; 'A note low in pitch,' he wrote, 'or a note played *piano*,
requires a slow vibrato, a higher note, or a note played forte and passion-
ately, requires a rapid vibrato'.[45] Van der Straeten, similarly recommending that the motion be modified to suit tempo and phrasing, was
nevertheless of the opinion that 'the student cannot be warned too
earnestly against the abuse of the vibrato, as it is quite as objectionable on
an instrument as in a voice'.[46]

Portamento also created controversy among nineteenth-century performers. Classified as an expressive form of appoggiatura by late eighteenth-century players, 'expressive' shifting evolved into a fingering device
as melodies came to be contained within lengthy slur groupings. Romberg,
Dotzauer and Kummer considered portamento to be an emotional
enhancement similar to vibrato, with Romberg still categorising the technique as an ornament. To the following generations of cellists, portamento
became intimately connected to shifting technique, and the frequency
with which such fingerings were chosen was a matter of taste. There was
the strict, Classical school of Vaslin and Cossmann, who were restrained in
their use of 'glides'. According to Broadley, the finest players of this school
'are noted for their perfect intonation, but are also noted for their lack of
sentiment'.[47] In contrast, there were those who were described as playing
in an overly sentimental 'salon style'. Cellists such as Alexander Batta and J.
F. Mendes, who were especially popular with female Parisian audiences,
were frequently castigated by 'refined' male listeners for their emulation of
the popular tenor Giovanni Battista Rubini (1794–1854). Characteristics
of this style included rubato tempo fluctuations, portamento 'sobs', and
exaggerated use of *piano* and *forte*.[48]

In presenting what he considered to be the average view of portamento,
Broadley outlined specific guidelines detailing the effects with which he
was familiar. He stated that there were two 'active' methods of using portamento for expression: the 'glide' could be applied to pitches as a means of
preparing a cadence, or it could be introduced 'in imitation of that produced by vocalists when two notes are taken on a vowel sound; the only
difference to be observed by the cellist is that the interval, and consequently
the glide, must not be so strongly marked'.[49] 'Passive' forms of portamento,
according to Broadley, covered difficulties inherent to the instrument, for
instance bridging awkward leaps. He also remarked that some players
applied portamento to detached strokes, anticipating the bow change in
order to create an appoggiatura effect. Another exaggerated effect was
induced when a strongly marked 'glide' was completed with a *sforzando*, a
technique popularised in England by the violinist John Dunn.[50]

Ex. 11.8(a) P. Baillot, *Méthode*, p. 132
(b) H. Rabaud, *Méthode*, p. 71
(c) A. Broadley, *Chats*, p. 66

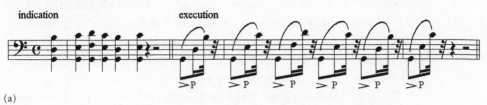

(a)

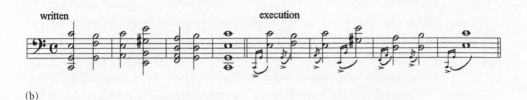

(b)

(c)

Techniques for playing chords also varied. Beginning with the lowest pitch, pizzicato chords could be arpeggiated with the thumb, but strings were also plucked simultaneously: Baudiot caught each string with a separate finger, while Romberg played the G and C strings with the thumb, the D string with the first finger, and the A string with the second finger.[51] Until the mid-nineteenth century, bowed chords were arpeggiated, with emphasis being placed on the lowest pitch (see Ex. 11.8a). Later nineteenth-century performers continued to articulate the pitches of the G and C strings separately, but, with emphasis moving to the upper notes through comparative length of note-values, they struck the A and D strings simultaneously (see Ex. 11.8b). By the beginning of the twentieth century, it was common to divide four-note chords by first playing the lowest two pitches, then sustaining the upper two pitches (see Ex. 11.8c).

Accompanimental skills

While most eighteenth- and nineteenth-century cello instructions address solo techniques, Schetky noted that proficiency in accompaniment

'should be the first Object of a Violoncellist, the Instrument being principally invented and intended for that purpose'.[52] For eighteenth-century
players, this involved continuo playing and the accompaniment of recitative. In assuming these duties, cellists were expected to be adept at either
leading or following a melody line with appropriately regulated rhythm,
metre and tempo. Before the advent of Maelzel's metronome, it was not
uncommon to keep time by tapping a foot.[53]

Throughout the middle of the nineteenth century, accompanists were
expected to be fully conversant with the rules of harmony. Not only was
such knowledge considered essential when determining how appropriate
nuances were to be applied to phrasing which followed harmonic structure, but, using arpeggio figurations or other chord-based patterns,
accompanists were often expected to realise figured-bass notation of the
continuo line or recitative when keyboard players were unavailable.[54]

Recitatives were most commonly accompanied by arpeggiation of the
chord, the key note being sounded by a double bassist. Added improvisation or embellishments, were also added by cellists, although these were
discouraged in instruction manuals. Such improvisation could be, as in
the case of Robert Lindley, an ego-enhancing demonstration of a player's
capabilities or, according to Baudiot, a means of filling in an awkward gap
in the performance when singers forgot their words or were slow to arrive
on stage.[55]

By the beginning of the twentieth century, as the piano became the
accompanimental instrument of choice and compositions dispensed with
both *secco* recitative and improvised cadenzas, improvisational skills came
to be considered anachronistic. 'It used to be customary for singers and
instrumentalists to take more liberty in the introduction of graces and
embellishments than is allowed in modern times', remarked Broadley in
1899. 'It is not now considered good taste to embellish a composition –
even the simplest melody – by the addition of anything to the written
notes', he continued, 'the modern artist, especially the instrumentalist,
must content himself with his individual treatment of what is before him,
depending solely on this, and the beauty of the composition for his
effect'.[56]

12 The development of cello teaching in the twentieth century

R. CAROLINE BOSANQUET

c. 1900–c. 1940

At the turn of the twentieth century the cello was usually considered a man's instrument, due largely to Victorian ideas of female decorum. General standards of playing were not particularly high – in 1890, Bernard Shaw had likened the sound of the cello to a 'bumble-bee buzzing inside a stone jar'![1] Much of the literature which was to provide the basis of cello instruction for the next hundred years either already existed or would appear within fifteen years. This literature was intended for the mature player, since young child beginners were rare. However, the availability of small cellos was increasing in the wake of the developing production of small violins,[2] and the metal, retractable cello spike,[3] though not in general use, was gradually gaining acceptance. Pablo Casals and Emanuel Feuermann helped to transform cello performance into an art of the highest order during the first half of the century, their playing incorporating a new ease and fluidity of physical movement as the basis of their technical command.

Early twentieth-century pedagogical material was logically presented, starting in the lower positions and working towards the higher ones, but often failed to take into account what was physically most appropriate for the player. It comprised systematic tutors, studies which focused on specific technical aspects, and short exercises for daily practice. Apart from Carl Fuchs' *Violoncello Method* (3 vols., London, 1906), this material was neither musically rewarding nor suitable for the young beginner,[4] most tutors being written by famous players who omitted to explain fully the reasons for their recommendations.

The first aspect discussed in both Piatti's revised *Violoncello Method*[5] and Fuchs's *Method* was whether or not to use the spike (see Fig. 12.1). Fuchs remarked: 'Although it is not advisable to allow beginners to play without a spike, I think it is useful to play without. The body must then of necessity be kept still, and anyone who has fallen into the habit of holding the legs in an ugly position, can remedy this evil by practising without the endpin'.[6] He continued: 'Ladies always use a spike. They can either cross the right leg over or put it back under the left leg and place the cello against

Fig. 12.1 Carl Fuchs's method of holding the cello (*Violoncello-Schule*)

the right side, or hold it as nearly as possible in the way men do'.[7] Beatrice
Harrison and Madame Suggia soon showed that the 'men's way' worked
best, and Fuchs later used a spike himself.[8] Piatti never used a spike,
although the posthumous revised edition of his treatise states that the
spike is 'generally adopted at the present'.[9]

Cello teachers of this period always started with long slow bows and

Ex. 12.1 The first item in Percy Such's *New School of Cello Studies*, vol. I

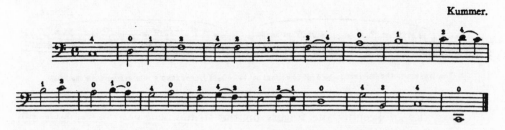

Ex. 12.2 Open-string bowing with accompaniment, from Carl Fuchs's *Violoncello Method*

encouraged the use of the whole bow. A study from Percy Such's collection of 1913 is typical (see Ex. 12.1). Fuchs was innovative in providing a piano part to accompany slow open-string bowing, making a simple thing into a rewarding musical experience (see Ex. 12.2). The slow bow-start, still used today, was rethought by Suzuki and Rolland after analysis of small children's natural, quick movements. The customary start with the notes of C major, as in piano playing, had its disadvantages; while the keyboard pattern of white notes repeats at the octave, a cello pattern repeats at the fifth with each new string. A C major start requires the pupil to finger 1 34 on the lower and 12 4 on the upper strings. However, the Dotzauer–Klingenberg treatise starts by giving the same patterns on all strings in a somewhat more modern manner.[10] Unlike Curwen's piano tutor of 1886, no cello method suggested singing first.

Cello pupils were expected initially to master first position, the potentially most uncomfortable part of the cello, where the hand is nearest to the scroll and the fingers are the most widely spaced.[11] Although prohibited for some time from making shifts, pupils were nevertheless expected to undertake various unnecessarily complex string-crossings and bowing patterns early on. They were also instructed to hold down as many fingers as possible, which, though useful for ingraining a mechanical map of the fingerboard, can cause undesirable tension. Example 12.3 spells agony for a near-beginner, particularly one with small hands. Nevertheless, the prac-

Ex. 12.3 A later excerpt from Percy Such's *New School of Cello Studies*, vol. I

The fingers on the **Minims** to be kept down, but not to be held longer than a semiquaver with the bow

tice of keeping the fingers on the strings whenever possible is still common, despite criticism from Eisenberg, Bunting and Pleeth.[12] Eisenberg observes: 'Formerly the lifting and hitting of the fingers was done mechanically like striking hammers on a piano. Corks were often placed between second and third fingers. This led to a well-drilled but inflexible hand'.[13]

When shifting was eventually allowed, the neck-positions (second, third, fourth) were studied in a similar manner; and because fifth, sixth, seventh and thumb-positions were so long delayed, many cellists either never reached them or constantly feared playing in the higher registers. In thumb-position, the thumb was required to be held firmly down across two strings; and instead of progressing gradually, writers prescribed complex patterns almost immediately, followed by octaves and thirds, as in Grützmacher's *Daily Exercises* (1909).

Cellists did not generally understand that the arm, indeed the whole body, naturally works as an entity, each movement of one part having a response elsewhere. Casals was taught to play with a book under his arm 'to improve forearm movement', while Piatti remarks, 'the change from one string to another is effected by the wrist, without moving the upper part of the arm'.[14] Fuchs, however, describes a long bow-stroke incorporating use of the upper arm, and observes that the so-called 'wrist movements' described in other tutors are in fact pendulum-like swings of the hand. But even he fell into the trap of isolating a limb for bow-changes at the heel and point: 'The beginning and the end of each bow should be played with the hand only . . . Practise long bows, stopping each one about four or five inches from the end and completing the bow with the hand alone'.[15] Piatti's physical description of vibrato also demonstrates the isolation of a part of the arm: 'vibrato consists of a wide movement of the left hand and should be acquired by practising a slow semi-circular movement coming from the wrist . . . The thumb should remain in contact with the neck'.[16] Nowadays, the resultant effect would be considered the vibrato of a poor amateur.[17] The technical exercises from this period constitute the backbone of training material for classical tonal music, and are still widely used, with the danger that old 'stiff' patterns are perpetuated despite modern advances in technical knowledge.

Ex. 12.4 An 'add-a-note' scale, from W. E. Whitehouse's *Half Minute Violoncello Studies*

Ex. 12.5 Scale with 'helping notes', from Becker's *Finger and Bow Exercises and Scale Studies*

Some albums of studies were graded in order of difficulty (e.g. Such's collection of 1913), while others were of one standard, such as Popper's advanced *High School of Cello Playing* (1901–5), the technical bible of the professional cellist. The most significant sets of short exercises include: Grützmacher's *Daily Exercises* (1909), starting with string-crossings, and ending with thumb-position; Cossmann's *Etudes* (1900), beginning with double-stop trills in combined rhythms, including two-against-three, and concluding with thumb-position involving unusually frequent use of the fourth finger; Whitehouse's *Half Minute Violoncello Studies* (1916), including 'add-a-note scales' (see Ex. 12.4) which foreshadow Margaret Rowell in the 1970s, a chromatic scale on one finger (again similar to Rowell), the 'add-a-note' principle applied in thumb-position, and useful exercises for travelling into and out of the thumb-position; and Becker's *Finger and Bow Exercises and Scale Studies* (1900), which utilise 'helping notes' for shifts involving a string-change and for descending shifts on the same string (see Ex. 12.5), Becker instructing that these helping notes should become increasingly shorter and lighter until they are inaudible.

The evidence of early recordings and other sources points to the fact that vibrato was not used continuously at the beginning of the century. Portamento, however, was a prominent stylistic element. This situation was to change as the century progressed.[18]

The most sought-after teachers were the Germans Becker and Klengel. Becker's most important publication was *Mechanik und Aesthetik des Violoncellspiels* (Vienna, 1929/R1971), written in collaboration with Dago Rynar. Klengel produced numerous pedagogical works and was remarkably flexible in his teaching. 'If you found a particular technique was comfortable for you, he let you use it', remarked Maurice Zimbler. 'He never interfered with a pupil's natural way of holding the bow or the cello'.[19]

Cello instruction in Britain was boosted by the work of the Waddell

Fig. 12.2 One hundred cellos: concert given by the London Violoncello School in 1925

School in Edinburgh, originally founded as a violin school by William Waddell in the late nineteenth century, and the London Violoncello School. On leaving the Royal College of Music in 1909, Waddell's daughter Ruth started teaching the cello at his school, with pupils being encouraged to begin at an early age. The school, still flourishing today, has moulded several distinguished cellists, notably Joan Dickson, Jane Cowan, Margaret Moncrieff and Moray Welsh.[20] Interestingly, Kitty Gregorson, a former pupil who later taught there until 1996, aged ninety, believes that Rolland's first string workshop in Britain (1974) was the most important event in the development of British string teaching. Rolland's theories are based on the free use of the whole body in relation to string playing.

In 1919 Herbert Walenn, a pupil of Becker, founded the London Cello School with the encouragement of Casals, who became its patron. The Walenn School, which flourished until its closure at Walenn's death in 1953, had a significant effect on the promotion of cello playing in England. Figure 12.2 depicts one of the school's regular concerts of massed cellos in 1925. The leader is the young John Barbirolli, who was a distinguished cellist before becoming conductor of the Hallé Orchestra, and the conductor is Walenn himself. Note the large number of female cellists, surprising for 1925, and all are using spikes. Many distinguished players were taught at the school, including Zara Nelsova and Jacqueline du Pré as children.

Casals founded the Ecole Normale in Paris in 1919, Diran Alexanian undertaking most of his teaching because of Casals's busy performing career. Alexanian's *Traité théoretique et pratique du Violoncelle* (Paris, 1922) is based on Casals's ideas, but its initial popularity did not last, because it over-emphasised very big stretches (of the interval of the fourth) and indulged in over-complex explanation. Casals observed in his introduction that the playing techniques of other instruments had 'gone through an evolution that violoncello 'Methods' alone have refused to follow'. He said that were Duport to come back to life he would be astonished at the lack of progress since his *Essai sur le doigté du violoncelle, et sur la conduite de l'archet* (Paris, 1806). Marjorie Enix confirms this: 'Scientific advancements in the study of anatomy, physiology, musical acoustics and engineering had produced a wealth of new and relevant information of potential value in instrumental performance and teaching. But unlike pedagogical systems for violin and piano, which had begun to accommodate to these musical and scientific changes, that of the cello had undergone no comprehensive revision'.[21]

The Ecole Normale in Paris was the centre to which cellists from all over the world came in the pre-war period for Casals's masterclasses. At the end of his life, he was giving similar masterclasses in America, and his countless technical and musical innovations provided the inspiration for books by Eisenberg and Bunting.[22] Casals never committed himself to paper because he believed he was developing constantly. He started from the premise that 'a score is like a straitjacket, whereas music, like life itself, is constant movement . . . spontaneous, free from any restriction'.[23] He caused a furore amongst the traditionalists by seeking to develop 'complete freedom of movement in the right arm, including the elbow . . . such free action making the whole bow technique stronger and easier'. He also 'undertook to revise the method of fingering and the action of the left hand', preserving his 'natural line of approach and observation of life and nature'.[24] In spite of small hands, he often chose 1 23 for tone–semitone rather than 1 34, and even extended 1 4 to the interval of the fourth. He later dropped this last idea because of unnecessary strain to the hand. The use of appropriate extensions served the ends of cleaner musical expressiveness, and eliminated inappropriate portamenti. As Carl Flesch remarked, 'Casals showed the difference between technical glissandi, and expressive and necessary glissandi . . . That's why, thanks to Casals, contemporary cellists give more artistic satisfaction than ever before'.[25]

Casals first formulated the concept of 'expressive intonation',[26] the emphasis for artistic purposes of the 'majorness' or 'minorness' of certain notes of a key, or of change of key. He advocated the individual use of the left-hand fingers instead of the conventional method of holding them down, thereby facilitating vibrato. Eisenberg, his pupil and also a teacher at the Ecole Normale, summarised the artistic potential of vibrato thus: 'Vibrato supplies a palette of colours from which to choose . . . and should be capable of producing as many shades and nuances as there are in a painting'.[27] Casals felt the diminuendo to be 'the life of music', and that 'the law of the diminuendo is as essential in the communication of music as it is in speech'.[28] He also differentiated between the dynamic accent and the agogic accent, and used an energetic percussive left-hand action and gentle plucking, giving additional clarity and forming the basis of the left-hand teaching of Eisenberg, Bunting and Stutschewsky.[29] Some, however, have found such percussive use of the fingers too aggressive.

Simultaneously with the developments at the Ecole Normale in Paris, the cellists Feuillard and Bazelaire were doing excellent pedagogical work at the Paris Conservatoire. Feuillard, teacher of Tortelier, produced a musical and well-constructed tutor for children *Méthode du Jeune Violoncelliste* (Paris, 1925). Like Romberg, whom he quoted, he believed that teachers should clarify their pupils' aims with the minimum means and back these up immediately by musical reward. He criticised the practice of setting endless studies of minimal musical content, like Mrs Curwen had done in piano pedagogy fifty years earlier. Feuillard's *Daily Exercises* of 1919 aim to achieve maximum result with minimum means. He also wrote many volumes of classical arrangements with piano, to be used in conjunction with *Le Jeune Violoncelliste*, and eight volumes of graded cello studies, inviting Tortelier to compose the final study of the last volume. He also adapted Ševčík's bowing exercises for the cello in 1905.

Bazelaire, like Feuillard, was a pupil of Delsart and he was a highly respected teacher and composer, writing several pedagogical texts.[30] Like Silva and Rudolf Matz, he disapproved of excessive stretching, considering it to be dangerous for all but the largest hands.[31] Guy Fallot reveals that Bazelaire gave all his cello lessons from the piano and described everything so clearly that demonstration at the cello was unnecessary.[32] Bazelaire's pupils had to go to his concerts to hear him play.

Three other cellists – Maurice Maréchal, Enrico Mainardi and Gaspar Cassadó – should be mentioned for their particular contribution to cello technique. Maréchal, a distinguished performer and teacher at the Paris Conservatoire (1921–42) and friend of Casals, is important because, unlike Casals and Feuermann, he championed works of his own time and extended cello technique in the process. Mainardi, himself a composer, also encouraged the performance of contemporary music, doubtless influencing his pupil Siegfried Palm in that regard. Cassadó, the compatriot and favourite pupil of Casals, was the first famous performer to use steel strings (as early as the twenties) in his search for a big sound. Steel strings were destined to become popular in the latter part of the century and also to be useful on very small instruments because their greater tension allowed a stronger sound, and they could be tuned by adjusters at the tailpiece.

The American string teacher Paul Herfurth's *A Tune a Day* (1937) for the cello[33] was the first publication intended for cello tuition in school classes; it was also appropriate for private instrumental lessons. Greatly ahead of its time, it comprised well-known folk tunes, graded in order of difficulty, and was a pioneer in making the early learning process consumer-friendly. Some well-graded albums of studies, such as that of Jacob Sakom (1931), were also published at about this time.

c. 1940 to the present

By the Second World War the model of the ideal cellist had been established: a musician, with technique based on fluid and natural movements completely at the service of the music. Some progress had been made in producing user-friendly teaching material, but it was not until after 1945 that innovative ways of teaching were evolved, particularly in communicating with young pupils and making the learning process pleasurable. The result has been an explosion in the final quarter of the century in both the number and quality of cellists.

After the Second World War, many people's wishes for artistic fulfilment were satisfied by listening to music and playing musical instruments. The radio and gramophone had only recently become widely available, so for the first time the sounds of musical instruments became familiar to almost everyone. Classical music had been enthusiastically received by the troops during the war, and evening classes in music appreciation had also taken place during that period. Along with artistic cravings came the socialist principle of 'opportunities for all', and in many parts of the world. In 1945, string programmes (in multi-string classes) were started in American public schools to match existing wind programmes.[34] Three years later, the USSR established elaborate and well-subsidised music talent programmes, involving selection of potential pupils for specialist training before the age of six. Those selected were considered potential international competition winners and were chosen for 'intelligence, coordination, flexibility and dexterity, aural acuity, their physical attributes and those of their parents ... their main attitudes in respect of "success achievement" ... and their personality type'.[35] Twenty years of specialist training would follow.

Also in 1948, Kodály introduced his 'Kodály System' of music education into Hungarian schools, and many talent schools were also established. Similar talent schools, offering free tuition, were founded in Bulgaria, Czechoslovakia and in most communist countries – about a thousand such schools evolved in the USSR. In Japan, Shin'ichi Suzuki, who had studied the violin in Germany with Klingler, started his 'Talent Education' at Matsumoto in 1945, first for the violin and then adapted for the cello by Sato, a student of Casals. Suzuki believed that every child has an inborn talent which needs to be nurtured from an early age and with the mother's collaboration. In 1948 Hideo Saito, the distinguished pupil of Feuermann, founded a Children's Music School, the Toho Gakuen High School for Music, later to become the first Japanese college of music. Saito (1902–74) was the teacher of many distinguished Japanese cellists, including Tsutsumi.[36]

In post-war England more child cellists were taught at the London Cello School and in the late 1950s and early 60s the state peripatetic system was initiated, offering chosen children, usually in classes, free instrumental tuition. This system grew and flourished during the 1970s and 80s, benefiting many,[37] but financial cutbacks have since resulted in its demise in some areas. In other districts the system has survived, but with children paying for lessons.

Saturday music courses for Juniors were introduced in England at various conservatoires from the 1920s, the children being taught first by students, and later by qualified teachers. Initially subsidised by the state, these have improved and flourished, but are now fee-paying. Talent schools have also been developed, the Menuhin School being the first, and the Purcell School, Chethams (Manchester) and Wells Cathedral School following; and most public schools now have flourishing music departments which offer scholarships for instrumentalists, cellists included. Private cello teaching has also blossomed world-wide, prompted by social factors such as the rise of the motor car (for cello transport) and the increased production of small instruments and bows. The Suzuki factory was a pioneer in the mass production of small instruments from 1945.[38] Initially, the quarter-size was the smallest model produced; but in the late 1970s, the first sixteenth-size violins and tenth-size cellos were manufactured for even younger beginners. Factory-made and part-factory-made cellos flourished in the then communist countries, the best ones for export coming from Romania and East Germany. Along with the mass production of instruments has come an increase in the making of quality instruments and bows by new generations of makers since the war.

In the 1950s, most cello pupils used gut strings tuned from the pegs. The latter were difficult to turn, and the 'raw' gut A and D strings frequently went out of tune, causing frustration to pupil and teacher. Steel strings tuned with adjusters were easier to deal with but very 'stiff' to keep down on the fingerboard. Such strings as Dominant, which are similar in tension to gut but remain in tune like metal, have been an important innovation since the early 1970s and have also been made for quarter, half and three-quarter sizes in the last decade. Quality metal strings which are less stiff to play on, and thus more comfortable, are now being produced (e.g. Jargar). Despite these improvements, cellists such as William Pleeth and Steven Isserlis consider that gut gives the only true cello sound.

Giving the beginner, and especially the young beginner, a really sound start has been an important post-war development. As mentioned earlier, children in Russian talent schools are given a fully professional training from the age of six, with two or even three one-hour lessons per week. In Japan, USA and England the early emphasis has been on carefully directed fun, which also aims at a quality musical result. In Hungary, and later Finland, the 'fun' and 'professional' aspects have been carefully balanced from the outset.

Both Suzuki and Kodály considered their ideas to be 'mother-tongue methods', starting with the premise that the learning method should be simple and should aim to build upon a secure aural base. They included eurhythmic games and introduced microscopic elements one at a time, in order to conquer technical problems gradually. More specifically, Suzuki's teaching system involved pupils in listening to recordings of the music to be played, playing the music several times over, undertaking pre-playing games and movements, and cultivating short and fast initial bowings in keeping with children's natural movements. The teaching of reading was delayed, emphasis being placed on aural development, musical memory and easy, relaxed movements. Children received several short individual lessons each week and a group lesson, all with parent participation.

Kodály considered folk song to be the 'mother-tongue' of a nation. Children started singing with the nursery teacher, and then learned to read music through the John Curwen system of sol-fa, hand-signs, and rhythm names, which transferred gradually to staff. Everything was undertaken vocally in classes for two years, so that children developed a good understanding of musical fundamentals and fluent sight-singing ability before embarking on playing instruments. All the initial music was pentatonic,[39] common in Hungarian folk music, with no semitones and therefore easy to sing.

Violinist Paul Rolland left Hungary for the USA shortly before the war. In 1946, he became a prime mover in founding ASTA (American String Teachers' Association), becoming the first editor of its magazine and later its president. ASTA aimed to provide string teachers with a forum for exchanging ideas and opportunities to participate in workshops and courses.[40] Rolland also developed a teaching method inspired by Suzuki's work and incorporating Suzuki's rhythms, but including elements of reading from the outset. His research project at the University of Illinois eventually resulted in his book and set of films, *The Teaching of Action in String Playing.* He also produced teaching material with Stanley Fletcher and his work had a profound effect on string teaching in the USA. In 1974 he gave the first of a number of annual workshops in England, with cellist Margaret Rowell, who had independently come to similar conclusions, and her assistant Irene Sharpe.[41] This had an equally significant effect on string teaching in the UK, developing an understanding of good string-playing movements and translating them into simple, everyday ideas for comprehension by children. In the later workshops, Joan Dickson adapted for the cello Rolland's demonstrations on the violin. Particularly impor-tant were total body action and balance, and the release of static tensions. Rolland considered 'the "freeze" of the left arm and shoulder', discussed earlier, to be the worst of these tensions, 'traceable to the traditional prac-tice of restricting the left arm of the beginner to first position'. From the outset, he advocated low, middle and high positions to be 'explored through simple shifting exercises using left-hand pizzicato and harmon-ics'.[42] Bowing was taught initially by big pizzicatos with a circling arm, fol-lowed by down-bows with a circling arm. The bow was held at the balance-point initially, so that it was lighter to hold and there was, there-fore, less potential tension. The balance of the right arm and bow was described as 'a teeter-totter [see-saw] whose fulcrum is the string and whose opposite ends are the elbow and bow tip'.[43] All movements of the arms were swings and curves, and the involvement of the whole arm was always emphasised. Repetitious movements such as *détaché, spiccato, sautillé, tremolo* and vibrato were shown to be made up of actions with their reflexes, and the film in which the movement of the upper arm can be seen to be a mirrored movement of the lower arm doing vibrato was a revelation to all who saw it for the first time.

Rolland's ideas were not universally accepted; after his death his work was followed up more in England than in the USA, led by violinist Sheila Nelson and her team. They have combined Rolland's ideas with Kodály's, and with additional innovations in the teaching of sight-reading. They give regular courses for teachers in England and abroad and much useful teaching material has developed from their work.[44]

Phyllis Young's work was also admired by Rolland. She, like Margaret Rowell, had evolved innovative ways of teaching children for the Texas String Project,[45] and harnessed the senses, particularly that of touch, in an imaginative and enjoyable way, promoting free movement. Her books are a goldmine of strategies for teachers using these principles and her workshops are enjoyed by cello teachers internationally, as are those of Irene Sharpe.

Evolved from the principles of Kodály, the 'Colour Strings Method' has been developed in Finland since 1971 by the Hungarian Szilvay brothers. Colour is used as an additional aid in the teaching of reading, and everything starts with the voice and inner hearing. Interval patterns, and harmonics, are used in different parts of the instrument from the start, and ensemble playing is encouraged early (see Fig. 12.3).

First recognised by actors, the work of F. M. Alexander (1869–1955), relating to postural balance and relaxation and enabling efficient use of the body, has been acknowledged by many (but not all) musicians since the 1970s.[46] Alexander teachers are now on the staff of all the major conservatoires in England, and many performers and teachers base their work on Alexander's principles.

Important books on cello playing have appeared in the second half of the century, including Eisenberg's *Cello Playing of Today* (1952) and Janos Starker's *An Organised Method of String Playing, Violoncello Exercises for the Left Hand* (1965). Starker divides the cello fingerboard into twenty-four positions and his exercises, designed for advanced cellists using double-stops, can be adapted for beginners. Their purpose is 'to strengthen fingers and to establish intonation within a given position ... constantly changing double-stops are parts of different harmonies, and so they require adjustments accordingly'.[47] Additionally, there are useful practice suggestions relating to famous concerto passages. Other notable publications include Paul Tortelier's *How I Play, How I Teach* (1975), Christopher Bunting's *Essay on the Craft of Cello Playing* (2 vols., 1982) and William Pleeth's *The Cello* (1982). Pleeth's volume is mostly text, the other two mostly exercises, but Bunting's detailed introduction also includes psychological information.

Like Starker, Bunting believes that the cello fingerboard needs redefining, but he does this by *reducing* the number of basic positions to four: First position, 'Neck' position, 'Viola' position, and 'Violin' position (and their offshoots); as these relate the most easily to open strings and harmonics, they encourage the concept of the string as a whole. Tortelier also treated the cello as a whole and particularly advocated the use of the thumb in the lowest part of the cello. Bunting and Tortelier both follow Casals's principle of finger percussion, but, conversely, Pleeth emphasises

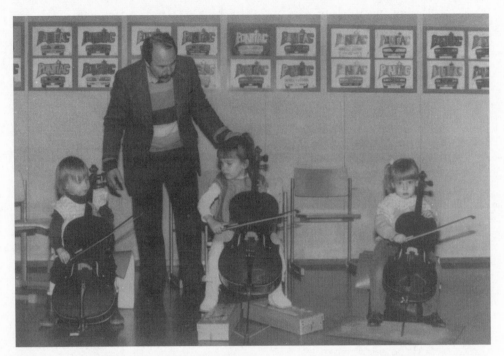

Fig. 12.3 Csaba Szilvay with a group of young pupils

'sensitivity of finger tread'.[48] All three consider 'expressive intonation' of great importance, and the need to adapt it to the piano's equal temperament when in the same octave. Pleeth also discusses intonation for playing in a string ensemble, and for playing with a wind instrument. He advocates a 'sloping' hand-position in all parts of the cello, but Tortelier recommends a 'square' one (relating, of course, to his use of the Tortelier endpin, which puts the cello on a more horizontal plane). Bunting also uses a 'square' position, which becomes more sloped as the hand ascends the cello and moves away from the player's body. Tortelier has innovative suggestions for fingering double-stopped octaves and thirds, and Bunting has many sliding exercises on one finger which train the ear and the spatial sense for pitching both easy and awkward intervals. All three of these books contain a wealth of ideas for the student and professional cellist, Bunting and Tortelier taking the view that the final goal of music is achieved only through technical mastery of the instrument, and Pleeth 'that technique *per se* cannot exist apart from the music it is meant to serve'.[49]

Regrettably, Joan Dickson did not publish a *magnum opus* before her death in 1994. However, her exercises *The Freedom of the Fingerboard* are extremely useful and can be taught aurally to pupils with no formal knowledge of positions, or equally can be used as warm-ups by advanced players. She also made a film on bowing, prior to working with Rolland, which included the concept of 'lanes', different points of contact for the bow in relation to a single pitch and various bow speeds to achieve different timbres. Pleeth likewise emphasises that 'Within the boundaries of that small space on the strings between fingerboard and bridge there dwells the richest variety of colours, textures and dynamics available'.[50] Both liken the bow to a paint brush, and Pleeth and Bunting are unanimously critical of the current unvariable and continuous vibrato.

The Yugoslav Rudolf Matz (1901–88), who collaborated briefly with Silva in the USA, produced much outstanding teaching material. His *The First Years of the Violoncello*, which comprises thirty-two sections, was begun in 1942 and took forty-five years to complete. As Matz was also a composer, his studies and pieces are particularly musical. His user-friendly teaching strategies aim to simplify each technique to its essence, treating each element of left- and right-hand technique in parallel contexts: abstract exercises, studies and pieces. The first book of thumb-position studies, for example, uses ϙ23 and ϙ13, before involving ϙ123 and even 4, a presentation advised by Silva which is more comfortable for the inexperienced hand. Another set of studies clarifies the relationship of thumb-position to first position by presenting the same music in both octaves.[51]

Recent developments in cello teaching have emphasised the instrument as a whole, aiming both to liberate the player physically by encouraging freer use of the hand-positions in the early stages and to remove phobias associated with playing in the higher registers. Technique has kept up with contemporary musical developments through, for example, the interval exercises of Bunting and Tortelier and Siegfried Palm's *Pro Musica Nova, Studies in Playing Contemporary Music* (1985), a pioneering collection of short commissions from twelve composers, demonstrating new notations, complex rhythm and pitch, and quick changes of technique. But there is still a pressing need for a systematic pedagogical approach to the technical problems posed by avant-garde composers. Concert pieces which incorporate contemporary techniques at a simple level are also required.

Two gaps in existing graded technical material, in double-stopping and harmonics, have recently been plugged. Novsak and Stein's accessible *Fun with Double Stops* (3 vols., 1988) gives musical enjoyment, progressing gradually (at least in the first two volumes). Bosanquet's *The Secret Life of Cello Strings* (1996) deals with cello harmonics using node maps, graded practice materials, and a suggested rationalisation of notation. Harmonics are useful from the earliest stages of technique, as pioneered by Rolland, George Vance[52] and the Szilvays.

Although cello teaching and technique have made great progress in this century, and the general level of playing and the number of good players

210 R. Caroline Bosanquet

have risen considerably, improvements are still needed, for stiff ways of playing unfortunately still exist, affecting both the quality of the players, and their physical comfort. On a mechanical level, the perfect cello case which fully protects the instrument but is light and comfortable to carry does not yet exist; nor do suitable chairs for cellists, which should have as wide a range of heights as a piano stool, and yet be light enough to be portable.[53] Many concert halls can offer only one type of chair to accommodate all heights of player, which is unacceptable. A longer spike is often required to counteract the increase in the average height of the younger generation; and it would be useful if longer bows were available too.

One of the most progressive developments in cello teaching in the twentieth century has been the increased opportunity for national and international interchange of ideas, pioneered through ASTA and ESTA, and more recently the great cello festivals of the USA and of Manchester in England. At these festivals delegates have the unique experience of hearing performances and observing masterclasses by a galaxy of international cellists. Another important development has been the change in attitude to the training of string teachers. In the majority of communist countries efficient training systems have been in place for a long time. In the USA, pioneering ventures such as the Texas String Project, from 1948, became the model for other ventures. However, only in the last five years have the major British conservatoires initiated appropriate courses for future teachers. One of the best courses for the training of string teachers is that of the Sibelius Academy in Finland, as demonstrated at the international ESTA conference in Spain in 1997.

Cello playing is currently growing in parts of the world not usually associated with a cello tradition. Since the death of Chairman Mao, a school of virtuoso cellists has been evolving in China. In India, Anup Biswas founded in 1994 a unique school in Calcutta where orphans and very poor children are given a specialist music education. The children are not chosen for their musical ability, as Biswas believes that 'everyone has music in them',[54] and the syllabus is special in that the children learn to play both Western and Indian classical music. The employment prospects for these children are said to be good. This pioneering venture is additionally interesting in that, through it, the expressive possibilities of the cello itself are being extended, Indian music often involving scordatura tuning, much complex sliding on one finger, no vibrato, microtonal intonation, melodic decoration and improvisation. Biswas is also developing a cello with sympathetic strings.

Cello teaching has progressed greatly since 1900. The extraordinary and expanding potential of the instrument will doubtless continue to be explored in ever-new circumstances throughout the twenty-first century.

13 The frontiers of technique

FRANCES-MARIE UITTI

The cello and its repertory have undergone radical transformations over the last seventy-five years. Whereas in former times musical styles and compositional conventions generally developed into an integral language over a period of some years, the proliferation of individual approaches to composition nowadays constantly challenges performers and their audiences to understand and assimilate new languages in rapid succession. Never before have instrumentalists been confronted with such difficulties as deciphering new notation for each different composer, mastering new technical requirements for each new piece, and transmitting often unnotatable sound-worlds convincingly to their audiences.

The left hand became liberated from its customary position-sense and the traditional diatonic framework, thanks to increased chromaticism, whole-tone, microtone and other scale patterns, glissandi and unusual non-consonant double- and multiple-stopping. Extreme applications of vibrato have been prescribed, including the ornamental vibrato-glissando, and traditional usages have been reversed, with demand for an intense, fast vibrato in soft passages, a wide, slow vibrato in loud passages, or even the use of *senza vibrato* for contrast or special effect. A wide variety of pizzicato effects has been developed, composers prescribing various pizzicato locations, specific plucking agents and other such instructions, and harmonics and scordatura have been exploited for their colouristic potential. Bowing technique developed in the twentieth century as a result of composers' demands on players to master awkward string-crossings, rapid changes and specific prescription of contact-point, speed and pressure, sudden or gradual changes in dynamic, often to extreme levels, and irregular slurrings and bow patterns. Percussive effects on various parts of the instrument and sounds extraneous to the cello, such as vocal and electronic effects, have also been added to the contemporary language, which has been further complicated by various notational and extra-musical factors.

As composers exploited the cello's wide range of colours and extensive tessitura, technical boundaries (assisted by the invention of steel strings) gradually dissolved to unveil a greatly expanded vocabulary of sounds. The story of this evolution is intertwined with the development of musical language and thought, hence my objective here to discuss the principal compositional trends together with select examples from the repertory.

The turning point

The first signs of change became evident *c.* 1915 with two contrasting works, Kodály's solo Sonata Op. 8 (1915) and Webern's *Three Little Pieces* Op. 11 (1914). Kodály's Romantic work with grand musical gestures requires a remarkable pyrotechnical prowess, 'orchestrating' the cello by employing double trills, and self-accompanied melodies. It exploits an extended range of five octaves as well as scordatura, enabling a unique harmonic expression otherwise unplayable within the constraints of the left hand. It set a new standard of virtuosity that was unmatched for the next fifty years.

In contrast, Webern's Op. 11 comprises probably the three shortest pieces ever written for cello. These crystalline structures are highly coloured through the use of *ponticello* and *sul tasto* contrasts as well as wide leaps, artificial and natural harmonics, and an extreme dynamic range from *ppp* to *fff*. The rhythms were considered complex for their time with, for example, triplet crotchets spread over the time of four crotchets.

Classicists

Conventional playing techniques were used by many composers in the 1940s and beyond, for example in the sonatas of Martinů, Prokofiev, Milhaud and Elliott Carter. However, in his Sonata (vc, pf, 1948), Carter introduced 'metric modulation'; a method of notating the gradual passing from one tempo to another, it is one of the major motifs of the whole work, relating all the movements in a coherent conception. Speeds are always in a state of flux, interweaving permutations throughout all the movements. Thus, while the physical cello techniques exploited by Carter are conventional, the mental frontiers have been extended to reveal new horizons of perception.

Serialism

With the increasing interest in serialism in the 1940s and 50s, melodies and rhythms became fragmented, creating a music that was ever more complex. This, along with the growing exploration of colouristic sonorities, influenced technical approaches to the instrument. The cello's range was also expanded, which, combined with melodic fragmentation, prompted performers to master wide leaps from one note to the next across distant octaves. Not least, performers accustomed to playing the traditional repertory by heart found themselves suddenly required to count! Metres changed constantly in order to equalise rhythmic energy and eliminate the 'tyranny of the beat', and metronome markings were in constant flux, requiring mastery of further mental gymnastics. In such idioms, perfect pitch was of great assistance not only to conductors but also to cellists, along with a memory for 'perfect tempo'.

Open forms

With ever more rigorous serialism, composers came to realise that attempts to control strictly all the musical parameters (pitch, rhythm, harmony) overloaded the system, causing chaotic elements to appear. The discovery of this chaotic behaviour interested several of them, opening the doors to 'open form' composition. These compositions of the early 1950s were written in such a way as to oblige the performer to assume some of the compositional decisions. In some cases, this was highly structured within the work; in others, it was trusted more freely to the performer's fantasy and taste.

The division between composer and performer was becoming ever less defined. Some scores were even notated graphically, as was the case with the early works of Earle Brown, who used dance blueprints as his inspiration, and left all interpretative decisions to the performer. His *Folio* (1952–3) comprises a series of loose pages resembling free abstract designs, available for realisation by any instrumentalist, dancer or actor. Brown's *Music for Cello and Piano* (1954) defines the instruments but only sketches the durations.

Cage, on the other hand, invented situations in which the performer was obliged to follow highly complex interpretative instructions. Some works were drawn on transparencies to be deciphered after superimposition upon each other, and still others were simply a list of addresses to be used as pinpoints on maps (or note placements on a staff). Most radical were those pieces which consisted only of instructions, and left the performer to work out an imaginary music. Feldman also wrote scores which only partially controlled music, assigning registers (high, middle and low) and specifying colours and articulations (*ponticello*, harmonic, pizzicato). Rhythms were notated graphically and dynamic indications tended to emphasise *piano* (see Ex. 13.1).

Ex. 13.1 Morton Feldman, *Intersection 4*

☐ = 80   *Morton Feldman*

The vogue for graphic notation caught on quickly in Europe. Penderecki's *Capriccio per Siegfried Palm* (1968) uses conventional notation as well as an invented system of symbols that represent certain performance instructions, explained in a detailed preface. It is a virtuoso showpiece, making use of *sul ponticello*, playing on the other side of the bridge, playing on the tailpiece, an extremely high range, and left-hand finger percussion, mixed with conventionally notated passages. Adventurous contributions also came from Sylvano Bussotti in the form of beautifully drawn graphic scores, some in an esoteric vein (*Sette Fogli Occulti*, 1959), and others more sensuous (*Autotono*).

Throughout history, composers have traditionally notated the idealised sound desired. However, Helmut Lachenmann invented a precise notational system in which his drawings dictate the cellist's physical actions. His *Pression* for solo cello creates an entirely new aesthetic wherein many of the sounds are produced on the body of the cello, and on the bow itself, resulting in a quiet, mysterious sound-world that is barely pitched. An interlude of chaotic grating sounds played behind the bridge explosively breaks this mood, only to return to the hypersensitive world at the end. The work is in no way arbitrary, but rather, a highly structured composition that is still considered radical today.

Theatre music and graphic notation

Theatre music was a logical offshoot from the new-found freedom of open-form music and graphic scores of the 1960s. Pieces in which musicians were required to act, sing and move onstage were composed by musicians, dancers and even directors. Nam June Paik wrote provocative works for Charlotte Moormon during the peak of the Fluxus movement in New York, requiring tiny video monitors to be strapped to her naked breasts. In other pieces she was required to play the cello underwater in a giant fish bowl. Vinko Globokar's *Janus,* a psychodrama between the inner male and female, involves the cellist, symbolically dressed as half male and half female, being seated on a rotating piano stool. The lights go up to reveal the male profile, and a rhythmic theme is played, punctuated by stamping feet.

Blackout. The cellist is next seen turned and lit on the feminine side, playing lyrically. The roles mix, conflict and finally resolve. Special cello techniques involve the use of two bows.

Posturo, by choreographer William Kirkpatrick, is one of the more daring works that exploit the cello's size and female form theatrically. The instrument becomes the hand of a clock and is required to be played in all positions, even upside-down, as a drama of madness is choreographed. Other works by Bussotti, *Sensitivo per Arco Solo* and *Variazione per Violoncello*, are also successful in their theatrical forms; and Mauricio Kagel's famous *Match* (2vc, perc, 1964) is a highly sophisticated analogy of a tennis game, casting the percussionist as referee. Gesticulations, text and a great variety of sounds issue forth from the players as they execute the most amazing virtuoso feats in competition with each other.

The voice

As the use of the voice became more widespread, composers required cellists to narrate texts, shriek and sometimes even snort, as in Gerald Plain's *Racoon Song*. Dieter Schnebel wrote various works using text, and Kagel featured heavy breathing, humming, screaming and groaning in his droll piece, *Siegfriedp*, written completely in harmonics. James Tenney used speech inflections as the basic source material for his flamboyant work, *Ain't I a Woman?* (vc, ch orch). The cellist first reads Sojourner Truth's text (with an American accent from the deep South), then plays the melodic transcription. This is followed by an orchestral extraction of the same, this time in harmonics. With each variation the work further reduces the material to its very essence.

One of the most sublime works is Louis Andriessen's *La Voce* (1981), named after the poem by Cesare Pavese. It opens with the cellist subtly miming unplayed sounds that gradually transform into long, vibratoless, minor and major seconds. The voice then enters, whispering the infinitely sad poem in Italian. Gradually as the work builds, the voice begins to sing in close harmony with the cello until, at the end, it rises to a full three-part chorale of stunning beauty. A special scordatura using two A strings is employed.

The idea of extreme scordature and restringings came to me in the early seventies through my own compositional and improvisational explorations. This made possible vastly different double-, triple- and quadruple-stops that in a normal tuning would not fit the left hand. I developed these ideas during 1970–9, composing over seventy-five *Ricercari* based on augmenting degrees of scordatura. Subsequent work with many composers led to this technique becoming a basis for some of their compositions, notably Luigi Nono (four G strings, four C strings in *Piario Polacco*), Klarenz Barlow (two C strings in *The Weather*), Richard Barrett (two C strings in *Dark Ages*), Giacinto Scelsi (four A strings in *Suah*, 1979) and Jonathan Harvey (two D strings in *Three Sketches*, 1989).

Microtones

Composers have recently turned to the cello as a favoured instrument for microtonal writing because of its string-length and clarity of timbre. Accurate performance of microtones involves a radical departure from centuries of traditional ear-training practices and their mastery requires a unique mental discipline, in addition to physical practice.

Mexican Julián Carrillo was one of the first to experiment with micro-tones. In his numerous cello works – which include six solo sonatas and a series of études employing microtones – he uses them mostly in a stepwise manner, dividing the tones in long scale figures. His Cello Concerto (1958) contrasts the cello's microtonal lines with the orchestra's diatonic system. Among others who experimented with microtones were Alois Hába, who divided the semitone into six parts in his solo Suite (1955); Belgian Henri Pousseur, who divides the octave into nineteen equal microtones in his evocative $19 \times \sqrt{8/4}$ (1977); and Horazio Radulescu, who bases his tunings on Pythagorean divisions of the string (the same tuning manifest when natural harmonics are played). Per Nørgård used the unstable harmonics that exist between the ones most commonly used to give a microtonal variance in his concerto *Between*. He also used the Indonesian scale, 'slendro', which contains six equidistant divisions of the octave.

Iannis Xenakis used microtones extensively as an integral part of his language. He has devised a precise manner of notating them by using 'beats per second', as the sounding of two almost-unisons will produce audible oscillations, which accelerate as the two pitches move further apart. Scelsi, meanwhile, based many of his compositions on the subtleties of slowly permutating microtone glissandi around a central pitch-mass. The cello's innate warmth lends an earthy sensuality to these powerful, abstract works.

New sonorities

In the 1960s, Germany's Darmstadt Summer School was the meeting place of some of the world's most fertile musical minds, notably Stockhausen,

Boulez, Nono and Bernd Alois Zimmermann, who collaborated with the Kontarsky brothers, Siegfried Palm and other leading instrumentalists in what was to become one of music history's most important developments. Seminal research in electronic music, as well as in-depth research into sonority, beyond the constraints of academic tradition, expanded the conception of music. There, for the first time, sound production from the whole instrument was accepted readily as valid material for the composer's use. The cello was played from the endpin to the scroll; it was treated as a percussion instrument; it invaded the range of the violin; and it was redefined as an instrument capable of great speed and of every expression known to music. Cellists were obliged to develop their techniques and reading skills to accommodate the resulting diverse personal languages and styles of a wide range of composers.

Complexity school

In the 1970s, a certain notoriety grew around some of the 'super virtuosi' who took on the challenge of the arcane, such as the Arditti String Quartet. Some composers revelled in challenging performers with the highest complexity imaginable, and an appreciative public responded with adulation. The mental rigours needed to decipher such scores were daunting. Brian Ferneyhough was one of the *enfants terribles*, writing multi-staffed scores with complex cross-rhythms that defied even the most dedicated performers. His work is extremely original in its musical thought and is possessed of a remarkable inner clarity and energy. For example, *Time and Motion Study II* (1973–6), for amplified cello, two tape loops and electronics, is a study in work efficiency. The performer is pitted against himself as this almost impossible score[1] takes him to the outer reaches of human capability (see Ex. 13.2). Two playback tape loops repeat in stereo the player's successes and failures, finally building and decaying into an hallucination. It is a virtuoso *tour de force* without precedent.

Among other composers who wrote outstanding works which use dense, complex forms are Richard Barrett (*Dark Ages*; *Praha*; *Ne Songe plus à Fuir*,), Michael Finnissy (*Andimironnai*; *Yalli!*), Roger Redgate (*Ecarte*) and James Dillon (*Parjanva-Vata*).

Minimalism

Minimalist composers constructed their music from elemental materials, often cellular scale and arpeggio fragments repeated in an ostinato. Some

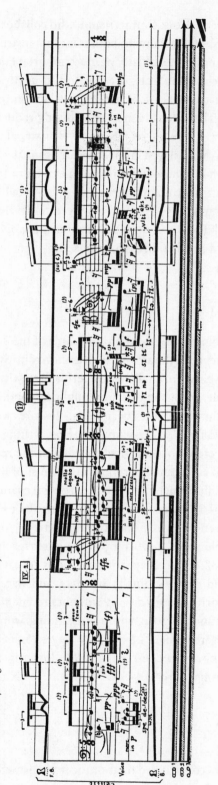

Ex. 13.2 Brian Ferneyhough, *Time and Motion Study II*

of their works are disarmingly beautiful in their simplicity. Dizzying patterns in seemingly infinite repetitions can produce trance-like states, and for the performer this can be disconcerting. Among the new challenges for instrumentalists, therefore, were those of counting bars, modules and patterns. Tom Johnson's *Rational Melodies* is an example of effective minimalism, as are László Sáry's *For Philip Glass*, Arvo Pärt's *Fratres III* and David Lang's *BitterHerb*.

Iconoclasts

Alongside the above stylistic developments came many pieces written by independent thinkers who composed for the instrument in highly individual styles. Xenakis's two landmark works, *Nomos alpha* (1964) and *Kottos* (1977), the latter named after the Greek mythological god with two hundred arms, establish him as a most original composer, basing his compositions on architectural forms and making use of stochastic processes and game theory. He was the first important musician to employ the computer, writing his own programme for the UPIC computer in Paris. Such techniques presaged much of the subsequent computer revolution and the use of computers as compositional tools and assistants. Xenakis used the cello in *Nomos alpha* to contrast stasis (through the use of near-unisons with subtly inflected microtones) with movement (rapid vertical movement of harmonic glissandi, normal glissandi, tremolos and moving fragments). Innovative, too, was his use of notation for beatings between micro-intervals, the measured glissandi in harmonics, slow glissandi defined against a beat which controls the exact speed, and extreme range made possible by the use of a gut C string (retuned throughout the work) extended to a low purring. He extends the upper range as well, through the use of artificial harmonics at the very top of the fingerboard. The last two lines depict two voices in rhythmic and linear juxtaposition, intersecting each other only to vanish at opposite ends of the fingerboard, a feat impossible with just one left hand but made possible either with a tape, or by very quick arpeggiation.

Kottos is even more radical, beginning literally on top of the bridge, *fff*, with a rich, dense sound filled with overtones. It is one of the most dramatic openings imaginable, invoking the 'terror of the gods'. The rest of the work balances blocks of contrasting material to create a magnificent form, its compositional elements comprising static harmonics, double glissandi of differing speeds, glissandi in artificial harmonics, fragmented microtonal melodic figures, fast passages of almost-repeating modules, of complex rhythmic chords spanning four strings, and *frappe-frotte* (vertical, repeated down-bows that beat and rub the string). A landmark in the cello repertory, it demands immense physical and mental power, as well as sheer stamina.

Galina Ustvol'skaya's five-movement *Grand Duet* (vc, pf, 1952) pushes performers to extremes of intensity. It is impressive in its relentless build-up of *ffff* rhythmic articulations on the cello, and its third movement requires the use of a bass bow for additional strength. Although its harmonic style is fairly traditional, its structure is both unusual and masterly. After four inexorably 'building' movements, the music finally resolves with the cello singing an extended melodic line that is transformed imperceptibly into a sublime one-note meditation; the piano futilely interjects material from the first movement.

Scelsi had composed most of his life's work before hearing any of it performed. He considered his fifty-five minute *Trilogy* for solo cello to be his autobiography in sound. The first work, *Triphon* (1957), is highly energetic and uses a custom-made metallic 'mute' (which straddles the bridge and lower two strings loosely) to divide the cello sonically into two halves. Passages of extreme speed challenge both the player and the instrument, as they are usually written for the slower-speaking low strings. His unexpected use of quarter-tones further divides the instrument. The second piece, *Diathome* (1957), divides the cello further through the use of 'almost-octaves', an interval whose upper note is a quarter-tone sharp. It begins with a dark menacing line that dissolves into fast legato oscillations between adjacent strings. The work accelerates to reach a sustained climax of unbearable tension in the upper positions. This is gradually released and the music descends to reiterate the slow melody on the C string. A mirror-image of the first section then follows, but this time it is distanced – a drama viewed through translucent glass. Technical innovations employed include legato-bowed tremolos between adjacent strings at extreme speeds, microtone alterations of consecutive octaves, and an extremely wide, pulsated vibrato. *Ygghur* (1961–4), the final movement, means 'catharsis' in Sanskrit. It is a fifteen-minute soliloquy revolving around a single tone centre, enabled by the descending scordatura g–B♭–G–B♭[1]. With this ingenious solution, the left hand can reach, in one position, unisons and octaves on all four strings. The work is notated at sounding pitches, thus requiring the cellist to accommodate them to the prescribed scordatura. Scelsi uses four staves, one for each string, to delineate the voices. Technical challenges involve execution of all the various pizzicati, scrapes and percussive sounds with the left hand against a sustained, but shifting, microtone chord held by the bow, *col legno tratto*, as in *Diathome*.

Cage's *Etudes Boreales* (1979) proved so formidable to execute that they were eventually abandoned in a drawer at Peters in New York. They

Ex. 13.3 John Cage, *Etudes Boreales*

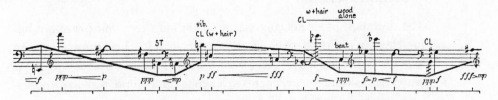

demand the utmost mastery of cello technique, particularly the ability to jump accurately to any point on the fingerboard and beyond (see Ex. 13.3). They are to be played without vibrato, magnifying the difficulty of leaping and allowing no possibility of correcting undesired inaccuracies. These etudes are controlled in every parameter – pitch, colour, duration and dynamic – and require an advanced knowledge of the instrument.

Electronics and computers

Although many years after Varèse's work, it was during the 1960s and 70s that great advances in electronic music took place. One of the pioneers was Mario Davidovsky, whose *Synchronisms No. 3* (1964) for cello and prerecorded tape is a milestone in the genre. Often, the cello is called upon to imitate synthesised sounds, which are realised through the use of pizzicati, *col legno*, harmonics and skittering passage-work. Among other compositions which explore the relationship between the cello and synthesised sound are Barry Truax's *Etude* and Rolf Gehlhaar's *Solipse* (1974). Gehlhaar enriches the work by using glissandi, percussive sounds, *col legno*, and sounds full with overtones. Jonathan Harvey added his profoundly beautiful *Ricercare una Melodia* (1985) to this repertory (scored for cello with quadrophonic tape), and his *Advaya* (1994) for cello, synthesiser and computer makes much use of quarter-tones. Ferneyhough's *Time and Motion Study II* also actually belongs to this category.

More recent works in this idiom are Tod Machover's *Electric Etudes*, and '*Begin again again . . .*' for an electronic cello called the 'hypercello'; four computers are used to drive the electronics, while Martin Bartlett's interactive computer program reacts to very specific parameters of pitch and timbre. The cello, by its very nature, is well suited to such electronic experiments, on account of its rich overtones, the colouristic potential of its long strings and its naturally deep resonance. In the late 1980s and 90s, amplification has become more fashionable as rock music has influenced composers in their quests for more powerful expressions. Michael Jordons' *Industry* is a notable example.

Free improvisation

The number of musicians participating in free improvisation has increased in recent years, as has the audience for it. These musicians open new musical horizons and add fresh insights into technical development with unconstrained experiments in language and sound. Instant composition may result in the element of surprise, with spontaneous creation of new themes and forms. Electronics have revolutionised improvisation through the use of amplification, sound-modifying tools, live sampling and computer programs. It is now possible for a single cello to produce all the sounds of the orchestra, with a dynamic range rivalling that of a rock band. Among those cellists who are at the forefront of this music are Aaron Minsky, whose jazzy pieces are not only humorous, but tightly composed; Tristan Honsiger, who adds his own special blend of intensity and raw passion to his sound; Ernst Reyseger, who delights with his jaunty approach; and Eric Friedman, who contributes his own special lyricism to this form.

The two-bow system

Many composers have written beautiful works using the two-bow technique, notably Nono (*Diario Polacco II*), Kurtág (*Message to Frances-Marie*; *Homage to John Cage*), Scelsi (*Sauh*; *Il Funerale di Carlo Magno*), Klarenz Barlow (*The Weather*), Jay Alan Yim (*Orenda*), James Clark (*Independence*), Horazio Radulescu (*Lux animae)* and Richard Barrett (*Dark Ages*; *Praha*), as well as works by Jonathan Harvey, Globokar, Guus Jansen and Frances-Marie Uitti. In the 1970s, while involved with improvisation, I felt the need to be able to play four-part chords (the cello could only sustain two-note chords, and at best manage a three- and four-note chord by rolling the bow quickly over the strings). In 1972 I commissioned a curved bow to be made to my specification but found that it was too limited for my musical needs as it could only play on adjacent strings. This gave rise to a sound that, in my opinion, became monotonously thick, given the low timbre of the cello. I later had the idea of using two bows in the right hand, one over and one under the strings, enabling four-part harmony to be played. The advantages of using two bows were many; first, any non-adjacent string could be played in combination with any others, thus giving performers the freedom to play any two- or three-part chords, as well as any single string. Furthermore, contrasting articulations, dynamics and colourings were made possible; for example, one bow can be legato while the other is staccato, one bow *sul ponticello* while the other *sul tasto*, and contrasting dynamics can be articulated simultaneously.

The twentieth century has witnessed a metamorphosis of compositional language coupled with the transformation of instrumental techniques and sound itself. The cello has emerged as a soloist and has won new territories in expression. As the world of music expands, new forms of presentation will influence technique and performance practice. Will concerts return to the salon with, perhaps, simultaneous internet broadcasts? Will the visual aspect of performance be emphasised, or even become a primary force? Will the cello itself, or the bow, be further improved? Whatever direction the future of music takes, it will probably result from a creative symbiosis between composers and instrumentalists, a wonderful and volatile union that has always sparked innovation.

Appendix: Principal cello treatises

The following pages provide bibliographical details of the principal treatises devoted specifically to the cello, arranged in chronological order by date of first edition, commencing with Michel Corrette's pioneering, if somewhat elementary, work of 1741. It is intended to supplement the text (of Chapters 11 and 12 in particular) and is in no sense a complete bibliography of treatises for the instrument.

1741   Corrette, Michel, *Méthode théorique et pratique pour apprendre en peu de tems le violoncelle dans sa perfection. Ensemble de principes de musique avec des leçons*, Op. 24 (Paris, 1741/*R*1972, 2nd edn 1783)

1764   Tillière, Joseph Bonaventure, *Méthode pour le violoncelle contenant tous les principes nécessaires pour bien jouer de cet instrument* (Paris, [1764]); Eng. edn *c.* 1795 as *New and Compleat Instruction*

1765   Crome, Robert, *The Compleat Tutor for the Violoncello* (London, [1765])

c. 1756–1767   Lanzetti, Salvatore, *Principes ou l'Application de Violoncelle, par tous les tons de la manière la plus facile* (Amsterdam, [*c.* 1756–67])

1772   Cupis, François, *Méthode nouvelle et raisonnée pour apprendre à jouer du violoncelle* (Paris, [1772])

1774   Baumgartner, Johann, *Instructions de musique, théorique et pratique, à l'usage du violoncelle* (The Hague, [1774])

c. 1778   Azais, Pierre-Hyacinthe, *Méthode de Basse* (Paris, [*c.* 1778])

c. 1780   Schetky, Johann, *Twelve Duetts for Two Violoncellos, with some Observations & Rules for playing that Instrument*, Op. 7 (London, [*c.* 1780])

      Thompson, C., *New Instruction for the Violoncello* (London, 1780)

1785   Hardy, Henry, *The violoncello preceptor, with a compleat set of scales for fingering in the various keys and the fingerboard properly delineated; also the octave accurately measured & divided, by which the student will be enabled to obtain a proficiency* (Oxford, [*c.* 1785])

1788   Kauer, Ferdinand, *Kurzgefasste Anweisung das Violoncell zu spielen* (Vienna, [1788])

1793   Gunn, John, *The Theory and Practice of Fingering the Violoncello* (London [1793, 2nd edn *c.* 1794])

1800   Reinagle, Joseph, *A Concise Introduction to the Art of Playing the Violoncello* (London, [1800])

      Müntzberger, Joseph, *Nouvelle méthode pour le violoncelle*, Op. 30 (Paris, [*c.* 1800])

1802   Alexander, Joseph, Jos., *Alexanders Anleitung zum Violoncellspiel* (Leipzig, [1802])

      Aubert, Pierre François Olivier, *Méthode ou nouvelles études pour le violoncelle*, Op. 9 (Paris, [1802])

      Bideau, Dominique, *Grande et nouvelle méthode raisonnée pour le violoncelle* (Paris, [1802])

Raoul, Jean Marie, *Méthode de violoncelle*, Op. 4 (Paris, [c. 1802]/R1972)

1804 Bréval, Jean-Baptiste, *Traité du violoncelle*, Op. 42
(Paris, [1804]); Eng. edn as *New Instruction for the Violoncello, Being a Complete Key to the Knowledge of that Instrument* (London, 1810)

1805 Baillot, P., Levasseur, J. H., Catel, C.-S., and Baudiot, C.-N., *Méthode de violoncelle et de basse d'accompagnement* (Paris, [1805]); Eng. edn as *Method for the Violoncello by Baillot, Levasseur, Catel & Baudiot, Adopted by the Paris Conservatory of Music* (London, c. 1855)

1806 Duport, Jean-Louis, *Essai sur le doigté du violoncelle, et sur la conduite de l'archet* (Paris, [1806])

1808 Fröhlich, Joseph, *Violoncellschule* (Cologne, 1808)

1811 MacDonald, John, *Treatise Explanatory of the Principles Constituting the Practice and Theory of the Violoncello* (London, 1811)

Schetky, Johann, *Practical and Progressive Lessons for the Violoncello* (London, 1811)

c. 1815 Vaillant Pierre, *Nouvelle méthode de violoncelle* (Paris, [c. 1815])

1826–8 Baudiot Charles, *Méthode pour le violoncelle*, Op. 25, 2 vols. (Paris, [1826–8])

1827 Crouch, Frederick W., *A Compleat Treatise on the Violoncello* (London, [1827])

1829 Hus-Desforges, Pierre Louis, *Méthode de violoncelle* (Paris, [1829])

Stiastny, Bernard, *Violoncell-Schule* (Mainz, [1829])

1830 Eley, Charles, *Improved Method of instruction for the Violoncello* (London, 1830)

1832 Dotzauer, Justus Johann Friedrich, *Violonzell-Schule* (Mainz, [1832])

1837 Rachelle, Pietro, *Breve Metodo*, Op. 14 (Milan, [1837])

1839 Kummer, Friedrich August, *Violoncell-Schule*, Op. 60 (Leipzig, [1839])

1839–40 Romberg, Bernhard, *Violoncell Schule von Bernhard Romberg* (Berlin, [1840]); Eng. edn as *A Complete Theoretical and Practical School for the Violoncello* (London, 1839)

Gross, Johann Benjamin, *Elemente des Violoncellspiels*, Op. 36 (Leipzig, 1840)

Hamilton, James Alexander, *Complete Preceptor for the Violoncello* (London, 1840)

1839–46 Offenbach, Jacques, *Ecole du Violoncelle*, Opp. 19–21, 34 (Paris, 1839–46)

1842 Lee, Sebastian, *Méthode pratique pour le violoncelle*, Op. 30 (Mainz, [1842]; Eng. edn, Mainz [c. 1875])

1843 Borher [Bohrer], F., *Méthode de violoncelle* (Paris, [1843])

1845 Kastner, Jean-Georges, *Elementar-Schule für das Violoncell mit einem Anhang von Übungsstücken* (Leipzig, 1845)

1846 Phillips, W. Lovell, *New and Complete Instruction for the Violoncello* (London, 1846)

1847 Offenbach, Jacques, *Cours méthodique de duos*, Opp. 49–54 (Paris, 1847)

1850 Depar, Ernest, *Méthode élémentaire pour violoncelle à l'usage des collèges et pensions* (Paris, 1850)

Lebouc, Charles Joseph, *Méthode complète et pratique de violoncelle* (Paris, 1850)

Chevillard, Pierre Alexandre François, *Méthode complète de violoncelle* (Paris, [c. 1850])

c. 1854 Miné, Jacques-Claude-Adolphe, *Méthode de violoncelle* (Paris, [before 1854])

c. 1855 Lindley, Robert, *Lindley's Handbook for the Violoncello* (London, [before 1855]) *c.* 1860 Dancla, Arnaud, *Méthode de violoncelle* (Paris, [*c.* 1860])

    Leutgen, H., *First Lessons for the Violoncello* (London, 1860)

    Warot, Adolphe, *Méthode progressive pour le violoncelle* (Brussels, 1860)

  1864 Henning, Karl, *Kleine Violoncello-Schule*, Op. 37 (Leipzig, 1864)

  1872 *Ryan's True Violoncello Instructor* (Cincinnati, 1872)

  1874 Winner, Septimus, *Winner's Primary School for the* Violoncello (Cleveland, 1874)

c. 1875 Benito, Cosme de, *Nouvelle méthode élémentaire de violoncelle* (Madrid, [before 1875])

    Tolbecque, Auguste, *Gymnastique du violoncelliste* (Paris, 1875)

c. 1876 Forino, Ferdinando, *Metodo completo per violoncello addottato vari Instituti. Musicali d'Italia* (Rome, [*c.* 1876])

    Schröder, Karl (Carl), *Neue, grosse, theoretisch-praktische Violoncell-Schule in vier Abteilungen*, Op. 34 (Leipzig, 1876–7)

  1877 Banger, G., *Praktische Violoncellschule*, Op. 35, 3 vols. (Offenbach, 1877)

    Quarenghi, Guglielmo, *Metodo di Violoncello* (Milan, 1877)

  1878 Braga, Gaëtano, *Metodo per Violoncello intieramente riformato* (Milan, 1878)

    Piatti, Alfredo, *Violoncello-Schule* (London, 1878)

    Rabaud, Hyppolite, *Méthode complète de violoncelle*, Op. 12 (Paris, [*c.* 1878])

    Junod, Laurent, *New and Concise Method for the Violoncello*, Op. 20 (London, 1878)

    Schröder, Karl (Carl), *Praktischer Lehrgang des Violoncellspiels* (Brunswick, 1878)

  1879 Zimmer, Franz, *Theoretisch-praktische Violoncellschule*, Op. 20 (Quedlinburg, 1879)

    Fries, Wulf, and Suck, August, *Practical Violoncello Instruction Book* (Boston, 1879)

  1880 Werner, Joseph, *Praktische Violoncell-Schule*, Op. 12 (Leipzig, 1880)

    Schröder, Karl (Carl), *Führer durch den Violoncell-Unterricht* (Leipzig, 1880)

    Jackson, G., *New Instructor for the Violoncello* (London, 1880)

    Tietz, August Ferdinand, *Praktischer Lehrgang für den ersten Unterricht des Violoncellspiels* (Brunswick, [*c.* 1880])

    Tietz, Heinrich, *Praktischer Lehrgang für den ersten Unterricht im Violoncellspiel* (Dresden, [*c.* 1880])

  1881 Siedentopf, C., *Violoncellschule*, Op. 16 (Magdeburg, 1881)

  1882 Forberg, Friedrich, *Violoncellschule*, Op. 31 (Leipzig, 1882)

    Stransky, Joseph, *Elementarschule des Violoncellspiels* (Berlin, 1882)

  1884 Vaslin, Olive, *L'art du violoncelle conseils aux jeunes violoncellistes sur la conduite de l'archet* (Paris, [1884])

    Langey, Otto, *Tutor for the Violoncello* (Pennsylvania, 1884; 2nd edn New York, 1891)

  1887 Heberlein, Hermann, *Violoncellschule, neueste, praktische und leicht verständliche Methode für Schul- und Selbstunterricht*, Op. 7 (Leipzig, 1887)

    Roth, Philipp, *Violoncell-Schule*, Op. 14 (Leipzig, [*c.* 1887])

  1888 Davidoff, Carl, *Violoncell-Schule* (Leipzig, 1888)

    De Swert, Jules, *Gradus ad Parnassum ou le mécanisme moderne du violoncelle*, Op. 50 (Leipzig, [*c.* 1888]); Eng. edn, London, *c.* 1890 as *Novello's Music Primers &*

Educational Series: The Violoncello by Jules De Swert

1890 Massau, A., *Cours préparatoire de violoncelle* (Brussels, [*c.* 1890])
    Schröder, Karl (Carl), *Katechismus des Violoncell-Spiels* (Leipzig, 1890)

1891 Grützmacher, Friedrich, *Hohe Schule des Violoncellspiels* (Leipzig, 1891)

1896 Giese, Fritz, *Scale and Technical Studies* (Boston, 1896)

1898 Van der Straeten, Edmund, *The Technics of Violoncello Playing*, vol. V of 'The Strad' Library (London, 1898)

1899 Broadley, Arthur, *Chats to 'Cello Students*, vol. VII of 'The Strad' Library (London, 1899)

1900 Bürger, Sigmund, *Technische Studien für das Violoncello*, Op. 4 (Leipzig, [*c.* 1900])
    Abbiate, Louis, *Nouvelle méthode de violoncelle théorique et pratique* (Paris, 1900)
    Van Lier, Jacques, *Violoncell-Bogentechnik frei bearbeitet nach Casortis Violin-Bogentechnik, vom Ende* (Cologne and Leipzig, [*c.* 1900])

1901 Heger, R., *Praktische Violoncell-Schule mit Benutzung von Werken klassischer Meister* (Bremen, 1901)

1901–05 Popper, David, *Hohe Schule des Violoncellospiels*, Op. 73, 2 vols. (Leipzig, 1901–5)

1906 Fuchs, Carl, *Violoncello Method*, 3 vols. (London, 1906)

1909 Langey, Otto, *Practical Tutor for the Violoncello* (London, 1909)

1920 Bazelaire, Paul, *Quelques Notes sur différents points importants de la Technique Générale du Violoncelle* (Paris, 1920)

1922 Alexanian, Diran, *Traité théorique et pratique du violoncelle/The Technique of Violoncello Playing* (Paris, 1922)

1925 Feuillard, Louis, *Méthode du Jeune Violoncelliste* (Paris, 1925)

1929 Becker, Hugo, and Rynar, Dago, *Mechanik und Aesthetik des Violoncellspiels* (Vienna, 1929/R1971)

1929–38 Stutschewsky, Joachim, *Die Kunst des Cellospiels*, I–II (Mainz, 1929), III–IV (Vienna, 1938)

1942–87 Matz, Rudolf, *The First Years of the Violoncello* (New York, 1987)

1944 Bazelaire, Paul, *L'enseignement du Violoncelle en France* (Paris, 1944)

1952 Bazelaire, Paul, *Pédagogie du Violoncelle* (Paris, 1952)

1957 Eisenberg, Maurice [with M. B. Stanfield], *Cello Playing of Today* (London, 1957)

1961 Starker, Janos, *An Organised Method of String Playing: Violoncello Exercises for the Left Hand* (New York, 1961)

1964 Potter, L. A., *The Art of Cello Playing* (Evanston, Ill., 1964)

1972 Mantel, G., *Cello Technik* (Cologne, 1972)

1973 Stanfield, M. B., *The Intermediate Cellist* (London, 1973)

1974 Rolland, Paul, *The Teaching of Action in String Playing* (New York, 1974; 2nd edn, 1986)

1975 Tortelier, Paul, *How I Play, How I Teach* (London, 1975)

1980– Suzuki, Shin'ichi, *Cello School*, 7 vols. (Tokyo, 1980–)

1982 Bunting, Christopher, *Essay on the Craft of Cello-playing: I, Prelude, Bowing, Coordination; II, the Left Hand* (Cambridge, 1982; rev. 2nd edn 1988, ed. D. C. Pratt)
    Doppelbauer, R., *Der frühe Cellounterricht* (Wilhelmshaven, 1982)
    Pleeth, William, *The Cello* (London, 1982)

1984 Adeney, M., *Tomorrow's Cellist: Exploring the Basis of Artistry* (Oakville, Ont., 1984)

1988 Pratt, D. C. (ed.), *Cello Technique 'From One Note to the Next'* (Cambridge, 1988) [rev. edn of Bunting, 1982]

1992 Szilvay Csaba, *Cello ABC – Colour Strings* (Espoo, 1992)

1996 Bosanquet, R. Caroline, *The Secret Life of Cello Strings* (*Harmonics for Cellists*) (Cambridge, 1996)

Glossary of technical terms

Acer: genus of trees, including the Norwegian maple (*acer platanoides*) and the sycamore (great maple or plane, *acer pseudoplatanus*), notable for its hardness, close grain and light colour.

Adjuster: a metal device located where the string is secured to the tailpiece; when operated by a screw mechanism, it facilitates fine tuning of strings (especially steel strings).

Alla gamba: see *Sul ponticello*.

Amplitude: the maximum displacement of a waveform.

Annular rings: red growth lines of impacted resin in the wood which are crucial to an instrument's sound production.

Antinode: a point of maximum vibration.

Archings: the curved shapes of the table and back of a stringed instrument.

Arpeggio: the notes of a chord played in rapid succession, in ascending or descending order.

Atonality: a term for music in which no principal key is perceptible.

Back-plate: the strip of metal on the bow that extends along the back of the frog, ending on the underside next to the slide.

Bariolage: a slurred or separate bow-stroke comprising repeated notes played alternately on two different strings, one stopped and one open.

Bass-bar: a thin, curved strip of spruce or pine set lengthways down the inside of the bass side of the instrument by the left foot of the bridge opposite the soundpost. Its length is approximately three-quarters that of the table and its function is to assist the table in resisting and responding to the pressure exerted by the bridge.

Basso continuo: see *Continuo*.

Batteries: a note-pattern requiring the bowing of alternating, adjacent strings.

Beats: a 'warbling' sound created by two notes of almost identical frequency. The beat rate is equal to the frequency difference.

Bee-sting: the small projection of the black part of the purfling into the corner beyond the mitre; also, the fine cut which ends the spiral of the scroll by the eye.

Belly: the table, or top of a stringed instrument; it is normally arched and has two f-holes cut into it on either side of where the bridge is positioned.

Binary form: a bipartite structure which follows the scheme A–B, with each section repeated.

Bitonality: the simultaneous use of two different keys.

Blocks: six blocks of softwood (normally pine) glued inside the cello, one each in the four 'corners' for added strength, one at the top into which is inserted the shoulder of the neck, and one at the bottom, through which a hole is bored to accommodate the plug which holds the endpin. See also *Corner-block*.

Bottom-block: see *Blocks*.

Bouts: an inward curve or bend in a rib or ribs of a cello. The curves of the waist of the cello are called 'middle bouts' or 'C bouts'; those at the top of the instrument are called 'upper bouts'; and those at its base 'lower bouts'.

Bridge: a fairly thin piece of wood (usually maple) which supports the strings at the appropriate height above the table and fingerboard. Its two feet rest on the table, to which the vibrations are conveyed. The table acts as a soundboard and in turn transmits the vibrations through the soundpost to the back of the instrument and to the column of air within.

Brisure: a note-pattern requiring the bowing of alternating, non-adjacent strings.

Button: the small half-round projection of the top end of the back, to which the bottom, or shoulder, of the neck is glued.

Cadenza: a virtuosic passage in improvisatory style (normally drawing on some prominent thematic material) provided by a performer (generally a concerto soloist or soloists) near the end of a movement or composition and closing with an extended trill on the dominant chord.

Canon: a musical structure in which at least one line imitates another after a gap in time.

Chaconne: a kind of continuous variation (in moderately slow triple metre) in which the 'thematic material' comprises a harmonic sequence whose first and last chords are generally stable even though the intermediaries may be substituted.

Coda: a concluding section of a movement or piece which confirms the impression of finality. In movements in sonata form the coda sometimes serves as a section for further development of material.

Col legno: Italian for 'with the wood' – a direction to strike the strings with the bowstick as opposed to the hair.

Concertino: (1) the group of soloists in a concerto grosso; (2) a composition in concerto style but usually in a somewhat freer one-movement form.

Concerto grosso: a type of concerto common in the Baroque era, characterised by the contrast of a small group of solo instruments (commonly two violins and continuo), called *concertino* or *principale*, with the full orchestra, called *concerto*, *tutti* or *ripieni*.

Con sordino: literally, 'with the mute' – the direction to position the mute on the bridge.

Contact-point: see 'Point of contact'.

Continuo: abbreviation for 'basso continuo', a bass line which may be 'figured' (hence 'figured bass') and which implies to the accompanying keyboard player (generally harpsichord, but possibly organ, fortepiano etc.; or possibly, in some contexts, a plucked instrument – lute, guitar, harp etc.) the harmonies he is expected to play above it. The bass line was normally doubled by a bass stringed instrument (cello or gamba, violone etc.).

Corner-block: the wooden block at each corner of the cello to which are attached the table, back and ribs.

Counterpoint: the art of making two or more musical lines fit together satisfactorily at the same time; or a musical passage exemplifying this technique.

Crémaillère: an early bow-type with a movable frog. When the desired hair tension was attained, the frog was held in place by an iron catch or loop set into one of several indentations in the bowstick.

Curls: the waves in the veined wood.

Damping: mechanisms by which vibration energy is lost.

Détaché: literally, a 'detached', broad and vigorous bow-stroke; in the eighteenth century the *détaché* was synonymous with staccato.

Development: see *Sonata form*.

Down-bow: Drawing the bow so that its point of contact with the string moves from the frog end towards the tip.

D-ring: see *Ferrule*.

Dynamic: loudness.

Endpin: a retractable steel spike fixed to the lower part of the cello to support the instrument and to regulate its playing height from the floor.

Exposition: see *Sonata form*.

Eye: (1) the circular inset on the sides of the frog or nut of the bow, often of mother-of-pearl; (2) the 'ears' of the scroll, which project on either side and at which point the spiral of the volute ends.

Ferrule: the metal (commonly silver) band, or D-ring, around the lower front of the nut which strengthens the wedge area and spreads the hair into a uniform ribbon.

F-holes: the f-shapes cut in the table.

Figured bass: see *Continuo*.

Fingerboard: the long piece of ebony, flat underneath but curved on top, against which the strings are pressed when the player's finger(s) contact them. It extends from the end of the pegbox over and above the table to roughly the beginning of the f-holes, and it is generally narrower at the pegbox end.

Fluting: a concave channel or groove, especially on the back of the scroll; or on numerous pre-Tourte bowsticks.

Frequency: the number of oscillations per second (Hz).

Frog: see *Nut* (2).

Fundamental: the lowest-order mode of a system.

Glissando: literally 'sliding'. A method of sliding up or down the string with a finger of the left hand, distinguishing in so doing each semitone of the slide.

Grain: the arrangement or direction of the fibres of the wood.

Ground bass (basso ostinato): a kind of continuous variation. A short melodic phrase is repeated continually as a bass line (but not necessarily unvaried), while one or more melody instruments exploit the principle of variation to good effect.

Harmonic: usually used to describe modes of vibration which have natural frequencies related by integer multiples of the fundamental. So-called 'natural' harmonics are produced by touching the string lightly (not pressing firmly) with a single finger at the appropriate 'nodal' point. 'Artificial harmonics' are produced by two fingers, the first finger of the left hand stopping the required note firmly (acting in effect as the nut of the fingerboard), while another finger (usually the fourth) produces the harmonic by touching the string lightly at the appropriate point.

Input admittance: amplitude of the velocity per unit excitation force.

Lapping: the protective band of leather, whalebone or silver wire that covers the bowstick at and just above the frog. It assists the fingers in gripping the bowstick and protects the stick from wear.

Linings: the thin strips of softwood glued to the side ribs and plates inside the instrument to provide sufficient glue area to hold securely the table and back to the side ribs.

Martelé: literally 'hammered'. In modern terminology this refers to a type of percussive bow-stroke characterised by its sharp initial accent and post-stroke articulation. It was used interchangeably with staccato by many eighteenth- and early nineteenth-century musicians.

Microtone: an interval smaller than a semitone.

Mode: vibration pattern in which all points on the surface move in the same direction or in opposite directions.

Mortice: a cavity cut into the wood into which another part fits or through which another part passes.

Moto perpetuo: a movement or piece which proceeds from beginning to end in the same rapid motion.

Mute: a device (metal, ivory, bakelite or wood), often in the form of a two-, three-, or five-pronged clamp which is placed on the bridge in order to absorb some of the vibrations and thus reduce the volume and alter the timbre of the sound produced.

Node: stationary point on a vibrating surface.

Nuances: the subtler, finer shades of expression.

Nut: (1) a small block of ebony attached to the neck of a cello and placed between the fingerboard and the pegbox to support and separate the strings as they are led from the tailpiece over the bridge and the nut to the pegs; (2) the heel of the bow where the tension of the bow-hair is adjusted.

Open string: an unstopped string which sounds its full 'open' length.

Ostinato: literally 'obstinate', 'persistent'. A phrase which is repeated persistently throughout a composition or section thereof.

Passacaglia: a kind of continuous variation based on a clearly distinguishable ostinato, normally in the bass but sometimes occasionally in an upper voice.

Peg: one of four substantial tapered wooden (ebony or rosewood) 'pins' which are inserted into holes in the pegbox to secure the strings and regulate their tension, and hence pitch. Each string is threaded through a hole in the shaft of the relevant peg, the shank of which is at right angles to the string.

Pegbox: the part of the neck extending from chin to scroll into which holes are reamed to receive the pegs.

Period: the time-lapse between identical features in a waveform.

Piqué: literally 'pricked' or 'spurred'. In eighteenth- and early nineteenth-century cello methods, this term refers to the bowing of dotted-rhythm note patterns.

Pizzicato: a direction to pluck the string (or strings) with the fingers, usually of the right hand (but sometimes with the left).

Plates: the table and back of the cello.

Plug: the device at the bottom of the cello into which the endpin is inserted.

Point of contact: the place where the bow touches the strings.

Polyphony: music in which two or more lines are sounding at the same time.

Ponticello: see *Sul ponticello*.

Portamento: a continuous slide between two pitches which does not distinguish the intermediate semitones.

Portato: a bowing in which two or more notes are played in the same bow-stroke, but detached.

Position: refers to the place taken by the left hand along the fingerboard in order for its fingers to stop the string and produce the notes required by the music.

Purfling: a narrow inlay of wood set into a channel carved around the border of the table and back of a cello. It normally comprises three narrow strips, the outer two of a white or yellowish wood sandwiching one of ebony. It helps to protect the edges of the instrument and is also ornamental.

Quarter-cut: wood cut radially from a tree so that the grain (annular growth rings) runs perpendicularly through the thickness of the specimen.

Quarter-tone: interval comprising half a semitone.

Recapitulation: see *Sonata form*.

Resonance: the enlarged motion which occurs when a vibrating system is excited at its natural frequency of vibration.

Ribs: the sides (generally of maple or of equivalent hardwood) that connect the table and back of the instrument.

Ricochet: involves at least two notes being played in the same 'bow-stroke' (either up or down), the bow being 'thrown' on to the string and the relevant notes articulated (usually in the upper third) through the natural 'bounce' of the stick.

Ripieno: the full orchestral forces in a concerto grosso.

Ritornello 'form': a type of structure commonly employed in the first, and sometimes the last, movements of Baroque concertos. It comprises an alternation of sections for tutti and soloist(s), in which the tutti sections (in a variety of closely related keys) are based for the most part on similar material (the so-called ritornello) while the content of the solo sections is freer and more varied.

Rosin: a hard, brittle material obtained from the distillation of oil of turpentine. It is applied to the bow-hair, giving it the requisite 'bite' to set the string(s) in vibration.

Rubato: see *Tempo rubato*.

Saddle: the small piece of hardwood (usually ebony) over which the tailgut is fitted to protect the bottom of the table edge.

Sautillé: a short, rapid bow-stroke taken around the middle of the bow so that the bow rebounds lightly off the string.

Scordatura: refers to any tuning of string instruments other than the established tuning (C–G–d–a in the case of the modern cello).

Scroll: the curved head at the end of the neck, beyond the pegbox of a cello, usually carved to resemble a scroll.

Secco recitative: operatic recitative which limits accompaniment to the basso continuo.

Senza sordino: literally 'without the mute'; a direction to remove the mute from the bridge.

Serialism: a technique of composition in which the twelve notes of the chromatic scale are arranged in an order that is binding for the work.

Shifting: the act of moving from one left-hand finger-position to another.

Siciliano: a seventeenth- and eighteenth-century dance of Sicilian origin in moderate 6/8 or 12/8 metre.

Slide: the rectangular plate of mother-of-pearl that covers the bow hair on the lower face of the frog, between the ferrule and the back-plate.

Sonata form: broadly speaking, this comprises three principal sections: (1) exposition, which introduces the (normally contrasting) thematic material; (2) development, in which the potential of that material is freely explored and expanded (via techniques such as melodic fragmentation, modulation, contrapuntal combination etc.); (3) recapitulation, in which material of the exposition is repeated with tonal and other modifications. A coda normally concludes a movement in sonata form.

Soundpost: a small piece of wood (generally of pine or spruce), about 11 mm in diameter, which fits vertically between the table and the back of the instrument (without being glued), directly in line with and slightly below the right-hand foot of the bridge.

Spectrum: a graph showing the relative proportions of the different frequencies making up a waveform.

Spiccato: in eighteenth-century terminology, a bowing which produces a dry, detached sound, not necessarily executed off the string. In the nineteenth century, it came to mean a relatively slow, bouncing stroke.

Spike: see *Endpin*.

Staccato: a detached, well-articulated stroke, normally indicated by a dot (or stroke) over (or under) a note. In modern violin playing, staccato involves the playing of several *martelé* strokes taken rapidly in one bow-stroke (either up or down). When the bow is allowed to spring slightly from the string, the stroke is known as 'flying staccato'.

Sul ponticello: Italian for 'on the bridge'; a direction to play with the bow very near to the bridge, in order to produce a nasal sound-quality. Another designation for this effect was *alla gamba*.

Sul tasto: Italian for 'on the fingerboard'; a direction to play with the bow further up the strings than usual, over the fingerboard.

Table: the belly or top-arched portion of the cello, with two f-holes cut in it and with an outline similar to the back.

Tailgut: a loop of gut, wire or nylon attached to the tailpiece, which is in turn anchored to the button.

Tailpiece: a piece of ebony (or metal for high-tension metal strings) fastened by a loop (tailgut) to the button at the lower end of a cello and to which the four strings are attached before they pass over the bridge and to the pegbox.

Tailpin: see *Endpin*.

Tempo rubato: literally 'robbed (or borrowed) time', denoting the flexible execution of appointed time-values. Notes may be held longer than their notated value, with others being shortened to compensate.

Ternary form: a tripartite structure which follows the scheme A–B–A(or A'), where A and B are often thematically independent, and the recurrence of A is sometimes modified (A'), possibly by additional ornamentation or, more radically, by a redevelopment of the same material. A coda based on material of either A or B, or both, may conclude the piece or movement.

Transient: the initial, non-periodic part of a waveform.

Twelve-tone: see *Serialism*.

Una corda: literally 'one string'; employed when a composer/performer wishes to exploit the uniformity of timbre offered by the execution of a particular passage on one string.

Underslide: a thin metal plate attached to the upper surface of the frog. It protects the bowstick from wear from friction between the movable frog and the stick.

Up-bow: 'Pushing' the bow so that its point of contact with the string moves from the tip towards the frog.

Vibrato: an oscillation in pitch within a small range produced by 'rocking' the finger which is stopping a string.

Volutes: the spiral-shaped sections of the scroll.

Wedge: the small block of wood that secures the hair in the frog and the head of the bow.

Wolf-note: a note or notes on an instrument, which, owing to that instrument's structure, are too loud or too soft or difficult to play precisely in tune compared with other notes. The phenomenon is caused by an irregularity in the resonance of the instrument which either enhances or damps one particular note, or to a strong and sharply defined resonance frequency that is slightly sharper or flatter than some note of the scale. The most likely wolf-notes on the cello are around e–f♯; these may sometimes be rectified by squeezing the body of the instrument with the knees when playing or by attaching a 'wolf mute' to the G string behind the bridge.

Notes

1 The cello: origins and evolution

1 See S. Bonta, 'Terminology for the Bass Violin in Seventeenth-Century Italy', *Journal of the American Musical Instrument Society*, 4 (1978), pp. 5–42. See also Chapter 10, pp. 160–2.

2 M. Agricola, *Musica instrumentalis deudsch* (Wittenberg, 1528; 2/1529/R1969, rev. 6/1545), p. x.

3 For example, by G. M. Lanfranco, *Scintille di musica* (Brescia, 1533/R1969) and L. Zacconi, *Prattica di musica* (Venice, 1592–1622/R1967).

4 This tuning was first mentioned by Hans Gerle in his *Musica teusch, auf die Instrument der grossen und kleinen Geygen, auch Lauten* (Nuremberg, 1532, rev. enlarged 3/1546/R1977).

5 For information about strings see E. Segerman, 'Strings of the Violin Family – Summary of Historical Information', *Fellowship of Makers and Restorers of Historical Instruments Quarterly* (October, 1982) and S. Bonta, 'From Violone to Violoncello: a Question of Strings?', *Journal of the American Musical Instrument Society*, 3 (1977), pp. 64–99, and *Idem*, 'Catline Strings Revisited', *Journal of the American Musical Instrument Society*, 14 (1988), p. 38.

6 Observations and measurements compiled by James Talbot in the late seventeenth century, currently housed in Christ Church Library, Oxford, Shelfmark Music MS 1187.

7 For further information about the Guarneri family see W. H., A. F. and A. E. Hill, *The Violin Makers of the Guarneri Family* (London, 1931; rev. 2/ 1965).

8 For further information about Antonio Stradivari see W. H., A. F. and A. E. Hill, *Antonio Stradivari: his Life and Work* (London, 1902; rev. 2/1909/R1963).

9 Cristofori is best known for his invention of the piano.

10 One of the most popular models, the Dolphin Electric Cello, has been developed by Mike Anderson of Starfish Designs, North Ballachulish, Scotland.

2 The bow: its history and development

1 François Tourte's father.

2 According to Fétis (*Antoine Stradivari, Luthier célèbre* (Paris, 1856, Eng. trans. 1864/R1964), p. 116), Tourte standardised the overall length of the cello bow at 72–3 cm, with a playing length of hair of 60–2 cm and a balance-point 17.5–18 cm above the frog.

3 Cello acoustics

1 Non-technical texts on musical acoustics are available for the general reader. The following books are particularly recommended: A. H. Benade, *Fundamentals of Musical Acoustics* (London, 1976); D. M. Campbell and C. Greated, *The Musician's Guide to Acoustics* (London, 1987); and C. A. Taylor, *Exploring Music: the Science and Technology of Tones and Tunes* (Bristol, 1992). Several standard reference works exist, which give references to contemporary scientific literature, e.g. N. H. Fletcher and T. D. Rossing, *The Physics of Musical Instruments* (New York, 1991); L. Cremer, *The Physics of the Violin* (Cambridge, Mass., 1984); C. M. Hutchins, *Musical Acoustics Parts 1 and 2, Benchmark Papers in Musical Acoustics Vols. 5 and 6* (Stroudburger, Penn., 1977); C. M. Hutchins, *Research Papers in Violin Acoustics 1975–1993* (New York, 1996).

2 Hermann von Helmholtz was an influential nineteenth-century physicist whose work on musical instruments and aural perception are described in his book *Die Lehre von den Tonempfindungen als physiologische Grundlage für die Theorie der Musik* (Brunswick, 1863; Eng. trans. 1875/R1954 as *On the Sensations of Tone*).

3 The frequency of concert A (or a^1) is usually taken as 440 Hz. Doubling or halving a particular frequency produces an increase or decrease of one octave (see also Ex. 3.1).

4 It is vital to distinguish between the meaning of 'harmonics' in the musician's sense and in a scientific context. The latter simply means a collection of simple tones whose frequencies have integer, or harmonic, relationships. To avoid confusion in this text these related tones are referred to as overtones. However, it is equally correct, and very common, to refer to the fundamental and its overtones as harmonics.

5 Fortunately, the perceived loudness of the sound does not vary as much as might be expected from casual observation of the

response curve. Loudness is subjective and determined by some sort of aggregate of the intensities of the overtones of the note, and it is unusual for all or none of the overtones to coincide with body resonances, so the loudness variations are not so great. It is not uncommon, however, for adjacent notes on a cello to be perceived as doubling or halving in loudness. Substantial changes in loudness like these are inevitably accompanied by obvious changes in tone-quality.

6 E. Bynum and T. D. Rossing, 'Holographic Studies of Cello Vibrations', *Proceedings of the Institute of Acoustics*, 19/5 (1997), pp. 155–61.

7 A fascinating technical insight into the world of the luthier is given by Carleen Hutchins, 'The Acoustics of Violin Plates', *Scientific American*, 245 (1981), pp. 170–86.

8 Body vibrations and the function of the soundpost and bridge are covered in a little more detail in R. Stowell (ed.), *The Cambridge Companion to the Violin* (Cambridge, 1992), pp. 30–45.

9 See Cremer, *The Physics of the Violin*, p. 220.

10 Scaling of violins and the susceptibility of the cello to wolf-notes is discussed in detail by John Schelleng in his paper 'The Violin as a Circuit', *Journal of the Acoustical Society of America*, 35 (1963), pp. 326–38.

11 Further details of the physics of wolf-notes are beyond the scope of this text. Interested readers are advised to consult Cremer's *The Physics of the Violin*.

12 Current details of the Violin Octet and principal references to earlier work are given by Carleen Hutchins, 'A 30-Year Experiment in the Acoustical and Musical Development of Violin Family Instruments', *Journal of the Acoustical Society of America*, 92 (1992), pp. 639–50. There are currently six complete sets in existence (and numerous individual instruments). Three of the sets are permanently housed at the University of Edinburgh collection of Historic Musical Instruments, the Stockholm Musik Museum and the Metropolitan Museum of Art in New York City. The Octet has also attracted new compositions and the instruments are used to give occasional concerts.

13 See, for example, J. Woodhouse, ' Stringed Instruments: Bowed', in M. J. Crocker (ed.), *Encyclopedia of Acoustics*, 4 vols. (New York, 1997), IV, pp. 1619–26, and references therein.

14 See K. Guettler, 'Bow Notes', *Proceedings of the Institute of Acoustics*, 19/5 (1997), pp. 1–10, and references therein.

4 Masters of the Baroque and Classical eras

1 P. Nettl, *Forgotten Musicians* (New York, 1951), p. 303.

2 C. Burney, *A General History of Music from the Earliest Ages to the Present Period* (London, 1776–89), ed. F. Mercer, 2 vols. (London, 1935/R1957), II, p. 1005.

3 S. Sadie (ed.), *The New Grove Dictionary of Music and Musicians*, 20 vols. (London, 1980), III, p. 755 *s.v.* 'Caporale, Andrea'.

4 Crome, *The Compleat Tutor for the Violoncello*, p. 1.

5 E. S. J. van der Straeten, *History of the Violoncello, the Viola da Gamba, their Precursors and Collateral Instruments* (London, 1914/R1971), p. 229.

5 Nineteenth-century virtuosi

1 Letter from Ignace Pleyel to Muzio Clementi (2 April 1802).

2 In E. S. J. van der Straeten, *History of the Violoncello, the Viola da Gamba, their Precursors and Collateral Instruments* (London, 1914/R1971), p. 293.

3 F. J. Fétis, *Biographie universelle des musiciens et bibliographie générale de la musique* (Brussels, 1835–44, 2/1860–5/R1963), *s.v.* 'Müntzberger, Joseph'.

4 E. Blom (ed.), *Grove's Dictionary of Music and Musicians*, 9 vols. (London, 1954), V, p. 1000.

5 W. J. von Wasielewski, *Das Violoncell und seine Geschichte* (Leipzig, 1889; Eng. trans. London, 1894/R1968), p. 193.

6 Van der Straeten, *History of the Violoncello*, p. 250.

7 M. Gorovitch, 'Charles Davidoff, a Great Cellist', *The Strad*, 62 (1952), p. 276.

8 Wasielewski, *Das Violoncell*, Eng. trans., p. 111.

6 Masters of the twentieth century

1 M. Campbell, *The Great Cellists* (London, 1988), p. 260.

2 *Ibid.*, p. 201.

3 Eisenberg, with co-author M. B. Stanfield, gives a full exposition of Casals's left-hand technique in *Cello Playing of Today* (London, 1957).

4 E. S. J. van der Straeten, *History of the Violoncello, the Viola da Gamba, their Precursors and Collateral Instruments* (London, 1914/R1971), p. 599.

5 S. S. Dale, 'Contemporary Cello Concerti LXX; Trexler and Klengel', *The Strad*, 89 (1978), p. 523.

6 Campbell, *The Great Cellists*, p. 214.

7 B. Jones, 'Concert Notes', *The Strad*, 94 (1984), p. 838.
8 Campbell, *The Great Cellists*, p. 233.
9 *Ibid.*

7 The concerto

1 E. S. J. van der Straeten (*History of the Violoncello, the Viola da Gamba, their Precursors and Collateral Instruments* (London, 1914/R1971), p. 374) claims that Della Bella's cello concerto was published in Venice in 1705.
2 Among Vivaldi's other concertante works involving cello are one concerto for two cellos (RV531), three concertos for violin and cello (RV544, 546, 547), one concerto for violin and two cellos (RV561), and two concertos for two violins and two cellos (RV564, 575).
3 In which all or part of the theme of the opening tutti returns in different keys between solo episodes, providing structural punctuation and formal unity.
4 Concerto composed in collaboration with his brother Giuseppe Maria.
5 The manuscripts of Canavas' concertos are housed in the Nationalbibliothek, Vienna, those of Vandini's concertos in the Wissenschaftliche Allgemeinbibliothek, Schwerin, and those of Molter's concerto in Karlsruhe's Badische Landesbibliothek.
6 The manuscripts of Lanzetti's concertos can be accessed in the Musikwissenschaftliches Institut der Philipps-Universität, Marburg an der Lahn, and those of Platti's in the Musiksammlung des Grafen von Schönborn-Wiesentheid in Wiesentheid.
7 See M.-G. Scott, 'Boccherini's B flat Cello Concerto: a Reappraisal of the Sources', *Early Music*, 12 (1984), pp. 355–7.
8 E. Lewicki, 'Die Spur eines Violoncell-Konzerts von Mozart', *Mitteilungen für die Mozart Gemeinde in Berlin*, 4 (1912), pp. 62–3.
9 Shostakovich reorchestrated the work in the 1960s, subtly expanding its sonority and range of colours without violating Schumann's style.
10 R. Schumann, 'Neue Bahnen', *Neue Zeitschrift für Musik*, 39 (1853), p. 185.
11 This second theme is closely related rhythmically to a theme from the opening movement of Viotti's Violin Concerto No. 22, a favourite of both Joachim and Brahms, and alluded to here probably as part of the reconciliation process.
12 In L. Ginsburg, *History of the Violoncello* (Moscow, 1950–78; Eng. trans. 1983), p. 117.
13 In D. Tovey, *Essays in Musical Analysis*, 7 vols. (London, 1935–9/R1972) III, p. 126.
14 Rediscovered in 1925, this work was

completed by Günter Raphael (1929), who, according to John Clapham, all but recomposed it, making extensive alterations. See Cowling, *The Cello* (London, 1975, 2/1983), p. 138. Another edition has been made by the Czech cellist Miloš Sádlo and Jarmil Burghauser.
15 Later published as Op. 82 No. 1.
16 The revised conclusion was completed on 11 June 1895. On discovering that Hanus Wihan, the work's dedicatee and Dvořák's adviser on various technical details, had not only proposed but actually composed a cadenza for insertion at this point, Dvořák threatened to withold the work altogether unless his publisher, Simrock, assured him that no such intervention would be permitted.
17 Sullivan's continuous three-movement work has recently been rescued from oblivion by Sir Charles Mackerras's fairly faithful reconstruction. A fire at the premises of Chappell and Co. in 1964 had destroyed the autograph score and the entire stock of orchestral and solo parts.
18 Its orchestral forces include saxophone, mandolin, guitar, 'glass harp', electronic bass and a vast battery of percussion.
19 Cowling (*The Cello*, p. 150) also writes of a Monn–Schoenberg concerto in G minor.
20 As in Britten's Violin Concerto (1939 rev. 1958).
21 Translated as 'A Whole Distant World'.
22 Pseudonym Vernon Duke.
23 S. Sadie (ed.), *The New Grove Dictionary of Music and Musicians*, 20 vols. (London, 1980), VII, *s.v.* 'Glazunov, Alexander Konstantinovich'.
24 Improvements in the reworked version include altering the structure of the first movement from a rondo to a ternary design with coda, extending the central scherzo and offering further opportunity for solo display, and completely revising the structure of the final variation movement in the interests of greater coherence.
25 A more delicate reorchestration for cello and chamber orchestra by Russian musicologist Vladimir Bok was premièred by Steven Isserlis in Cardiff (BBC National Orchestra of Wales/Mark Wigglesworth) in April 1997.
26 Including electric guitar, drum kit, piano, celesta, harpsichord, tubular bells *et al.*
27 Sadie (ed.), *The New Grove Dictionary*, XI, *s.v.* 'Lutosławski, Witold'.
28 Quoted in C. B. Rae, *The Music of Lutosławski* (London, 1994), p. 119.
29 Cassadó did much to promote the cello in

his country and internationally; he even arranged Mozart's Horn Concerto K.447 for cello and orchestra.

8 The sonata
1 Such is the theoretical definition. But in practice the two types are not always clearly differentiated; many 'church sonatas' conclude with one or more dance movements (not always so designated), while many 'chamber sonatas' include an opening movement which is not a dance.
2 Op. 1 Nos. 7 and 8, and Op. 3 Nos. 9 and 10. Op. 3 No. 10 reappeared with various modifications in an anthology entitled *Sonate a tre di vari autori* (Bologna, c. 1700).
3 Published posthumously in the same anthology mentioned in note 2.
4 See E. Cowling, *The Cello* (London, 1975, 2/1983) pp. 79–81.
5 RV40, 41, 43, 45–7 were published in Paris, c. 1740.
6 See Cowling, *The Cello*, pp. 87–8.
7 *Ibid.*, Appendix A, pp. 223–6. The cellist Nona Pyron also published some lesser-known works in her series for Grancino International Ltd., emphasising the volume and richness of the repertory.
8 A manuscript in the Biblioteca Conservatorio G. Verdi in Milan is a possible holograph by Alessandro, but the same sonatas in a much neater hand, and possibly a copy, are housed in the Biblioteca Communale in Bologna, attributed to Domenico.
9 Pergolesi's work is actually entitled *Sinfonia in F*; it comprises four movements and some of its themes were used by Stravinsky for his *Pulcinella*.
10 Known as Jean-Pierre Guignon.
11 Comprising six sonatas for vn, vle, hpd and six for 2vc.
12 See E. Barsham, 'Six New Boccherini Cello Sonatas', *Musical Times*, 105 (1964), pp. 18–20.
13 W. S. Newman, *The Sonata in the Classic Era* (Chapel Hill, 1963; rev. 2/1972), p. 770.
14 The Chevalier de Leaumont's *Duo Concertant Pour le Clavecin ou le Forte Piano et Violoncelle* (1787) has been cited by Cowling (*The Cello*, p. 81) as possible inspiration.
15 Cowling, *The Cello*, p. 129. Apparently, Casals often included this in his recitals. A version for cello and piano (published in 1807 as Op. 64) of the String Trio Op. 3 has also survived; an example is apparently housed in the Beethoven Archives in Bonn.
16 The dedication did not appear until the work's Vienna edition of 1819.
17 A. F. Schindler, *Beethoven as I Knew Him*,

ed. D. W. MacArdle, trans. C. S. Jolly (London, 1966), p. 213.
18 See *Allgemeine musikalische Zeitung* 20 (11 November 1818), cols. 792–4, and 26 (1 April 1824), cols. 213–25.
19 See *Allgemeine musikalische Zeitung*, 23 (21 March 1821), col. 185.
20 The work remained in manuscript until 1871, when it was published with an alternative cello part, soon followed by arrangements for viola and guitar. See F. Avellar de Aquino, 'Six-stringed Virtuoso', *The Strad*, 109 (1998), pp. 500–7.
21 The work was listed as being by Karl Würth, a pseudonym used by the teenage Brahms when he was not entirely satisfied with a composition. See S. Avins, 'An Undeniable Gift', *The Strad*, 107 (1996), pp. 1048–53.
22 Geiringer has demonstrated the fugue subject's close affinity with that of Contrapunctus 13 in J. S. Bach's *The Art of Fugue*.
23 In the same way in which Brahms transcribed his Sonatas Op. 120 Nos. 1 and 2 for violin and piano. See 'Uncovered Masterpiece' *Time* (5 August 1974), pp. 77–8.
24 See G. Bozarth, 'Leider nicht von Johannes Brahms', *The Strad*, 99 (1988), pp. 146–50.
25 R. Specht, *Richard Strauss und sein Werk*, 2 vols. (Zurich, 1921), p. 111, demonstrates the influence of Schumann and Mendelssohn.
26 J. Harding, *Saint-Saëns and his Circle* (London, 1965), p. 124.
27 J. Bonnerot, *Camille Saint-Saëns (1835–1921): sa Vie et son œuvre*, 2nd rev. edn. (Paris, 1922), p. 69.
28 See W. S. Newman, *The Sonata since Beethoven* (Chapel Hill, 1969; rev. 2/1972), p. 518.
29 E. Bernsdorf, *Signale für die musikalische Welt* (27 October 1883), col. 996.
30 Newman (*The Sonata since Beethoven*, p. 697) points out that Brahms provides a precedent for this arrangement in the finale of his Quartet Op. 67.
31 Shostakovich's Viola Sonata Op. 147 has been arranged for cello by Russian cellist Daniil Shafran.
32 Denisov also composed a Sonata for Alto Saxophone and Cello (1994).
33 The other two are the Sonata for Violin and Piano and the Sonata for Flute, Viola and Harp.
34 Debussy gave the work the unofficial subtitle 'Pierrot, angry with the moon'.
35 He had written and destroyed two violin sonatas (1919, 1924) before his one surviving example (1942–3) for Ginette Neveu.
36 S. Sadie (ed.), *The New Grove Dictionary of*

Music and Musicians, 20 vols. (London, 1980), XV, *s.v.* 'Poulenc, Francis'.

37 An affinity has been observed between the turbulent opening of Barber's Sonata and that of Brahms's Sonata in F Op. 99. The first movement's second theme is also very Brahmsian.

38 Sonata No. 1 (1941) was withdrawn by the composer.

39 R. F. Goldman, 'The Music of Elliott Carter', *Musical Quarterly,* 43 (1957), p. 161.

40 Sadie (ed.), *New Grove Dictionary,* X, *s.v.,* 'Lessard, John (Ayres)'.

41 Modelled on his Violin Sonata (1941).

42 Originally Sonata in D minor.

43 Printed as Op. 6.

44 Newman, *The Sonata since Beethoven,* p. 694.

45 Cassadó also composed a Cello Sonata without any declared nationalistic associations.

9 Other solo repertory

1 See E. Cowling, *The Cello* (London, 1975, 2/1983), p. 77.

2 The MS is entitled *Balli e Sonate a 2 violoni e basso, / a violino e basso ed a basso solo,/con b. c.* and comprises thirty pieces for two violins and continuo, two for violin and continuo, and one for basso and continuo.

3 The Cöthen cellist Christian Bernhard Linigke is also suggested as a possible recipient of these suites.

4 Available space will only allow discussion of the major twentieth-century works for the medium.

5 Not forgetting the 'Sacher variations' of Boulez and Dutilleux.

6 Xenakis provides a mathematical analysis in his article 'Vers une Philosophie de la Musique', in *Musiques Nouvelles. Revue d'esthétique* (Klincksieck, 1968), pp. 173–210.

7 This lyrical movement has been completed from Prokofiev's rough drafts by Vladimir Bok.

8 A shamisen was a Japanese long-necked plucked lute.

9 E♭ = the German note Es (or 'S'), A, C, B (called 'H' in German), D = R, as in the solfa note 're'.

10 Bruch also arranged this piece for violin and orchestra; viola and piano; piano and harmonium; piano solo; cello and organ; and organ solo.

11 Don Quixote is also portrayed by a solo violin, while Sancho Panza's characterisation is also shared by tenor tuba and bass clarinet.

12 S. Sadie (ed.), *The New Grove Dictionary of*

Music and Musicians, 20 vols. (London, 1980), XI, *s.v.* 'Maconchy, Elizabeth'.

13 J. Tavener in sleeve notes for CD entitled *Svyati* (RCA Victor Red Seal 09026 68761 2) featuring Steven Isserlis (cello).

14 See R. Orledge, 'Fauré's Pelléas et Mélisande', *Music and Letters,* 56 (1975), pp. 170–9.

15 Incidentally, variations 1, 2 and 6 can be found in Weber's *Grand Pot-pourri* in a more or less identical form.

16 Wilhelm Fitzenhagen, who premièred the work, subsequently made substantial revisions to Tchaikovsky's score, altering solo dynamics, phrasing and some notes, adding repeat marks to both halves of the theme, omitting the eighth variation completely and changing the order of the remaining variations. His version, generally that familiar to players and audiences nowadays, was published by Pyotr Jurgenson on the understanding that Tchaikovsky had approved the revision, but this was not the case. Tchaikovsky's original version was not published until 1956.

17 See also 'Sacher' Variations, pp. 143–4.

18 Some of Franchomme's variations and fantasias are for solo cello and string quintet.

10 Ensemble music: in the chamber and the orchestra

1 S. Bonta, 'Catline Strings Revisited', *Journal of the American Musical Instrument Society,* 14 (1988), p. 51.

2 See S. Bonta, 'Terminology for the Bass Violin in Seventeenth-Century Italy', *Journal of the American Musical Instrument Society,* 4 (1978), pp. 5–42.

3 This chapter discusses neither the repertory for cello and keyboard nor the concerto, which are treated elsewhere in this volume.

4 S. Bonta, 'From Violone to Violoncello: a Question of Strings?' *Journal of the American Musical Instrument Society,* 3 (1977), p. 89.

5 O. Gambassi, *La cappella musicale di S. Petronio* (Florence, 1987), p. x.

6 W. Klenz, *Giovanni Maria Bononcini of Modena* (Durham, N C, 1962), p. 19.

7 Bonta, 'Terminology', p. 27.

8 S. La Via, '"Violone" e "violoncello" a Roma al tempo di Corelli', *Studi Corelliani IV. Atti del Quarto Congresso Internazionale (Fusignano, 4–7 settembre, 1986)* (Florence, 1990), p. 169.

9 *Ibid.,* p. 171.

10 A. Planyavsky, *Der Barockkontrabass Violone* (Salzburg, 1989), pp. 73–8.

11 This is the conclusion of H. Burnett in 'The Bowed String Instruments of the Baroque Basso Continuo (ca. 1680—ca. 1752) in Italy

and France', *Journal of the Viola da Gamba Society of America*, 8 (1971), p. 29.

12 The repertory of Italian ensemble music is surveyed in P. Allsop, *The Italian 'Trio' Sonata* (Oxford, 1992).

13 Besides those articles already mentioned, Bonta's arguments are further developed in 'Corelli's Heritage: the Early Bass Violin in Italy', *Studi Corelliani IV. Atti del Quarto Congresso Internazionale (Fusignano, 4–7 settembre, 1986)* (Florence, 1990), pp. 217–23.

14 See P. Allsop, 'The Role of the Stringed Bass as a Continuo Instrument in Italian Seventeenth-century Music', *Chelys*, 8 (1978–9), p. 31.

15 This is discussed fully in T. Borgir, *The Performance of the Basso Continuo in Italian Baroque Music* (Ann Arbor, 1987).

16 'The most complete accompaniment to a Solo, and the one to which no possible exception can be taken, is a keyboard instrument in combination with a Violoncello', C. P. E. Bach, *Essay on the True Art of Playing Keyboard Instruments* (Berlin, 1762), II, p. 8.

17 D. Watkin, 'Corelli's Op. 5 Sonatas: 'Violino e Violone o Cimbalo'?" *Early Music*, 24 (1996), pp. 645–63.

18 See O. Iotti, *Violin and Violoncello in Duo without Accompaniment*, Detroit Studies in Music Bibliography 25 (Detroit, 1972).

19 See E. I. Amsterdam, 'The String Quintets of Luigi Boccherini', Ph.D. diss., University of California at Berkeley (1968).

20 *Ibid.*, p. 82.

21 C. Burney, *A General History of Music* (London, 1776–89), p. 573.

22 A. Sandberger, 'Zur Geschichte des Haydnschen Streichquartetts' (1900), rev. *Ausgewählte Aufsätze zur Musikgeschichte* (Munich, 1921–4), I, pp. 224–65.

23 J. Webster, 'Towards the History of Viennese Chamber Music in the Early Classical Period', *Journal of the American Musicological Society*, 27 (1974), pp. 221–47, esp. 243–6.

24 W. Kirkendale, *Fugue and Fugato in Rococo and Classical Chamber Music* (Durham, NC, 1979), p. 42.

25 *The Monthly Magazine*, 2 (London, 1796), p. 981, reprinted by C. Cudworth in *Music and Letters*, 36 (1955), p. 158. William Drabkin discusses possible relationships between 'ancient' and 'modern' music in 'Corelli's Trio Sonatas and the Viennese String Quartet: Some Points of Contact', *Studi Corelliani V. Atti del Quinto Congresso Internazionale (Fusignano, 9–11 settembre, 1994)* (Florence, 1996), pp. 119–38.

26 Included in *Cobbett's Cyclopedic Survey of Chamber Music*, 2nd edn (Oxford, 1963), I, p. 533.

27 In his earliest chamber music even the use of the cello itself has been questioned; see J. Webster, 'The Scoring of Mozart's Chamber Music for Strings', in *Music in the Classic Period: Essays in Honor of Barry S. Brook*, ed. A. W. Atlas (New York, 1985), pp. 259–96. Similar conclusions are drawn by Carl Bar in respect of the Serenade in 'Zum Begriff des "Basso" in Mozarts Serenaden', *Mozart-Jahrbuch* (1960/61), pp. 133–55.

28 K. Marx, *The Violin Family: the New Grove Musical Instrument Series* (London, 1989), p. 178.

29 T. F. Dunhill, *Chamber Music* (London, 1913), p. 116.

30 On the Classical string quintet, see T. Seiber, *Das Klassische Streichquintett* (Bern, 1983).

31 C. Brown, *Louis Spohr: a Critical Biography* (Cambridge, 1984), p. 164.

32 A. Copland and V. Perlis, *Copland since 1943* (New York, 1989), p. 301.

33 For a discussion of these, see B. Smallman, *The Piano Quartet and Quintet* (Oxford, 1994), pp. 8–9.

34 A. C. Bell, 'An Introduction to Haydn's Piano Trios', *The Music Review*, 16 (1955), p. 193.

35 B. Smallman, *The Piano Trio* (Oxford, 1990), pp. 86–7.

36 F. Brand, 'Das neue Brahms-Trio', *Die Musik*, 32 (1938–9), p. 321.

37 *Gazette musicale de Paris*, 1 (1834); trans. O. Strunk, *Source Readings in Music History* (New York, 1950), p. 810.

38 Klengel also wrote some works for four cellos, notably his *Variationen über ein eigenes Thema* Op. 15, *Thema mit Variationen* Op. 28 and *Zwei Stücke* Op. 5.

39 See G. Read, *Compendium of Modern Instrumental Techniques* (Westport, Conn., 1993). See also Chapter 13, pp. 211–23.

40 Read, *Compendium*, p. 223.

11 Technique, style and performing practice to *c.* 1900

1 R. Crome, *The Compleat Tutor for the Violoncello* (London, [1765]), p. 1.

2 R. G. Edwards, 'The Violoncello, a Solo Instrument', *The Musician*, 18 (13 May 1913), p. 345.

3 *Mercure de France* (April 1762), quoted in C. Pierre, *Histoire du Concert Spirituel 1725–1790* (Paris, 1975), p. 127.

4 'Einige Worte bezüglich des Violoncells',

Allgemeine Wiener Musik-Zeitung, 2/29 (8 March 1842), p. 115.

5 'Is the Cello the Real King of String Instruments?' *Current Opinion*, 65 (18 August 1918), p. 97.

6 M. Corrette, *Méthode théorique et pratique pour apprendre en peu de tems le violoncelle dans sa perfection. Ensemble de principes de musique avec des leçons* Op. 24 (Paris, 1741/R1972), p. 1.

7 'On the Rise and Progress of the Violoncello', *The Quarterly Musical Magazine and Review*, 6/23 (1824), p. 353.

8 See E. Anderson (ed. and trans.), *The Letters of Beethoven*, 3 vols. (London, 1961), II, pp. 594–5, for Beethoven's explanation of this system of notation to Sigmund Steiner.

9 B. Romberg, *A Complete Theoretical and Practical School for the Violoncello* (London, 1839), p. 65.

10 V. Walden, *One Hundred Years of Violoncello: a History of Technique and Performance Practice, 1740–1840* (Cambridge, 1998), pp. 74–8.

11 A. Broadley, *Chats to 'Cello Students* (London, 1899), p. 6.

12 For information regarding the development of the endpin, see T. A. Russell, 'The Development of the Cello Endpin', *Imago Musicae*, 4 (1987), pp. 335–56, and 'New Light on the Historical Manner of Holding the Cello', *Historical Performance*, 6/2 (Fall, 1993), pp. 73–8.

13 Broadley, *Chats*, p. 7.

14 C. Baudiot, *Méthode pour le violoncelle*, 2 vols. (Paris, [1826–8]), I, pp. 5–6.

15 'Etwas über den berühmten französischen Violoncellisten Lamare,' *Berlinische musikalische Zeitung* 26 (1806), p. 102.

16 E. S. J. van der Straeten, *The Technics of Violoncello Playing* (London, 1898), p. 18.

17 Vaslin had a weak, double-jointed third finger. For a comparison of the hand-shapes of Janson and Duport, see *Correspondance des Amateurs Musiciens*, 45 (1 October 1803), p. 1; Romberg, *School*, p. 7; O. Vaslin, *L'art du violoncelle conseils aux jeunes violoncellistes sur la conduite de l'archet* (Paris, [1884]), p. 3.

18 J. Gunn, *The Theory and Practice of Fingering the Violoncello* (London, [1793]), pp. 60–1; J.-L. Duport, *Essai sur le doigté du violoncelle, et sur la conduite de l'archet* (Paris, [1806]), p. 8.

19 P. Baillot, J. H. Levasseur, C. S. Catel, and C. N. Baudiot, *Méthode de violoncelle et de basse d'accompagnement* (Paris, [1805]), p. 80; Romberg, *School*, pp. 51–2.

20 *Allgemeine musikalische Zeitung*, 3 (16 October 1799), cols. 33–7.

21 G. Muffat, *Florilegium secundum für Streichinstrumente*, ed. H. Rietsch in *Denkmäler der Tonkunst in Österreich*, IV (Graz, 1959), p. 21; Corrette, *Méthode*, p. 8.

22 A comparison of recommended bow-grips for French violinists and cellists is provided in *Correspondance des Amateurs Musiciens*, 14 (26 February 1803), p. 1, and 46 (8 October 1803), p. 1; the earliest extant description of Romberg's bow-grip is found in the letter of 27 April 1807 to Friedrich Kunst, reproduced in H. Schäfer, *Bernhard Romberg: sein Leben und Wirken* (Münster, 1931), appendix.

23 This is illustrated in a photograph of 1907, reproduced in P. Casals, *Joys and Sorrows: Reflections by Pablo Casals as Told to Albert E. Kahn* (London, 1970).

24 Corrette, *Méthode*, pp. 33, 35.

25 Duport, *Essai*, p. 17.

26 Baudiot, *Méthode*, I, p. 21.

27 Corrette, *Méthode*, p. 41.

28 Boccherini's use of clef changes to specify changes in hand-settings is discussed by Romberg, *School*, p. 65.

29 This attribute of Romberg's playing necessitated that he reshape the fingerboard underneath the C string in order to accommodate the wide string vibrations. It is possible that the comparatively low pitch-standard used in Paris until after the Restoration contributed to French cellists' discontent with their lowest string on the smaller instruments used for solo playing.

30 The concertos of Bréval and Lamare were consequently sold to violinists. In the 1786 catalogue, Richomme advertised Bréval's first two concertos as being for violin or violoncello; Lamare's concertos, published under his name but composed by D. Auber, are discussed in this context in *Berlinische musikalische Zeitung*, 45 (1805), p. 178.

31 L. Ginsburg, *History of the Violoncello*, ed. H. R. Axelrod, trans. T. Tchistyakova (Neptune City, NJ, 1983), p. 25.

32 Corrette, *Méthode*, p. 12.

33 Duport, *Essai*, pp. 170–1.

34 J. J. Rousseau, *Dictionnaire de musique* (Paris, 1768/R1969), p. 449. It was likewise remarked in the *Musikalische Real-Zeitung* (8 October 1788), col. 115, that French performers had a greater affinity for harmonics than either Italian or German players.

35 Romberg, *School*, p. 73.

36 J. J. F. Dotzauer, *Violonzell-Schule* (Mainz, [1832]), p. 27.

37 Baillot *et al.*, *Méthode*, p. 128.

38 Duport, *Essai*, p. 171.

39 *Allgemeine musikalische Zeitung* (November, 1803), cols. 86–7.

40 Baillot *et al.*, *Méthode*, p. 128.
41 Dotzauer, *Violonzell-Schule*, p. 47.
42 F. Geminiani, *A Treatise of Good Taste in the Art of Musick* (London, 1749/R1969), p. 3.
43 Romberg, *School*, p. 87.
44 Vaslin, *L'art*, p. 18.
45 Broadley, *Chats*, p. 76.
46 Van der Straeten, *Technics*, p. 135.
47 Broadley, *Chats*, p. 56.
48 F. Blanchard, 'Die Violoncellisten', *Allgemeine Wiener Musik-Zeitung* (17 November 1842), p. 554; E. S. J. van der Straeten, *History of the Violoncello, the Viola da Gamba, their Precursors and Collateral Instruments* (London, 1914/R1971), p. 562.
49 Broadley, *Chats*, pp. 57–8.
50 *Ibid.*, p. 60.
51 Baudiot, *Méthode*, II, p. 227; Romberg, *School*, p. 82.
52 J. G. C. Schetky, *Twelve Duetts for Two Violoncellos, with some Observations & Rules for Playing that Instrument* Op.7 (London, *c.* 1780), p. 1.
53 Instructions for beating time with the foot are included in Crome, *Compleat Tutor*, pp. 12–13, and J. Baumgartner, *Instructions de musique, théorique et pratique, à l'usage du violoncelle* (The Hague, [1774]), pp. 6–7.
54 Baumgartner, *Instructions*, p. 25; D. Watkin, 'Corelli's Op. 5 Sonatas: 'Violino e Violone o Cimbalo?' *Early Music*, 24 (1996), pp. 645–63.
55 Lindley's enjoyment of adding embellishments to an accompaniment received negative comment in *The Harmonicon*, 2 (May 1824), p. 99, and 5 (April 1827), p. 74; Baudiot, *Méthode*, II, p. 193.
56 Broadley, *Chats*, pp. 73–4.

12 The development of cello teaching in the twentieth century

1 Cited by Tully Potter in his notes for *the Recorded Cello: the History of the Cello on Record* (Pearl GEMM 9981–9985).
2. Quarter-, half and three-quarter sized cellos were advertised in the 1910 catalogue of J. Thibouville-Lamy (Mirecourt) but had to be specially ordered.
3 The cello spike, 'invented' around the middle of the nineteenth century, had been used earlier, but was not common. There is, for example, a Meissen pottery figure of a cellist with a spike (*c.* 1740) in the Fitzwilliam Museum, Cambridge.
4 Although Mrs Curwen had already produced such books for the piano in 1886. She used her father-in-law John Curwen's tonic sol-fa and hand-sign system to train the

inner ear through the voice, and as a prelude to reading staff notation; she also incorporated Aimé Paris's rhythm time names: ♩=ta; ♪ ♪=ta-te etc. These ideas later became part of the Kodály Method in Hungary. She advised that exercises in arm, hand and finger training be done away from the instrument and also advocated free gymnastics, ideas which pre-echo Suzuki and Rolland.
5 A. Piatti, *Méthode du Violoncelle* (London, 1882), rev. W. E. Whitehouse and R. V. Tabb as *Violoncello Method* (London, 1910), Preface.
6 William Pleeth (*The Cello* (London, 1982), p. 146) also points out that the modern way of holding the cello grows from the 'Baroque' manner.
7 E. S. J. van der Straeten, in his *Technics of Violoncello Playing* (London, 1898), gives a similar description. In 1965 I met a female member of the New Orleans Symphony Orchestra who had been taught this way in the late thirties at a Convent in Australia!
8 As corroborated by Carl Fuchs' grand-daughter Delia Fuchs, also a cellist, when interviewed by the present author.
9 Piatti, *Violoncello Method*, rev. Whitehouse and Tabb, Preface.
10 The Dotzauer–Klingenberg Method is a compilation by Klingenberg of Dotzauer's best material from several sources, with additional selections from Duport, Romberg and Gross, all arranged in progressive order.
11 For example, the first 105 exercises of the Dotzauer–Klingenberg Method are in first position.
12 M. Eisenberg [with M. B. Stanfield], *Cello Playing of Today* (London, 1957), p. 12; C. Bunting in conversation with the present author and in masterclasses; W. Pleeth, *The Cello* (London, 1982), p. 162.
13 Eisenberg [with Stanfield], *Cello Playing of Today*, p. 12.
14 J. M. Corredor, *Conversations avec Casals: souvenirs et opinions d'un musicien* (Paris, 1955; Eng. trans., 1956), p. 24; Piatti, *Violoncello Method*, rev. Whitehouse and Tabb, p. 28.
15 Fuchs, *Violoncello Method*, I, p. 19.
16 Piatti, *Violoncello Method*, rev. Whitehouse and Tabb, p. 28.
17 It should be noted that Piatti's vibrato movement related to a cello without a spike, hence supported by the thumb; but his text does not make this clear.
18 See R. Philip, *Early Recordings and Musical Style* (Cambridge, 1992), pp. 95–108, 141–204.
19 M. Zimbler, cited by Tully Potter in his notes for *the Recorded Cello: the History of the Cello on Record* (see n. 1).

20 Joan Dickson: performer and teacher; professor at RSAM and RCM, teacher at the Purcell School, founder member and key figure in ESTA, British Branch. Jane Cowan: teacher and Director of the International Cello Centre from the late 1960s, first in London, then in Scotland. Margaret Moncrieff: performer, and teacher at Wells Cathedral School, RCM and RNCM. Moray Welsh: teacher at RNCM and Co-Principal cellist of LSO.
21 M. Enix, *Rudolf Matz, Cellist Teacher, Composer* (Ottawa, 1996), p. 152.
22 Eisenberg [with Stanfield], *Cello Playing of Today*; C. Bunting, *Essay on the Craft of Cello Playing* (London, 1982).
23 D. Blum, *Casals and the Art of Interpretation* (London, 1977), p. 70.
24 J. M. Corredor, *Conversations avec Pablo Casals*, cited in L. Ginsburg, *History of the Violoncello* (Moscow, 1950–78; Eng. trans., 1983), p. 144.
25 Quoted in Ginsburg, *History of the Violoncello* (Eng. trans.), pp. 161–2.
26 Blum, *Casals and the Art of Interpretation*, pp. 102–9.
27 Eisenberg [with Stanfield], *Cello Playing of today*, p. 108.
28 Blum, *Casals and the Art of Interpretation*, pp. 103 and 104.
29 Stutschewsky's *Die Kunst des Cellospiels*, vols. I–II (Mainz, 1929), vols. III–IV (Vienna, 1938) contained many useful exercises, but emphasised extensions that were too great for the average hand.
30 Bazelaire's pedagogical works include: *Quelques Notes sur différents points importants de la Technique Générale du Violoncelle* (Paris, 1920); *L'enseignement du Violoncelle en France* (Paris, 1944); and *Pédagogie du Violoncelle* (Paris, 1952).
31 Silva, who performed and taught in Italy and the USA, including at Juilliard and Yale, started working on a history of cello technique. His unfinished work is housed at the University of North Carolina at Greensboro. He also arranged Kreutzer's violin studies for cello. Other collections at Greensboro are those of Matz, Milly Stanfield, and Eisenberg.
32 G. Fallot, a former Bazelaire pupil now based in Switzerland, in conversation with the present writer.
33 *A Tune a Day* for violin was published in New York in 1927, followed by the cello and viola versions in 1937. The series expanded to woodwinds, brass and percussion.
34 Some string programmes had existed earlier – see, for example, the *A Tune a Day* series (referred to in n. 33) – but were rare.

35 E. Andrews, *Healthy Practice for Musicians* (London, 1997), p. 29.
36 Tsutsumi later studied with Janos Starker in the USA, and is now his colleague at Bloomington, Indiana.
37 The peripatetic system grew from the pioneer work of the Rural Music Schools Association in the 1930s which provided cheap violin and some cello lessons in classes. Lessons were given in village halls, private houses and schools after hours.
38 Suzuki's father, Masakichi, founded a violin factory in 1885. 'When things went well . . . the factory could turn out 400 violins and 4,000 bows a day' (S. Suzuki, *Nurtured by Love* (New York, 1969), p. 59). The factory still exists today.
39. Pentatonic = five-note scale. The most common one, used in two forms, can be considered a major or natural-minor scale, without the semitones. In the Kodály Method semitones are added later.
40 Followed twenty-five years later by ESTA (European String Teachers Association, and since 1989 including countries from Eastern Europe), and finally AUSTA (Australian Strings Association Ltd).
41. Margaret Rowell (1904–95) evolved her whole-body cello technique in the 1930s, after suffering tuberculosis. In the words of Irene Sharpe 'Margaret believed in teaching "from the inside out". She wanted us to feel what it is like to produce an expressive tone and a beautiful phrase, not just fit yourself into a prescribed position with the hope that things will come out sounding all right.' (*American String Teacher* (Summer, 1995)). Irene Sharpe, the protégée of Margaret Rowell, has taught at the San Francisco Conservatory for over twenty years, and has given many masterclasses and teacher workshops around the world.
42 P. Rolland, *The Teaching of Action in String Playing* (New York, 1974), p. 75.
43 *Ibid.*, p. 130.
44 For example, Sheila Nelson's *Tetra Tunes* series.
45 The Texas String Project (est. 1948) was unique in that it both taught young children to play and trained future teachers. It became the model for many other string training programmes. Phyllis Young became its director in 1965. Her books *Playing the String Game* (Texas, 1978) and *The String Play* (Texas, 1986) are published by Texas University Press.
46 In addition to Alexander's books – *The Use of Self* (London, 1932) is the best known – there are many recent books on the Alexander

Technique. The main training centre for Alexander Teachers in London, England, is directed by Walter Carrington.

47 J. Starker, *An Organised Method of String Playing* (New York, 1965), p. 7.

48 Pleeth, *The Cello*, p. 23.

49 Most of it was published during his lifetime in Yugoslavia but is not well known elsewhere. Dominus Music (Montreal) is at present republishing his cello teaching material.

50 Pleeth, *The Cello*, p. 58.

51 Rudolf Matz, *Twelve Etudes: Introduction to Thumb Position*, and *Twenty Four Etudes Relating Neck Positions to Thumb Position*.

52 George Vance, an innovative teacher of young bass players, from Washington, DC.

53 My teaching studio houses three adjustable piano stools. One stool has cut-down legs to suit pupils using quarter- and half-size instruments, one is of normal height, and one has extra-long legs to suit the increasing number of pupils who are over six feet tall.

54 Anup Biswas in conversation with the present writer.

13 The frontiers of technique

1 It has a staff for each hand, a notated line of phonemes, and notations for each foot with respective volume indications to be controlled by two foot-pedals.

Select Bibliography

Note: The reader is also referred to the Appendix 'Principal cello treatises', pp. 224–8.

Adas, J., 'Le célèbre Berteau', *Early Music*, 17 (1989), pp. 368–80

Agricola, M., *Musica instrumentalis deudsch* (Wittenberg, 1528; 2/1529R1969, rev. 6/1545)

Allsop, P., 'The Role of the Stringed Bass as a Continuo Instrument in Italian Seventeenth-Century Instrumental Music', *Chelys*, 8 (1978–9), pp. 31–7
  The Italian 'Trio' Sonata (Oxford, 1992)

Bächi, J., *Von Boccherini bis Casals* (Zurich, 1961)

Bacon, A. C., 'The Evolution of the Violoncello as a Solo Instrument', diss., Syracuse University (1962)

Barsham, E., 'Six New Boccherini Cello Sonatas', *Musical Times*, 105 (1964), pp. 18–20

Beare, C., *Capolavori di Antonio Stradivari* (Milan, 1987)

Benade, A. H., *Fundamentals of Musical Acoustics* (London, 1976)

Blees, G., *Das Cello-Konzert um 1800: Eine Untersuchung der Cello-Konzerte zwischen Haydns Op. 101 und Schumanns Op. 129* (Regensburg, 1973)

Bonetti, C., *A Genealogy of the Amati Family of Violin Makers 1500–1740*, trans. G. G. Champe (New York, 1989)

Bonta, S., 'From Violone to Violoncello: a Question of Strings?' *Journal of the American Musical Instrument Society*, 3 (1977), pp. 64–99
  'Terminology for the Bass Violin in Seventeenth-Century Italy', *Journal of the American Musical Instrument Society*, 4 (1978), pp. 5–42

Boomkamp, C. Van Leeuwen, and Van Der Meer, J. H., *The Carel Van Leeuwen Boomkamp Collection of Musical Instruments* (Amsterdam, 1971)

Boyden, D. D., *Catalogue of the Hill Collection of Musical Instruments in the Ashmolean Museum, Oxford* (Oxford, 1969)
  The History of Violin Playing from its Origins to 1761 (Oxford, 1965)

Bozarth, G., 'Leider nicht von Johannes Brahms', *The Strad*, 99 (1988), pp. 146–50

Bragard, R., *Musical Instruments in Art and History* (London, 1968)

Broadley, A., *Chats to 'Cello Students* (London, 1899)
  The Violoncello: its History, Selection and Adjustment (London, 1921)

Brook, B. S., *La symphonie française dans la seconde moitié du XVIIIe siècle*, 3 vols. (Paris, 1962)

Buchanan, J. M., *see* Firth, I. M.

Burnett, H., 'The Bowed String Instruments of the Baroque Basso-Continuo (ca. 1680–ca. 1752) in Italy and France: the Various Meanings of the Term "Violone"', *Journal of the Viola da Gamba Society of America*, 8 (1971), pp. 29–63

Bynum, E., and Rossing, T. D., 'Holographic Studies of Cello Vibrations',
    Proceedings of the Institute of Acoustics, 19/5 (1997), pp. 155–61
Campbell, D. M., and Greated, C., *The Musician's Guide to Acoustics* (London,
    1987)
Campbell, M., *The Great Cellists* (London, 1988)
Casals, P., *Joys and Sorrows: Reflections by Pablo Casals as Told to Albert E. Kahn*
    (London, 1970)
Childs, P., 'The Bows of Etienne Pajeot', *The Strad*, 104 (1993), pp. 372–5
Condax, L. M., *Final Summary Report of Violin Varnish Research Project* Mellon
    Institute No. 3070 (Pittsburgh, Penn., 1970)
Corredor, J. M., *Conversations avec Casals: souvenirs et opinions d'un musicien*
    (Paris, 1955; Eng. trans., 1956)
Cowling, E., *The Cello* (London, 1975, 2/1983)
  'The Italian Sonata Literature for the Violoncello in the Baroque Era' diss.,
    Northwestern University (1962)
Cremer, L., *The Physics of the Violin* (Cambridge, Mass., 1984)
Cyr, M., 'Basses and Basse Continue in the Orchestra of the Paris Opéra,
    1700–1764', *Early Music*, 10 (1982), pp. 155–70
Dilworth, J., 'Mr Baker the Fidell Maker', *The Strad*, 106 (1995), pp. 475–81
Dioli, A., *L'arte violoncellistica in Italia* (Palermo, 1962)
Donington, R., 'James Talbot's Manuscript', *The Galpin Society Journal*, 3 (1950),
    pp. 27–45
Doring, E., *The Guadagnini Family* (Chicago, 1949)
Dräger, H. H., *Die Entwicklung des Streichbogens* (Kassel, 1937)
Eckhardt, J., *Die Violoncellschulen von J. J. F. Dotzauer, F. A. Kummer, und B.
    Romberg* (Regensburg, 1968)
Eitner, R., *Biographisch-bibliographisches Quellen-Lexikon der Musiker und
    Musikgelehrten*, 10 vols. (New York, 1898)
Elsen, Josephine, 'The Instrumental Works of Peter Ritter', diss., Northwestern
    University (1967)
Eras, R., *Über das Verhältnis zwischen Stimmung und Spieltechnik bei
    Streichinstrumenten in Da-gamba-Haltung* (Leipzig, 1958)
Farish, M. K., *String Music in Print* (New York, 1965; suppl. 1968)
Fauquet, J. M., *Les sociétés de musique de chambre à Paris de la restauration à 1870*
    (Paris, 1986)
Fender, P., 'The Rebec: a Comprehensive Survey', *The Strad*, 94 (1983), pp. 28–9,
    109–11, 174–7, 257–60
Fétis, F. J., *Antoine Stradivari, luthier célèbre* (Paris, 1856; Eng. trans., John Bishop,
    London, 1864/R1964)
  Biographie universelle des musiciens et bibliographie générale de la musique, 2nd
    edn, 8 vols. and supplement (Paris, 1887–8)
Firth, I. M., and Buchanan, J. M., 'The Wolf in the Cello', *Journal of the Acoustical
    Society of America*, 53 (1973), pp. 457–63
Fletcher, N. H., and Rossing, T. D., *The Physics of Musical Instruments* (New York,
    1991)
Forino, L., *Il violoncello, il violoncellista ed i violoncellisti* (Milan, 1905, 2/1930)

Geminiani, F., *A Treatise of Good Taste in the Art of Musick* (London, 1749/R1960)

Gerber, E. L., *Historisch-Biographisches Lexikon der Tonkünstler und Neues Historisch-Biographisches Lexikon der Tonkünstler*, 4 vols. (Graz, 1977)

Ginsburg, L., *History of the Violoncello*, ed. H. R. Axelrod, trans. Tanya Tchistyakova (Neptune City, NJ, 1983)

Istoriya violonchel 'nogo iskusstva, kniga vtoraya, [*History of the Art of the Cello*], I–IV (Moscow, 1950–78)

Greated, C., see Campbell, D. M.

Guettler, K., 'Bow Notes', *Proceedings of the Institute of Acoustics*, 19/5 (1997), pp. 1–10

Halfpenny, E., 'The Berkswell Cello', *Galpin Society Journal*, 37 (1984), pp. 2–5

Harich, J., 'Das Haydn-Orchester in Jahr 1780', trans. E. Hartzell, *The Haydn Yearbook*, 8 (1971) pp. 5–69

Hart, G., *The Violin: its Famous Makers and their Imitators* (London, 1875)

Helmholtz, H. L. F., *Die Lehre von den Tonempfindungen als physiologische Grundlage für die Theorie der Musik* (Brunswick, 1863); Eng. trans. 1875/R1954 as *On the Sensations of Tone as a Physiological Basis for the Theory of Music*

Henley, W., *Universal Dictionary of Violin and Bow Makers*, vols. I–V (Brighton, 1959–60); vol. VI ed. C. Woodcock as *Dictionary of Contemporary Violin and Bow Makers* (Brighton, 1965)

Heron-Allen, E., *Violin-Making As It Was and Is* (London, 1885)

Hill, W. H., A. F. and A. E., *Antonio Stradivari: his Life and Work* (London, 1902; 2nd edn 1909/R1963)

The Violin Makers of the Guarneri Family (London, 1931, rev. 2/1965)

Huggins, M. L., *Gio. Paolo Maggini, his Life and Work* (London, 1892)

Hutchins, C. M., 'Founding a Family of Fiddles', *Physics Today*, 20 (1967), pp. 23–7

Musical Acoustics Parts 1 and 2: Benchmark Papers in Musical Acoustics Vols. 5 and 6 (Stroudburger, Penn., 1977)

'The Acoustics of Violin Plates', *Scientific American*, 245 (1981), pp. 170–86

'A 30-Year Experiment in the Acoustical and Musical Development of Violin-Family Instruments', *Journal of the Acoustical Society of America*, 92 (1992), pp. 639–50

Research Papers in Violin Acoustics 1975–1993 (New York, 1996)

Iotti, O., *Violin and Violoncello in Duo without Accompaniment*, Detroit Studies in Music Bibliography 25 (Detroit, 1972)

Jambe de Fer, P., *Epitome musical* (Lyons, 1556); repr. in Lesure (1958–63)

Kinney, G. J., 'The Musical Literature for Unaccompanied Violoncello', diss., Florida State University (1962)

Kohlmorgen, F., *Die Brüder Duport und die Entwicklung der Violoncelltechnik von ihren Anfängen bis zur Zeit B. Rombergs* (Berlin, 1922)

La Borde, J. B. de, *Essai sur la musique ancienne et moderne*, 4 vols. (Paris, 1780)

Lanfranco, G. M., *Scintille di musica* (Brescia, 1533/R1969)

Lassabathie, T., *Histoire du Conservatoire Impérial de Musique et de Déclamation* (Paris, 1860)

Le Blanc, H., *Défense de la basse de viole contre les entreprises du violon et les prétensions du violoncelle* (Amsterdam, 1740/R1975); repr. in *La Revue Musicale*, 9 (1927–8)

Lesure, F., 'L'Epitome musical de Philibert Jambe de Fer (1556)', *Annales Musicologiques*, 6 (1958–63), pp. 341–86

Lewicki, E., 'Die Spur eines Violoncell-Konzerts von Mozart', *Mitteilungen für die Mozart Gemeinde in Berlin*, 4 (1912), pp. 62–3

Liégeois, C., and Nogué, E., *Le violoncelle: son histoire, ses virtuoses* (Paris, 1913)

Lindeman, F., 'Dutch Violin Making Down the Centuries', *The Strad*, 106 (1995), pp. 782–91

Littlehales, L., *Pablo Casals* (London, 1929)

Lutgendorff, W. L. F. von, *Die Geigen- und Lautenmacher vom Mittelalter bis zur Gegenwart* (Tutzing, 1975)

Lützen, L., *Die Violoncell-Transkriptionen Friedrich Grützmachers* (Regensburg, 1974)

Malusi, L., *Il Violoncello* (Padua, 1973)
  L'arco degli strumenti musicale: storia, tecnica, costruttori, valutazioni (Padua, 1981)

Markevitch, D., 'A Lost Art? The Use of the Thumb in 18th- and Early 19th-Century Cello Works', *Strings*, 7 (1992), pp. 16–18
  'A New Sound for Familiar Music: the Cello as an Accompanying Instrument in the 18th-Century', *Strings*, 6 (1991), pp. 18–21
  Cello Story (Princeton, NJ, 1984)
  The Solo Cello: a Bibliography of the Unaccompanied Violoncello Literature (Berkeley, 1989)

Marx, K., *Die Entwicklung des Violoncells und seiner Spieltechnik bis J.-L. Duport (1520–1820)* (Regensburg, 1963)

Merseburger, M., see Vadding, M.,

Mersenne, M., *Harmonie universelle* (Paris, 1636–7/R1963; Eng. trans., 1957)

Millant, R., *J. B. Vuillaume: sa vie et son oeuvre*, trans. A. Hill (London, 1972)

Milliot, S., 'Réflexions et recherches sur la viole de gambe et le violoncelle en France', *Recherches sur la Musique Française Classique*, 4 (1964), pp. 179–238
  Le violoncelle en France au XVIIIe siècle (Lille, 1981)

Mirandolle, W., *De violoncel: haar bouw, geschiedenis en ontwikkelingsgang* (The Hague, 1943)

Monical, W., *Shapes of the Baroque* (Illinois: American Federation of Violin and Bow Makers, 1989)

Moore, L., 'The Duport Mystery', *Dance Perspectives*, 7 (1960), pp. 12–17

Moran, J., 'Fingering in Beethoven's Cello Music: an Evaluation of the Historical Sources', Diplomarbeit, Schola Cantorum Basiliensis (1994)

Morrow, M. S., *Concert Life in Haydn's Vienna: Aspects of a Developing Musical and Social Institution* (Stuyvesant, NY, 1989)

Muffat, G., *Florilegium secundum für Streichinstrumente*, ed. H. Rietsch in Denkmäler der Tonkunst in Österreich IV (Graz, 1959)

Newman, W. S., *The Sonata in the Baroque Era* (Chapel Hill, 1959, rev. 1966)
  The Sonata in the Classic Era (Chapel Hill, 1963; rev. 2/1972)
  The Sonata since Beethoven (Chapel Hill, 1969; rev. 2/1972)

Niecks, F., 'Recollections of Violoncellists', *Monthly Musical Record*, 49 (1919), pp. 122–3 and 145–7

Nogué, E., see Liégeois, C.,
  La littérature du violoncelle (Paris, 1925, 2/1931)
  Le violoncelle, jadis et aujourd'hui (Paris, 1937)

Palm, S. 'Wo steht das Violoncello heute?' *Neue Zeitschrift für Musik*, 130 (1969), pp. 419–23

Pape, W., 'Die Entwicklung des Violoncellspiels im 19. Jahrhundert, diss., Universität des Saarlandes, Saarbrucken (1962)

Philip, R., *Early Recordings and Musical Style* (Cambridge, 1992)

Pierre, C. V. D., *Bernard Sarrette et les origines du Conservatoire national de musique et de déclamation* (Paris, 1895)
  Le Conservatoire National de Musique et de Déclamation: Documents Historiques et Administratifs (Paris, 1900)
  Histoire du Concert Spirituel 1725–1790 (Paris, 1975)
  Der Barockkontrabass Violone (Salzburg, 1989)

Pleeth, W., *The Cello* (London, 1982)

Pohl, C. F., *Mozart und Haydn in London*, 2 vols. (Vienna, 1867)

Praetorius, M., *Syntagma musicum*, I (Wittenberg and Wolfenbüttel, 1614–15/R1968), II (Wolfenbüttel, 1618; 2/1619/R1958 and 1980, Eng. trans., ed. D. Z. Crookes, 1986); III (Wolfenbüttel, 1618, 2/1619/R1958 and 1976)

Quantz, J. J., *On Playing the Flute*, trans. E. R. Reilly (London, 1966)

Racster, O., *Chats on Violoncellos* (London, 1907)

Rapp, E., *Beiträge zur Frühgeschichte des Violoncellkonzerts* (Würzburg, 1934)

Regazzi, R., *The Complete Luthier's Library* (Bologna, 1990)

Reindorf, M., 'Authentic Authorship', *The Strad*, 101 (1990), pp. 546–50

Retford, W. C., *Bows and Bow Makers* (London, 1964)

Roda, J., *Bows for Musical Instruments of the Violin Family* (Chicago, 1959)

Rossing, T. D., see Bynum, E. and Fletcher, N. H.

Roth, P., *Führer durch die Violoncell-Literatur* (Leipzig, 1888, 2/1898)

Rothschild, G. de, *Luigi Boccherini: his Life and Work*, trans. N. Dufourcq (Oxford, 1965)

Rühlmann, J., *Die Geschichte der Bogeninstrumente* (Brunswick, 1882)

Russell, T. A., 'The Development of the Cello Endpin', *Imago Musicae*, 4 (1987), pp. 335–56
  'New Light on the Historical Manner of Holding the Cello', *Historical Performance*, 6/2 (Fall, 1993), pp. 73–8

Sacconi, S. F., *The Secrets of Stradivari*, trans. A. Dipper (Cremona, 1979)

Sadie, S. (ed.) *The New Grove Dictionary of Music and Musicians* 20 vols. (London, 1980)

Sadler, M., *The Retford Centenary Exhibition* (London, 1975)

Saint-George, H., *The Bow: its History, Manufacture and Use* (London, 1896, 2/1909)

Sandys, W. and Forster, S. A., *The History of the Violin* (London, 1864)

Schäfer, H., *Bernhard Romberg: sein Leben und Wirken* (Münster, 1931)

Schelleng, J. C., 'The Violin as a Circuit', *Journal of the Acoustical Society of America*, 35 (1992), pp. 326–38

Scott, M. G., 'Boccherini's B flat Cello Concerto: a Reappraisal of the
    Sources', *Early Music*, 12 (1984), pp. 355–7
Segerman, E., 'Strings Through the Ages', *The Strad*, 99 (1988), pp. 52–5, 195–201,
    295–9
Sensbach, S. W., 'French Cello Sonatas, 1871–1931', diss., University of Texas,
    Austin (1996)
Shaw, G. J., 'The Violoncello Sonata Literature in France during the Eighteenth
    Century' diss., Catholic University of America, Washington, DC (1963)
Stowell, R. (ed.), *The Cambridge Companion to the Violin* (Cambridge, 1992)
Taylor, C. A., *Exploring Music: the Science and Technology of Tones and Tunes*
    (Bristol, 1992)
Trevelyan, P., 'A Quartet of String Instruments by William Baker of Oxford (circa
    1645–1685)', *The Galpin Society Journal*, 49 (1996), pp. 65–76
Vadding, M. and Merseburger, M., *Das Violoncell und seine Literatur* (Leipzig,
    1920)
Valentin, E., *Cello: Das Instrument und sein Meister Ludwig Hoelscher* (Pfullingen,
    1955)
Van Der Meer, J. H., see Boomkamp, C. Van Leeuwen
Van der Straeten, E. S. J., *History of the Violoncello, the Viola da Gamba, their
    Precursors and Collateral Instruments* (London, 1914/R1971)
Vatelot, E., *Les archets français* (Nancy, 1976)
Vidal, A., *Les instruments à archet, les faiseurs, les joueurs d'instruments, leur
    histoire*, 3 vols. (Paris, 1877/R1961)
Vollmer, W., *Über die Erscheinung des Wolftons bei Streichinstrumenten,
    insbesondere beim Cello* (Karlsruhe, 1936)
Waegner, G., *Die sechs Suiten für das Violoncello allein von J. S. Bach* (Berlin, 1957)
Walden, V., 'An Investigation and Comparison of the French and Austro-German
    Schools of Violoncello Bowing Technique', diss., University of Auckland
    (1993).
    *One Hundred Years of Violoncello: a History of Technique and Performance
    Practice, 1740–1840* (Cambridge, 1998)
Wasielewski, J. W. von, *Das Violoncell und seine Geschichte* (Leipzig, 1889,
    enlarged, 3/1925/R1970; Eng. trans., I. S. E. Stigend (London, 1894/R1968))
Watchorn, I., 'Baroque Renaissance', *The Strad*, 95 (1985), pp. 822–7
Watkin, D., 'Corelli's Op. 5 Sonatas: Violino e Violone o Cimbalo?' *Early Music*, 24
    (1996), pp. 645–63
Weber, H., *Das Violoncellkonzert des 18. und beginnenden 19. Jahrhunderts*
    (Tübingen, 1933)
Webster, J., 'Violoncello and Double Bass in the Chamber Music of Haydn and his
    Viennese Contemporaries, 1750–1780', *Journal of the American Musicological
    Society*, 29 (1976), pp. 413–38
Weigl, B., *Handbuch der Violoncell-Literatur* (Vienna, 1911, 3/1929)
White, R., 'Eighteenth-Century Instruments Examined' (National Gallery Report
    on Varnish), *The Strad*, 95 (1984), pp. 258–9
Winternitz, E., *Musical Instruments and their Symbolism in Western Art* (Yale,
    1979)

Gaudenzio Ferrari, his School and the Early History of the Violin (Varallo Sesia, 1967)

Witten, L.C. Jr, 'Apollo, Orpheus and David: a Study of the Crucial Century in the Development of Bowed Strings in North Italy 1480–1580 as seen in Graphic Evidence and some Surviving Instruments', *Journal of the American Musical Instrument Society,* 1 (1975), pp. 5–55

Woodfield, I., *The Early History of the Viol* (Cambridge, 1984)

Woodhouse, J., 'Stringed Instruments: Bowed', in M. J. Crocker (ed.), *Encyclopedia of Acoustics,* 4 vols. (New York, 1997), IV, pp. 1619–26

Zacconi, L., *Prattica di musica* (Venice, 1592–1622/R1967)

Zemitis, M. R., *Violin Varnish and Coloration* (New York, 1981)

Zingler, U., 'Studien zur Entwicklung der italienischen Violoncellsonate von den Anfängen bis zur Mitte des 18. Jahrhunderts' diss., University of Frankfurt (1966)

Index

cello (*cont.*)
    unaccompanied, 137–45; national styles of
    playing, 178–80; notation, 179–80,
    214–15, 242n8; origins and antecedents, 7;
    principal makers and centres of making,
    14–25; scaled, 45, 237n10; six-string, 137,
    142, 239n20; sizes, 9, 15, 18, 20, 22–3, 46,
    160, 195, 204, 205, 243n2; teaching,
    195–210; technique, style and
    performance practice, 178–94, 211–23;
    terminology, 7, 160–2; treatises, 179,
    195–210, 224–8; tunings, 9, 236, with
    sympathetic strings, 210
Cermak, Johann (*c.* 1710–*c.* 1795), 59
Cervetto, Giacobbe Basevi (*c.* 1682–1783),
    53, 57, 118, 165
Cervetto, James (1747–1837), 53, 57, 66
Chailly, Luciano (*b.* 1920), 135
Chaminade, Cécile (1857–1944), 155
Charles IX (of France), 7, 14–15
Chausson, Ernest (1855–99), 173
Chávez, Carlos (1899–1978), 132
Chethams School (Manchester), 204
Chevillard, Pierre Alexandre François
    (1811–77), 64, 225
Childs, J. B., 177
Chopin, Fryderyk Franciszek (1810–49), 68,
    126, 127, 140–1, 152–3
chords (techniques of playing), 193
Cima, Giovanni Paolo (*c.* 1570–after 1622),
    161
Cirri, Giovanni Battista (1724–1808), 53, 93,
    118
Clark, James, 222
Clarke, Rebecca (1886–1979), 132
Coenen String Quartet, 66
Cohen, Robert (*b.* 1959), 75
Cole, Orlando, 78
col legno, 220, 221, 230
Colombi, Giuseppe (1635–94), 138
Colour Strings Method, 207
computers, 145, 219, 221, 222
concertino, 97, 98, 99, 101, 105, 106, 107, 109,
    110, 111, 112, 114, 115, 116, 230
concerto 92–115, 119, 123, 147, 190
Concert of Antient Music, 57, 66
concerto grosso, 112, 230
Concerts du Conservatoire, 62
Concert Spirituel, 54, 55, 58
con sordino, 230; see also mute
contact-point, see point of contact

continuo, 116, 117, 118, 119, 120, 121, 138,
    162, 167, 194, 230
continuo playing, see accompanimental
    skills
Cooke, Arnold (*b.* 1906), 104, 133
Copland, Aaron (1900–90), 172
Corelli, Arcangelo (1653–1713), 28, 66, 117,
    118, 160, 161, 164, 165, 167
Corrette, Michel (1709–95), 56, 118, 179–80,
    184, 185, 186, 188, 224
Cossmann, Bernhard (1822–1910), 67, 68,
    75, 95, 192, 199
Coulthard, Jean (*b.* 1908), 131
Couperin, Louis (*c.* 1626–1661), 142
Cowan, Jane, 200, 244n20
Cowell, Henry (1897–1965), 130, 154
Cowling, Elizabeth, 118, 121, 238n18,
    239n15
Cramer, Wilhelm (1745–99), 28–9, 32
Cremona, Civic Museum, 11, 17, 32;
    principal luthiers of, 14–18; school of
    violin making, 18; Triennale Competition,
    26
Cristofori, Bartolomeo (1655–1731), 4, 22,
    236n9
Crome, Robert, 57–8, 64, 178, 179, 189, 224
Crosdill, John (1755–1825), 57
Crosse, Gordon (*b.* 1937), 148
Crouch, Frederick William (*b.* 1808), 66, 225
Crumb, George (Henry) (*b.* 1929), 142
Cudmore, Richard (1787–1840), 66
Cummings, Douglas (*b.* 1946), 78
Cupis, François (1732–1808), 55, 94, 120,
    179, 189, 224
Curtis Institute (Philadelphia), 78, 84–5
Curwen, John, 205, 243n4
Curwen, Mrs., 202, 243n4
cutting 'on the quarter', 3, 4, 5; 'on the slab',
    3, 4
Czech String Quartet, 69

Dahl, Ingolf (1912–70), 131
Dall'Abaco, Evaristo Felice (1675–1742), 92,
    165
Dall'Abaco, Giuseppe (*c.* 1710–1805), 118, 165
Dallapiccola, Luigi (1904–75), 141–2, 150
Dammen [Dahmen], Johan Arnold
    (1760–94), 65
Dancla, Arnaud Phillipe (1819–62), 156, 226
Danzi, Franz (Ignaz) (1763–1826), 94, 156
David, Ferdinand (1810–73), 173